Are All Politics Nationalized?

Edited by
Stephen K. Medvic, Matthew M. Schousen,
and Berwood A. Yost

Are All Politics Nationalized?

Evidence from the 2020 Campaigns
in Pennsylvania

TEMPLE UNIVERSITY PRESS
Philadelphia • *Rome* • *Tokyo*

TEMPLE UNIVERSITY PRESS
Philadelphia, Pennsylvania 19122
tupress.temple.edu

Library of Congress Cataloging-in-Publication Data

Names: Medvic, Stephen K., editor. | Schousen, Matthew M., 1960– editor. |
 Yost, Berwood A., editor.
Title: Are all politics nationalized? : evidence from the 2020 campaigns in
 Pennsylvania / edited by Stephen K. Medvic, Matthew M. Schousen, and
 Berwood A. Yost.
Description: Philadelphia : Temple University Press, 2023. | Includes
 bibliographical references and index. | Summary: "Uses the 2020
 elections in Pennsylvania as a case study to gauge American election
 nationalization and to explore little-understood aspects of the
 phenomenon"— Provided by publisher.
Identifiers: LCCN 2022017987 (print) | LCCN 2022017988 (ebook) | ISBN
 9781439922545 (cloth) | ISBN 9781439922569 (pdf)
Subjects: LCSH: Elections—Pennsylvania—History—21st century. | Political
 campaigns—Pennsylvania—History—21st century. | Political
 culture—Pennsylvania—21st century. | Pennsylvania—Politics and
 government—21st century.
Classification: LCC JK3693 2020 A73 2020 (print) | LCC JK3693 2020
 (ebook) | DDC 324.9748—dc23/eng/20220805
LC record available at https://lccn.loc.gov/2022017987
LC ebook record available at https://lccn.loc.gov/2022017988

To our students:
the next generation of citizens, scholars,
activists, and politicians

Contents

     Partisan Incentives Shape Nationalization in Northwestern
     Pennsylvania / ANDREW BLOESER AND TARAH WILLIAMS   163

8   Campaigns in the Seventeenth Congressional District:
     Handling Pressure from National Eyes while Maintaining
     Local Ties / KRISTEN COOPIE AND OLIVIA O'DONNELL   186

9   Conclusion: What Have We Learned about Nationalization?
     / STEPHEN K. MEDVIC, MATTHEW M. SCHOUSEN,
     AND BERWOOD A. YOST   215

     Contributors   233

     Index   235

Acknowledgments

The project upon which this book is based has been a wonderful collaboration from its inception. The three of us have the good fortune to work together at Franklin & Marshall College, in a department and in centers that are extraordinarily collegial, and in which endless conversations take place in the halls and in one another's offices. We've collaborated, in various combinations, many times in the past but this project was uniquely rewarding. In large part, that's because of how enjoyable it was to work with colleagues from around the Commonwealth of Pennsylvania. To a person, they were diligent, thoughtful, and good-natured, and their case studies were carefully conducted and insightful. Their contributions are the nucleus of the book, and we are grateful to them for their hard work and collegiality.

The use of AdImpact data was vital to this project and was made possible by research support from the Provost's Office and the Center for Politics and Public Affairs at Franklin & Marshall. At AdImpact, Mandie McILvaine was instrumental in making the data available and comprehensible. We want to thank President Barbara Altmann and Provost Cameron Wesson at Franklin & Marshall for continuing to support the Franklin & Marshall Poll, which provides indispensable data about the state's voters. We also wish to thank the team at the Center for Opinion Research who administer the survey, led by Project Manager Jackie Redman, for their hard work and dedication. As academic department coordinator for the Government Department at Franklin & Marshall, Paulina Erazo Ayala provided indispensable administrative support, as always. Our friend and colleague Amy Moreno offered invaluable editing assistance.

For his support and guidance, we thank Aaron Javsicas, editor-in-chief at Temple University Press. His patience was much appreciated and his wise counsel significantly improved the book. The rest of the team at Temple, and in particular Will Forrest, made the production process a pleasure.

Finally, and most importantly, we want to thank our spouses, Laura, Missy, and Christina. We could never have completed this book without their support, encouragement, and feedback. We're better people, and this project is a better study, because of them.

Are All Politics Nationalized?

1

Introduction

Studying Nationalization

STEPHEN K. MEDVIC, MATTHEW M. SCHOUSEN,
AND BERWOOD A. YOST

In 2021, state and local elections throughout the United States were sites of contention over issues that appear to have been generated at the national level in the last years of the Trump presidency. Candidates from Maine to Hawaii, and for offices from governor to school board, ran ads about "critical race theory" and pledged opposition to, or support for, mask mandates in schools. Notably, there were no campaigns for national offices in 2021. Nevertheless, national issues were thought to have predominated. So nationalized were these off-year elections that the first "lesson" identified in a Brookings Institution postelection analysis was that "All Politics Is No Longer Local" (Kamarck 2021).

The belief that American politics has become nationalized in recent decades is widely held. According to the conventional understanding of this phenomenon, politics at even the most local level is focused heavily on national issues and debates, and voters make decisions about state and local candidates based on their views of the national parties and presidential candidates. However, nationalization as a concept, and the process by which politics becomes nationalized, are not well understood. Too often, for example, the terms *nationalization* and *polarization* are used interchangeably, despite the fact that a political system could be nationalized but not polarized and vice versa.

Furthermore, the vast majority of the work that has been done on nationalization is concerned with voting behavior. As a result, we know very little about elite behavior and the degree to which—and the ways in which—

politicians are encouraging nationalized behavior among the voters. This book attempts to address this gap in our understanding of nationalization. Beyond introducing the motivation behind the book and defining the term *nationalization*, this chapter reviews the literature on the nationalization of American politics, describes the case study methodology we have employed, and provides some background on recent Pennsylvania electoral history.

The Research Question

Scholars agree that congressional and even state-level elections have become nationalized, but does that mean that congressional and state-level *campaigns* have become nationalized as well? If claims of nationalization are correct, and voters are selecting candidates up and down the ballot based on their views of the national parties and their presidential voting preferences, then down-ballot campaigns are likely to be affected. Have congressional and state-level campaigns rejected the notion that "all politics is local" and transformed their candidates into nationalized team players? Do these candidates focus on national issues and tie themselves to their presidential candidate?

The central question this book asks is whether campaigns at the congressional and state legislative levels show signs of nationalization, and if so, to what degree have they become nationalized? This overarching question gives rise to other questions: Do down-ballot candidates coordinate their messages and resources in order to run as part of a unified ticket? Are other entities, such as political parties and outside groups, nationalizing these down-ballot races? Are presidential campaigns working with congressional and state-level candidates to ensure a unified message? Are political parties tying together elections at different levels in an effort to create a single, coherent message for voters?

Given the widespread acceptance of the nationalization thesis, it is surprising that few scholars have examined the implications of the thesis for congressional and state-level candidates and their campaigns. In a highly nationalized political environment, one would expect congressional and state house candidates to adopt messages containing national themes. Do they? This book uses Pennsylvania as a case study to explore this question and to help us better understand how nationalization influences candidates and campaigns at the congressional and state levels.

Nationalization Defined

Nationalization has been the subject of quite a bit of research by scholars of comparative politics (see, for example, Jones and Mainwaring 2003; Caramani 2004; Chhibber and Kollman 2004; Morgenstern, Swindle, and Castagnola 2009; Hicken and Stoll 2011; Lago and Montero 2014; and Morgenstern 2017). However, the focus of such work is almost entirely on party systems and the extent to which they encourage "the replacement of local parties with national parties" or "homogenous electoral results of parties across sub-national units" (Lago and Montero 2014, 194). Lago and Montero (2014) note that, generally speaking, there are two dimensions to the concept of nationalization: dispersion and inflation. The first of these is concerned with "the extent to which parties receive similar levels of electoral support throughout the country," and the second emphasizes "the extent to which the number of parties at some level of aggregation may be higher than the number of parties at another level of aggregation" (195). There are, of course, several ways to measure dispersion and inflation, but the details of the various measurements are beyond the scope of this review.

While still concerned with the nationalization of party systems, Morgenstern (2017) identifies a different pair of dimensions. For him, *static nationalization* accounts for "the degree of homogeneity in a party's vote across a country *at a particular point in time*," while *dynamic nationalization* is "the consistency in the change in a party's vote in each district *across time*" (5, emphasis in original). This is similar to the distinction, discussed in the literature review below, that Claggett, Flanigan, and Zingale (1984) make between the convergence of a party's level of support nationally and the uniformity of its electoral response to political forces from one time period to the next.

The comparative scholarship on nationalization relies exclusively on the electoral performance of the parties in a given system. That is, the evidence for nationalization is found in election results and the patterns of vote choice in the electorate. In *The Increasingly United States*, the most comprehensive treatment of the nationalization of American politics to date, Daniel Hopkins (2018) expands the conceptualization of nationalization. He recognizes that an essential element of nationalization is the "overlapping bases of political mobilization and division, with politics considered nationalized when voters face and make similar choices across the levels of government" (34–35). However, another critical aspect of nationalization, according to Hopkins, is "engagement, with mass politics considered more nationalized when citizens allocate disproportionate time and attention to the national level" (35).

In the conceptualizations that have been employed in scholarship to this point, nationalization is to be found in the behavior of citizens. In this book, we prefer a broader understanding of nationalization, one that can incorporate the actions of political elites, including candidates for office. Our conceptualization focuses on elite messaging and signaling. That is, we are concerned with the way politicians, party operatives, and interest group activists frame politics for citizens.

We believe nationalized politics places an emphasis on ideology and partisanship, including appeals to negative partisanship, and it focuses on issues that are debated nationally, among presidential candidates, in Congress, and on cable news. Nationalized politics will not emphasize issues that are salient in only a specific state or locale, nor will it stress the performance of local or state government. In the campaign context, incumbency and unique candidate traits are local themes because they apply to particular candidates in particular areas.

We propose to operationalize this concept as follows:

- A piece of campaign communication (e.g., a television ad or a piece of direct mail) is *nationalized* to the extent that the words and images can be used for/against any candidate, anywhere in the country. Names could simply be changed and the remaining content would be the same.
- A piece of campaign communication is *localized* to the extent that the words and images can be used only for/against a specific candidate or in a particular locality. None of the content could be applied to another race (or more than a limited number of races) in exactly the same way.

This operationalization allows us to look for signs of nationalization in the actions of elites. As we see in the following review of the literature, the vast majority of the evidence in support of the nationalization thesis has been found, to this point, in mass political behavior. The extent to which elected officials and candidates are encouraging nationalization is an open question.

Nationalization among Voters, Parties, and Candidates

Research on the nationalization of politics in the United States began over sixty years ago. A review of that scholarship reveals some important insights into the changes that have occurred in American politics over that period of time.[1] It also suggests that more research is needed to fully understand the process of nationalization.

Voters

This is not the first era in which American politics has been said to be nationalized. E. E. Schattschneider (1960) was perhaps the first scholar to posit a period of nationalization. For him, "a profound change in the agenda of

American politics" occurred in 1932, as Franklin Roosevelt's New Deal fundamentally altered the nature of government in the United States (88). The result, according to Schattschneider, was that elections after 1932 "substituted a national political alignment for an extreme sectional alignment everywhere in the country except the South" (89) and had become "dominated by factors that work on a national scale" (90).[2] The evidence for this was increasingly competitive races in more parts of the country (again, outside the South).

Donald Stokes's (1965) early inquiry into nationalization began with the question "Where are the political actors whose performance is salient to the voter?" (63). As potential answers to that question, he noted that there are three sets of forces that might influence the voters' choices, namely, those at the national, statewide, and local (or "constituency") levels. In his initial analysis of the comparative impact of those forces on voting behavior in the 1950s, Stokes found that national factors explained 86% of the variance in turnout levels but just 32% of the variance in the two-party vote for the U.S. House, while district effects explained 49% of the House vote (75–78). Using a different methodological technique, however, Richard Katz (1973a) analyzed the House vote in the decade of the 1950s and found that the "American political system looks considerably more national, and less like a loose federation of unrelated local political systems, than Stokes's analysis would lead one to expect" (825). Indeed, Katz found that national forces explained nearly 55% of the variance in the House vote while district-level forces explained just 26% of such variance (823).[3] Furthermore, Democratic districts were more nationalized than Republican districts (with national factors accounting for at least 60% of the variance in Democratic districts), and competitive districts were more nationalized than noncompetitive ones (823–24).

In a subsequent study that extended the analysis back to the 1870s, Stokes (1967) found that the influence of local forces on voter turnout had declined steadily over time and reached a low point in the 1950s, while national forces began growing in influence after the first decade of the twentieth century and reached their peak in the 1950s (192–95). With respect to the impact of local forces on the party vote for the House, it began declining steadily after its peak in the 1920s, reaching a nadir in the 1950s (195–96). This implied an increase in the influence of national forces, although it could well have been state forces that superseded local ones. Although Stokes did not provide any evidence to settle the matter, Claggett, Flanigan, and Zingale (1984) would later do so using Stokes's method. They examined the impact of local and national forces through the 1960s and found that after a slight increase in national influence between 1920 and 1940, the impact of national forces declined a bit and then leveled off in the 1950s and 1960s (79). Thus, for the period of time between 1860 and 1970, Claggett, Flanigan, and

Zingale describe the influence of national forces on the House vote as "erratic and low" (80).

Still, Claggett and colleagues noted that the nationalization thesis is appealing. "Surely," they maintained, "improved communications, a national economy, national media, and nationwide campaigning by presidents for congressional candidates of their party *ought* to have produced more nationalized response by voters" (1984, 80). To explore that possibility, they examined two conceptualizations of the phenomenon in question. One such conceptualization treats nationalization as "*convergence in the levels of partisan support* across the nation" (80, emphasis in original). That is, when political behavior is becoming nationalized, different parts of the country begin to look similar in terms of their support for the two major parties. The second conceptualization views nationalization as "uniformity in the *response* of geographical units to the political forces in an election" (80, emphasis in original).

The analysis by Claggett, Flanigan, and Zingale (1984) differed in several ways from Stokes's analysis, including the fact that they used county-level, rather than congressional district, data and substituted regional forces for state forces. Although they altered Stokes's statistical model, Claggett, Flanigan, and Zingale still adopted a variance-components approach for their analysis of elections between 1842 and 1970. Their results indicated that for most of the twentieth century, national effects had roughly half the influence on voting in House races that local effects had (89). Indeed, they failed "to find any increase over the past 100 years in the nationalization of party voting in either a convergence in the levels of partisan support or in the uniformity of response" (89).

Extending such analysis to 1980, Kawato (1987) also sought to measure the influence of national factors in terms of the convergence and the movement (or response) of the electorate. His findings demonstrate that there "has never been a nationalization of the U.S. electorate in terms of convergence" (1245). Interestingly, the impact of district-level factors grew after 1940 and by 1980 were by far the most dominant force. In terms of the uniformity of response by the electorate to national forces, Kawato finds "a cyclical pattern . . . rather than the monotonic nationalization found in previous research" (1246). Specifically, he found minispikes in the impact of national forces in and around 1890 and 1940. Still, district-level factors were most influential throughout the time period under examination, and the impact of those factors grew tremendously after 1950.

In an attempt to avoid the shortcomings of previous studies that had examined nationalization in only one office, Vertz, Frendreis, and Gibson (1987) used variance-components analysis to isolate the influence of national, state, and local factors in presidential, U.S. Senate, gubernatorial, and

U.S. House races. Restricting their study to the period from 1962 to 1984, Vertz and colleagues found that national factors explained most of the variance (normalized variance of 0.56) around the mean Republican share of the two-party vote within counties. In U.S. Senate and gubernatorial races, however, state-level forces predominated (0.68 and 0.63, respectively). Finally, local factors explained most of the variance (0.64) in the vote for U.S. House during the period under examination (963). As the authors concluded, "The answer to the question whether the U.S. electorate is nationalized or not would seem to be, *it depends*" (964).

Based on analyses of voting behavior into the 1980s, then, there was little evidence of nationalization. What evidence did exist suggested that national forces had brief moments of prominence (e.g., around 1940) or were influential in presidential races but had relatively marginal impact elsewhere. Indeed, in House races, district-level factors predominated throughout the twentieth century and, perhaps, grew in influence after midcentury.

The latter conclusion coincides with a body of scholarship on congressional elections that showed an uptick in the electoral safety of incumbents beginning in the 1960s (Erikson 1971, 1972; Mayhew 1974; Alford and Hibbing 1981).[4] There were many explanations for this increase in the incumbency advantage, but perhaps the most common claim was that incumbent-specific information (e.g., personal traits and voting records) had become more salient to voters than the incumbent's party identification (see Ferejohn 1977; Nelson 1978–1979). Indeed, this was said to be a period in which the partisanship of voters was declining, campaigns were becoming candidate-centered, and split-ticket voting was on the rise (Wattenberg 1984). Incumbency, of course, is a district-level (or local) factor in congressional races. As such, the growing incumbency advantage strongly implied that national factors were declining in influence, at least in House elections.

More recently, Jacobson (2015a) and Erikson (2017) have shown that the incumbency advantage began to decline in the 1980s and 1990s and had fallen to 1950s levels by 2010 (82). Carson, Sievert, and Williamson (2020) corroborate that finding and show that, in the period from 1840 to 2016, the nationalization of elections influenced the degree to which congressional incumbents had an advantage over their opponents. Nationalization itself was, in the nineteenth century, a product of electoral procedures like the party-strip ballot, and in the twentieth century, a product of "voter choices and attitudes" (158).

Perhaps paramount among those choices and attitudes is the resurgent role in the late twentieth century of partisanship in voting decisions (Bartels 2000; Hetherington 2001; Green, Palmquist, and Schickler 2002). In particular, scholars note that partisanship exerts its influence through increasingly negative attitudes toward the opposing party and not necessarily warmer feelings toward one's own party, a phenomenon known as "negative partisan-ship" (see Abramowitz and Webster 2016). Nevertheless, much of the work on the nationalization of elections treats nationalization as nearly synony-mous with partisan voting behavior. To determine whether elections have been nationalized, one simply determines the extent to which aggregate outcomes in down-ballot races are correlated with the presidential vote in the state or district. Another way of putting this, following Brady, D'Onofrio, and Fiorina (2000), is to treat "presidential vote coefficients [in regression analyses] as indicators of nationalization, or the national component of the vote" (138).

There are a number of studies of aggregate election results that detect an increase in nationalization. Some of this work finds the influence of the presidential vote in U.S. House and Senate races to have increased in recent decades (Brady, D'Onofrio, and Fiorina 2000; Abramowitz and Webster 2016; Abramowitz 2018, 62–69). In their study of state legislative races, Zing-her and Richman (2019) find that presidential vote shares significantly influ-ence the partisan balance in state legislatures, "particularly when (relatively) national polarization is high" (1047).

Sievert and McKee (2019) found an increase since the 1980s in the effect of the presidential vote on U.S. Senate and gubernatorial outcomes, although the effect is larger on the former than the latter. Sievert and McKee also examine the percentage of races won by the same party at the presidential and Senate or gubernatorial levels. In 1980, the party that won the presiden-tial contest in a state won just over 50% of the Senate contests and 44% of gubernatorial races; by 2012, "these figures rose to approximately 84 percent and 69 percent, respectively" (1062). However, when they analyzed election results by region, they found that gubernatorial elections in the Midwest had become denationalized over time, a finding they are quick to note does not "strictly undermine the evidence of more nationalized gubernatorial elec-tions," particularly given the small number of cases (1067).

A few studies replace the presidential vote with another variable intend-ed to capture national forces. Knotts and Ragusa (2016), for example, meas-ure the effect of presidential approval on special elections to the U.S. House from 1995 through 2014. They find approval's influence to have grown throughout the period, "with the 2002 midterm representing an important juncture in the nationalization of special elections" (34). Similarly, Rogers (2016) gauges the impact of presidential approval on the likelihood that state legislators will attract challengers (as well as the impact of approval on voters' decisions, as discussed below). Rogers finds that, controlling for state and local conditions, legislators in the president's party are more likely to attract challengers, especially as the president's approval rating drops (213–16).

Among the aggregate studies of nationalization, Bartels's (1998) analysis of state-level presidential election results from 1868 to 1996 is unique. In it, he separates the impact of a partisan component "reflecting standing loyalties carrying over from previous elections" from national (and subnational) forces (277). He found that the relative influence of national and subnational forces had been balanced for much of the twentieth century. However, that balance had tipped "toward national forces at the beginning of the New Deal and in the most recent elections [i.e., the 1980s and 1990s] and toward sub-national forces during the racial sorting-out of the 1950s and '60s" (285).

In their study of polarization in the mass public and among 'U.S. senators, Caughey, Dunham, and Warshaw (2018) compile a data set of hundreds of poll results (and over one million respondents) from 1946 to 2014. Rather than study individual attitudes, the authors examine partisan subconstituencies (i.e., Democrats and Republicans as groups of voters within states). They find that Democratic and Republican subconstituencies have become increasingly polarized on economic, racial, and social issues and that state differences within parties have largely disappeared, a process they refer to as "ideological nationalization" (141–42). Furthermore, they show that ideological nationalization has occurred both for state-party publics and for senators in all three policy domains and that "the nationalizing trends in the Senate and the mass public parallel each other closely throughout the period" (144).

Although most aggregate studies exploring nationalized voting behavior find evidence of nationalization, a few do not. Gimpel's (1996) inquiry into autonomous state party systems, or "those where the local party coalitions are consistently different from national party coalitions" (3–4), found qualified support for nationalization. Comparing the mean presidential vote in a state with the state's mean votes for U.S. House, U.S. Senate, and governor between 1914 and 1990, he found that subpresidential outcomes in eastern and midwestern states were more congruent with presidential voting than were those in western states, which were more autonomous. The reason for the differences, he explained, is that the issues over which the national parties spar "have less salience in western state politics than in the East and Midwest" (31).

Gimpel's conclusion, that "the extent to which U.S. state politics is nationalized has been overblown," should be considered in light of the fact that he was writing in the mid-1990s (1996, 23). It is quite possible that signs of emerging nationalization were on the verge of becoming apparent just as Gimpel's study ended. Indeed, Renner's (1999) reexamination of the congruence between presidential results and Senate and gubernatorial outcomes between 1986 and 1996 in the states Gimpel studied came to a different conclusion. Using factor analysis, Renner finds "more evidence of congruence than incongruence" and notes that in "both the northern and western states, a single dominant factor emerges that explains comparable percentages of the variance. There do not appear to be consistently different electoral planes along which state elections are fought" (130).[5]

The results of a study by Kasuya and Moenius (2008) also cast doubt on claims of nationalization. Drawing on the comparative politics literature, they conceptualize nationalization as low levels of both "inflation" and "dispersion" within a party system. For Kasuya and Moenius, *inflation* is the degree to which party competition at the district level differs from party competition nationally. Obviously, the less the difference in levels of competition between districts and the nation as a whole, the lower the level of inflation. *Dispersion* is "the variation across districts of the extent of each districts' [sic] contribution to national-level party system inflation." (127). When all districts contribute to inflation equally, dispersion is low. Kasuya and Moenius apply these concepts to House elections from 1870 to 2002 and find "the American party system started from localization, and then became highly nationalized during the period from the 1930s to the 1960s, while more recent decades have seen more localized interparty competition" (133).

Similarly, in his study of party nationalization in dozens of countries around the world, Morgenstern (2017) found limited evidence for either static or dynamic nationalization in the United States. With respect to *static nationalization* (or the homogeneity of results across the country at a given point in time), Morgenstern found some variation over time but, in general, concluded that static nationalization in the United States is "very low" (97). For *dynamic nationalization* (or the consistency of change in party support across districts over time), the data suggest that this form of nationalization grew "from moderate levels in the 1950s to very high levels in the 1980s before falling back somewhat in the 1990s and 2000s" (97). "The takeaway," he maintains, "is still that the US parties have low DN, but there is evidence that localism is less severe than in earlier decades" (98).

Finally, Trounstine (2018) examined partisan representation at the local and national levels between 1990 and 2006. Nearly one-third of all county councils in the twelve states in her data set had partisan majorities that differed from the presidential majority in those counties. Trounstine considers the possibility that the number of representationally split counties has decreased over time and finds that it has done so. Furthermore, she finds that part of the explanation for representational splits is incomplete partisan realignment at the local level. Indeed, "the national vote did not become a better predictor of local seat shares over the course of [the] time series. It appears that unlike the state and congressional levels, local realignment was not more prevalent during this period" (38).

Using individual-level data—specifically the votes cast by 6.6 million voters in South Carolina between 2010 and 2018—Kuriwaki (2020) also shows that behavior in local elections often differs from the behavior of the same voters in national races. Ticket-splitting, which is often identified as a sign that local forces carry more sway than national forces, has decreased quite dramatically in congressional elections in recent years. However, Kuriwaki shows that the percentage of voters who split their tickets in races below the national level and the statewide level is routinely in the double digits. Indeed, in the time period under examination, nearly one-fifth of voters in South Carolina voted for a county sheriff candidate from a different party than their choice for president (17).

Several other scholars have attempted to explore nationalization at the individual level. Born (2008), for example, used American National Election Study (ANES) data from 1980 through 2004 to show that among a range of national forces—including ideology, retrospective economic evaluations, and assessments of presidential candidates' personal qualities—only party identification has become more determinative of voting for the House of Representatives. Recently, a number of studies of nationalized voting behavior have employed data from the Cooperative Congressional Election Study (CCES). Sievert and McKee (2019) rely on CCES data from 2008 to 2016 as well as exit poll data for the period 1990–1998 to gauge the level of same-party voting between presidential and subpresidential levels. They find that "voters in Senate elections not only exhibit high levels of partisan loyalty but also do so in an increasingly uniform manner" (1071). Voters in gubernatorial elections also show signs of increased partisan loyalty, although the changes over time are less pronounced and in some regions of the country (e.g., the Midwest) are hardly noticeable at all (1071–73). Rogers's (2016) analysis of CCES data finds that state legislators' electoral fates are largely connected to presidential approval. And Moskowitz (2021) relies on the CCES to show that local news coverage attenuates the nationalization of elections; that is, where there is more access to local news, there is more ticket-splitting.

Two scholars, relying on both aggregate and individual-level data, have done more than any others to advance the view that American politics has become nationalized in recent years. In a series of papers analyzing the last few election cycles, Jacobson (2015b; 2015c; 2017; 2019) shows that voting behavior, and thus election results, are increasingly influenced by national factors. "One simple measure of electoral nationalization," explains Jacobson (2019) "is the standard deviation of the change in major-party vote share from the previous election across stable, contested districts; the smaller the standard deviation, the more uniform the swing across districts, and thus the more nationalized the election" (23). In the 2014 and 2018 midterm elections, the standard deviation of the swing was 4.3, which Jacobson notes is less than half of the average standard deviation in the 1970s and 1980s. In addition, Jacobson finds that the correlation of the House and Senate vote with the presidential vote is now routinely in the mid- to high-90% and high-80% range, respectively. This is a much higher correlation than in previous decades.

Among his varied evidence for nationalization, Hopkins (2018) demonstrates that presidential voting and gubernatorial voting have become increasingly related since the 1980s (42–51). He also shows that the home state advantage that presidential candidates have long been thought to enjoy began shrinking at about the time the correlation between presidential and gubernatorial voting began growing (53). The implication here is that national considerations (e.g., partisanship) have started to override more localized factors such as where a candidate calls home. In a chapter that draws on a range of evidence—including survey, internet search, campaign contribution, and voter turnout data—Hopkins provides further support for the conclusion that

> Americans today are markedly more engaged with national and above all presidential politics than with state or local politics. And while there is evidence that Americans were more engaged with national politics than with state politics as far back as the late nineteenth century, it is also clear that the gap between national and subnational engagement has been growing in recent decades. . . . National politics—and above all the American presidency—seems to be the sun around which contemporary American political behavior revolves. (Hopkins 2018, 86)

This review of the literature provides fairly strong evidence for the thesis that American elections have become nationalized. There is, no doubt, evidence to the contrary, particularly when we look at elections for offices below the national and statewide levels. But the bulk of the scholarship, especially in more recent work, strongly suggests that national forces began to exert influence in the 1980s (if not earlier), grew more influential in the 1990s, and have, over the last two decades, become dominant.

However, all of the scholarship reviewed to this point focuses on voting behavior. The evidence for nationalization rests very heavily on the fact that voters have begun voting in similar ways for president and for Congress and, perhaps, for governor. Although an increase in partisan loyalty among voters is undoubtedly an essential element of nationalization, it is not the only one. Surely, if elections have become nationalized, we should see evidence in the behavior of other political actors.

Political Parties

In the World War II era, the political parties in the United States were highly decentralized. That is, state and local parties were largely autonomous and often were run by party bosses at the state or municipal level. Indeed, as E. E. Schattschneider (1942) wrote at the time, above the state and local party machines, "there are visible only the transparent filaments of the ghost of a party" (163). V. O. Key (1958) echoed that conclusion a few years later when he noted that "more than a tinge of truth colors the observation that there are no national parties, only state and local parties" (361). Given the lack of a national element, Key referred to American parties as "more nearly confederative than federal in nature" (368). And Hugh Bone (1958) would end his study of the national party committees by noting, "To a considerable degree the strength, role, and effectiveness of the national party agencies will be determined by the attitude of the state and local organizations and how important the national party as an entity is to them" (239; see also Cotter and Hennessy 1964).

This lack of central authority in the parties prompted a committee of the American Political Science Association (APSA), chaired by Schattschneider, to issue a report in 1950 calling for the parties to become more "responsible." That is, parties must offer voters a distinct choice so that the electorate can hold the party in power accountable for its actions, and parties must also recognize "that national, state and local party leaders have a common responsibility to the party membership" (APSA Committee on Political Parties 1950, 2). Among the recommendations the committee made were that national conventions should meet biennially and that a "party council" should be formed in each party to develop and enforce a national party agenda (5).[6]

No sooner had the APSA report been issued than Schattschneider (1956) himself recognized that increasing party competition in the post–World War II era was producing more robust party organizations in states that had previously been dominated by one party. The pressure to build stronger organizations, he maintained, was rooted initially in presidential elections (212). Indeed,

> in a nationalized political system, local party organization is never a purely local matter . . . because national interests may be defeated by weak local organizations anywhere in the country—a state may be lost because some small-town organizations did not mobilize

their vote, and the country may be lost because a close state is lost (Schattschneider 1956, 213).

Few others noticed the changes taking place in the party organizations, although David (1956) documented signs of the increasingly "tight" organization at the national level (346). He also identified the 1954 midterm elections as the first in American history in which "both major parties were actively and simultaneously led by their titular heads [i.e., Eisenhower and Stevenson] in a mid-term campaign" (347).

If stronger, more centralized parties were beginning to emerge in the 1950s, their full development would take time and face setbacks. By the 1970s, numerous scholars were describing "party decomposition," as Burnham (1970) called it. Volumes with titles like *The Party's Over* (Broder 1971) and *American Parties in Decline* (Crotty and Jacobson 1980) began to appear. The work in this camp detailed the parties' "inability . . . to sufficiently organize, represent, and compete" (Ladd 1978, xxi).

The basis of the "party decline" thesis, however, was not a deteriorating organizational capacity but the changing behavior of the American voter. Voters were becoming, so it was said, less partisan in their attitudes and behavior (among the vast literature on this topic, see Nie, Verba, and Petrocik [1976]). This led to, among other things, more candidate-centered decision-making and more split-ticket voting (Wattenberg 1991).

Parties exist, at least in part, to get politicians elected to office (Aldrich 1995). As such, we would expect parties to adapt to new circumstances like a decline in partisan voting behavior. Considerable evidence from the 1980s suggests that the parties were adapting at the very moment when some scholars were announcing their demise. Schlesinger (1985) heralded a "new American political party" that had become "more national in scope, more active, and with clear signs of greater linkage among its nuclei" (1162), a party nucleus being "the collective efforts to capture a single office" (1153). Herrnson (1988) showed that the national parties in the 1980s were "wealthier, more stable, better organized and better staffed than ever before" (121). Multiple studies by Cotter, Gibson, Bibby, and Huckshorn demonstrated the growing organizational strength of the parties between the 1960s and 1980s at the local (Gibson et al. 1985) and state (Bibby et al. 1983; Gibson et al. 1983) levels. These newly strengthened party organizations were bolstered by the development of stronger national party organizations and by the integration, or interdependence, of party organizations at all levels of government (Huckshorn et al. 1986; Cotter et al. 1989).

It is important to note that party adaptation took different forms in the two parties (Cotter and Bibby 1980). The Democrats underwent a process of "reform" that focused on party rules and procedures, such as delegate selection, while the Republicans engaged in "renewal" of the party's organizational capacities.[7] Democratic reform was provoked by the party's contentious 1968 national convention and was an attempt to address demands that the party's presidential nomination process be more representative of its rank-and-file supporters (Shafer 1983). However, this procedural reform was followed several years later by a renewal effort in the Democratic Party akin to the organizational transformation of the Republicans in the 1970s (Herrnson 1996). That transformation was prompted by the competitive disadvantage the GOP faced in the mid-twentieth century (Conway 1983), and it led to the creation of what many have called a "service party" capable of providing campaign assistance to Republican candidates around the country (Bibby 1979; Conley 2013).[8] The Democrats' party renewal project was similarly triggered by electoral considerations following President Carter's unsuccessful reelection bid (Herrnson 1996).

By the 1980s, then, both parties had centralized resource allocation and campaign support, as well as quite a bit of authority (e.g., over delegate selection rules), in their national committees (including the House and Senate campaign committees). Nevertheless, the process of nationalization was far from complete (Bibby 1986). As Esptein (1982) put it, "Despite the substantial nationalizing responses of the parties . . . their confederative structures have been modified rather than destroyed" (102). Several studies of the Democratic Party indicated that the party had obviously centralized in organizational and procedural terms, but was not capable of dictating presidential nominations, setting party policy, or enforcing party discipline (Hitlin and Jackson 1979; Longley 1980). Jackson and Hitlin (1981) showed that while in 1976 there was widespread support among Democratic national convention delegates for the reforms the party had recently made, there was also resistance to further centralization of power in the national party. As they concluded, "The old confederation is now gone and the new federal structure of the party would seem to be secure" (285).

Paddock's (1990; 1991) analyses of both parties' national and state platforms from 1956 to 1980 found that, despite the nationalization of many party functions during this period, the parties remained decentralized in terms of policy positions. However, in his examination of state party platforms from 1918 to 2014, Hopkins (2018) concluded, "Until around 1960, knowing what state a platform came from was critical in knowing the topics it was likely to highlight" (159). At that point, the parties' state platforms began to look more uniform throughout the country. Today, "there is increasingly a single national agenda to which the various state parties are responding. Far more than in the past, the state parties now shift their gaze in unison, from education to terrorism or gay marriage as national politics dictate" (159). In their extension of Hopkins's analysis through 2017, Hopkins, Schickler, and Azizi (2020) maintained that in the period after 1990, it has become "clear that cross-state differences in topic usage are declining," which is "consistent with the nationalization of the political agenda, as many states have increasingly given similar attention to a range of high-profile topics" (20).

Despite this nationalization of the parties' policy agendas, the parties have recently been described as "hollow." According to Schlozman and Rosenfeld (2019), the parties are "neither organizationally robust beyond their roles raising money nor meaningfully felt as a real, tangible presence in the lives of voters or in the work of engaged activists" (121).[9] Even the nationalized policy agenda may not be the result of the parties actively centralizing their programs. As Schlozman and Rosenfeld see it, "In place of programmatic formal parties are polarized networks of interest and advocacy groups, drawing on research and expertise from higher education and think tanks" (135). The result is "platform-by-proxy" (135), whereby the "platform-drafting process serves principally to gauge different factions' relative institutional clout within the party" (136). Nor can the parties control presidential nominations. Although there was a period of roughly twenty years (starting in 1980) when the party establishment was able to steer the nomination to its preferred candidate (Cohen et al. 2008), it now appears that such coordination is beyond the capacity of party insiders (Cohen et al. 2016).

Ultimately, while the parties are more nationalized (or centralized) than they were in the mid-twentieth century, they are far from fully nationalized entities. Their ability to establish a policy agenda—and, more importantly, to enforce it—and to influence nominations is limited. Still, they play a critical role in the campaigns of their candidates.

Candidates and Their Campaigns

Given the length and expense of American political campaigns, and the attention paid to them in the media, it is surprising that they have not been the focus of much nationalization scholarship. It seems natural to ask if campaigns have been nationalized. But very little research asks that question, and scholars interested in nationalization have largely ignored the role that campaigns play in advancing (or hindering) the process of nationalization.[10]

To our knowledge, only two recent studies directly explore the role of national issues in subnational campaigns. Holliday's (2020) study of 93 presidential and 312 gubernatorial election debates from 2000 to 2018 attempts to determine how much gubernatorial candidates focus on state, as opposed to national, issues and whether the focus has changed over time. He finds little evidence that gubernatorial campaigns are nationalized or that they are becoming more nationalized over time. "On the whole," Holliday maintains, gubernatorial candidates still talk about issues relevant to the state and have done so at about the same rate for the past two decades. While certain national topics do seem to find their way into gubernatorial campaigns, the share of time spent debating them is relatively small, and the degree to which such nationalized topics do come up is only weakly associated with subsequent nationalization of election results. (Holliday 2020, 15–16)

Of course, Holliday's data extends back only to 2000, but it is unlikely that gubernatorial campaigns were more nationalized before 2000 than they have been recently.

Down-ballot candidates in presidential election years have a strategic choice to make, namely, whether to tie oneself to the top of the ticket. Doing so, of course, is a way of nationalizing the campaign. That may be especially true when the candidate at the top of the ticket is unusually controversial. Liu and Jacobson (2018) examined Republican congressional candidates' embrace of Donald Trump in 2016 to understand both the decision to support Trump (or not) and the effects of that decision. They found that candidates in competitive districts were significantly less likely to support Trump than candidates in either safe Republican districts or safe Democratic districts. Women and incumbents were somewhat less likely to support Trump, but women incumbents were significantly less likely to do so. Interestingly, a candidate's decision to embrace Trump's candidacy or distance themselves from it had no noticeable effect on their electoral performance (because partisanship influenced the vote up and down the ballot).[11]

Just How Nationalized Is American Politics?

We are left with something of a blurry picture with respect to the nationalization of American politics. At the level of the electorate, there is abundant evidence that voting behavior has become nationalized. Of course, the voting patterns we have seen in recent years (e.g., a decline in split-ticket voting) may well be, as Morris Fiorina has long argued, the result of a constrained set of choices given to voters—at all levels of government, the choice is virtually always between a left-of-center Democrat and a right-of-center Republican (see, for example, Fiorina [2017]). Nevertheless, the rise of negative partisanship suggests a change in the attitudes of voters such that they increasingly view one party favorably and the other, at all levels of government, as unacceptable.

At the elite level, there is far less evidence that politics has become nationalized. Power within the political parties is undoubtedly more centralized in the national committees today than it was in the past, but those committees, nonetheless, appear "hollow" in many respects. Unfortunately, there are so few studies of candidates and their campaigns that we know very little about how nationalized campaign efforts have become.

The assumption, of course, is that those representing—or hoping to represent—states and local districts must have nationalized their appeals in recent years. Otherwise, what is the source of the nationalized behavior of the voters? While it is probably safe to assume that elites have contributed to nationalization at least to some extent, precisely how they have done so, and in what venues, has yet to be established. It could be, for example, that the rhetoric of governing differs in important ways from the rhetoric of campaigning, and that one but not the other has become nationalized.

To better understand the role of political elites in the process of nationalization, we believe campaigns are a good place to start. Media attention focuses on elections every two years and the electoral arena is highly partisan. If political elites are communicating national themes to voters, one would expect those themes to show up in campaigns.

Case Study Selection and Methods

If American elections have become nationalized, we should see clear signs of nationalization in the campaigns of candidates running in congressional and state-level races, but to date no one has studied these campaigns in that context. This work begins by accepting the premise that the electorate is indeed becoming more nationalized, which allows us to turn our focus toward the campaigns themselves. If electoral behavior suggests that voters conceive of congressional and state-level elections in nationalized terms, then down-ballot candidates and their campaigns either are structured in such a way as to present voters with nationalized choices, or these candidates and campaigns simply do not matter and voters are ignoring them in order to transform congressional and state legislative races into nationalized elections. While it may be tempting to assume that down-ballot candidates are nationalizing their campaigns, this work specifically examines whether and/or to what extent that is true and, in doing so, explores a component of nationalization that until now has been generally ignored by scholars: nationalization from the perspective of the candidates and their campaigns.

Because there is currently no theory of how nationalization operates in campaigns and there are very few studies that even consider nationalization in a campaign context, our approach is to observe numerous campaigns, guided by an overarching research question instead of engaging in any tests of specific hypotheses. We expect that this inductive approach will allow for theorizing and hypothesis development in future work. Our study is therefore exploratory and intended to generate findings that can later be turned into hypotheses to develop a theory of nationalization within the context of local campaigns.

Our work provides new insight into how candidates and campaigns operate in a nationalized environment, as well as examining these candidates and campaigns from a new and, we believe, better perspective. In addition to providing a comparative analysis of campaigns and elections for one particular office (e.g., congressional races), we also provide a vertical analysis of the potential reciprocal influences of simultaneous elections at the presidential, congressional, and state legislative levels in a given location (specifically, within congressional districts). We know of no previous study, for example, that has examined the impact of a presidential or U.S. House campaign on the strategies employed by state legislative candidates. The very idea of nationalization suggests that a vertical approach is essential in order to capture the potential nationalizing forces at work in down-ballot races. If congressional and state-level campaigns are part of larger nationalized forces, the only way to capture these influences would be to examine these elections within a wider context. In other words, an examination of statewide or congressional elections in isolation could miss the connections between elections at different levels—the very connections that make nationalization possible.

We begin our analysis of the 2020 Pennsylvania election cycle in Chapter 2, with an analysis of the presidential, congressional, and state legislative races throughout the state. Chapters 3 through 8 then provide case studies of six congressional districts. Using the congressional district as the unit of analysis, scholars selected because of their proximity to and knowledge of campaigns and elections in their geographic areas offer "nested" studies of campaigns and elections within their congressional districts. Each case examines the presidential, congressional, and state house legislative district races taking place within the boundaries of the congressional district. Consequently, each case can examine how races were conducted up and down the ballot and within the context of the other elections happening simultaneously. This approach provides us with analyses of elections at the state, congressional, and presidential levels and also with a more complete understanding of how state and congressional elections operate within the context of a broader general election environment.

The six congressional districts were selected based on competitiveness, partisanship, population density, incumbency, and geography. The goal was to have a wide variety of cases, from competitive to safe, liberal to conservative, urban to suburban to rural, including Democratic and Republican incumbents and elections in every part of the state. Nested within each congressional district are analyses of two state house legislative races. House races were selected to provide a similar variety of cases. See Table 1.1.

TABLE 1.1 OVERVIEW OF CASES

Congressional Districts				PA State House Districts	
District	Incumbent and Party	Location	Population Density	House Districts	Incumbent and Party
First	Fitzpatrick (R)	Southeastern	Suburban/ rural	143th 144th	Labs (R) Polinchock (R)
Fourth	Dean (D)	Southeastern	Urban/ suburban	150th 154th	Webster (D) Open
Eighth	Cartwright (D)	Northeastern	Rural	119th 120th	Mullery (D) Kaufer (R)
Tenth	Perry (R)	Mid-state	Rural/small town	105th 199th	Lewis (R) Gleim (R)
Sixteenth	Kelly (R)	Northwestern	Rural/small town	6th 9th	Roae (R) Sainato (D)
Seventeenth	Lamb (D)	Southwestern	Suburban	28th 30th	Open Mizgorski (R)

Our study does not include U.S. Senate or Pennsylvania state senate elections because, in the 2020 election cycle, there were no U.S. Senate races in Pennsylvania and the limited number of Pennsylvania state senate elections made comparisons across races difficult. In Pennsylvania, half of the fifty senate districts are up for election each election cycle. In 2020, only odd-numbered senate seats were being contested and thus the number of races that our study could have included was limited. In addition, although the Pennsylvania Supreme Court redrew Pennsylvania's congressional districts in 2018, state legislative districts were generally not affected. As a result, state legislative districts often do not follow congressional district lines. In practical terms for our study, this meant that some congressional districts did not have any state senate races being contested in 2020, others had only one state senate race (and some of these were not competitive or lacked a challenger), and for others the state senate districts were not nested within a single congressional district. Therefore, we decided to include two state house races in each congressional district, rather than have some state senate races mixed in with a majority of state house races.

We selected our chapter authors and matched them with their congressional districts in early 2020, but state house races were not selected until after the June 2nd primary election in order to ensure that all selected races had credible Democratic and Republican candidates and that we had a good mix of different types of races. Each of the chapters, using a Pennsylvania congressional district as the unit of analysis, simultaneously tracks presidential, congressional, and state legislative campaigns in an effort to provide unique insights into three different types of elections, while also exploring the potential localization and/or nationalization of elections at these different levels.

The goal of each case study is the same: to determine the degree to which U.S. House of Representatives campaigns and state legislative campaigns were nationalized with respect to resources, messaging, strategy, and tactics, and to examine how much coordination and incidental compatibility took place between campaigns at the presidential, congressional, and state legislative levels. Our case study authors closely monitored the presidential, congressional, and state legislative races and gathered data by interviewing political elites, tracking campaign communications (via media, social media, and direct mail), and attending campaign events and candidate debates. We were greatly assisted by AdImpact, a firm specializing in campaign media data analytics, which provided us with a list of every media ad buy (radio, cable, and TV) for every presidential, congressional, and state legislative race in real time. AdImpact was also able to provide the actual ads and a transcript of every TV ad aired for all presidential, congressional, and state legislative races in Pennsylvania.

Before going into the field, the case study authors were all given the same rubric to use when looking for nationalizing factors. According to the rubric,

- Nationalization in speeches, campaign communications, and so on emphasizes ideology and partisanship and is less likely to emphasize incumbency, unique candidate traits, local issues, and government services.
- When local topics and candidate characteristics are discussed in nationalized campaigns, they are framed symbolically to reflect national debates.
- Nationalized races emphasize negative partisanship.
- A piece of campaign communication (e.g., a television ad or a piece of direct mail) is nationalized to the extent that the words and images can be used for or against any candidate, anywhere in the country. Names could simply be changed and the remaining content would be the same.
- A piece of campaign communication is localized to the extent that the words and images can be used for or against only a specific candidate or a particular locality. None of the content can be applied to another race (or to more than a very limited number of races) in exactly the same way.

While each case study examined the presidential, congressional, and state races using the same data collection techniques and the same operationalized definition of *nationalization*, the authors did not share their findings with one another until after they had completed their analysis because we did not want any single case to influence the findings in any other case. It was important for our study that each case operated independently from the others.

Why Pennsylvania?

These case studies are situated within Pennsylvania not only because it is the state where we live but also because many of the patterns of nationalization and polarization evident across the United States during the past few decades are also evident within the Keystone State. Notably, Pennsylvania's mix of urban and rural communities, its relatively large share of white, working-class voters, and changes to its manufacturing base mirror important voting groups and economic changes that have helped drive these patterns of nationalization and polarization across the United States. Pennsylvania also happens to be a swing state that typically includes competitive congressional races. A state that is expected to have competitive races up and down the ballot with a mix of economic and demographic representation is a good place to begin trying to understand whether and how parties, campaigns, and interest groups cooperate and communicate with voters. This section—"Why Pennsylvania?"—provides background information about the changes that have taken place in Pennsylvania since the end of the twentieth century.

Pennsylvania has been a vigorously contested swing state for decades, and it was designated by many media outlets and political commentators as a vital swing state heading into 2020.[12] President Trump's 2016 victory in Pennsylvania appeared to change the state's recent statewide electoral habits, which were favorable to Democrats, but the 2018 midterm results raised questions about the durability of the president's electoral coalition. The 2018 midterms showed that voters in Trump counties, although equally motivated to vote in 2018 compared to 2016, were less monolithically supportive of Republican candidates, while the voters residing in the counties that Hillary Clinton won in 2016 were much more supportive of Democrats in 2018. The divergent results of 2016 and 2018 made Pennsylvania a priority for both campaigns in 2020.

Despite having a Democratic voter registration advantage from 1960 to 2000, the state had a Republican bias in electoral contests—Democrats won only 46% of statewide elections in the state during this time period (Treadway 2005). In fact, the Republicans' electoral success in this era made some people doubt that the state's voter registration statistics reflected the actual partisan disposition of the state's voters (Yost 2003).

Democrats performed better statewide between 2000 and 2018, winning five of six presidential races, four of five gubernatorial races, and three of seven Senate races. In total, Democrats won most (70%) statewide elections from 2000 to 2018, while Republicans controlled the majority of seats in congressional (eight of ten elections, one tie), state house (eight of ten), and state senate (ten of ten) elections. The state's partisan competitiveness is demonstrated by the 2106 presidential election: Republican Donald Trump carried the state, while all three state row offices—Attorney General, Auditor General, and Treasurer—were won by Democrats.

Social and Economic Change Since 2000

The social and economic changes underlying political change in Pennsylvania reveal a stressed and economically struggling state. The state had relatively slow population growth, growing only 4.1% since 2000,[13] with virtually every noncore and micropolitan county in the state experiencing population declines after 2001.

Median household income declined in the state, although income change tended to differ regionally. The median household income was $58,820 (in inflation-adjusted dollars) in 2000 and was $56,951 in 2018. Also, the poverty rate increased, from 11.0% to 13.1%. Income changes are notably different depending on the county, and most counties in small metros earned below the state median. It also seems that the smaller counties that showed growth in median household income are located in areas that have benefited from the shale gas boom in the state. This relationship may explain at least some of the movement toward Republican registration in southwestern Pennsylvania, as Republican policies are often more industry-friendly.

Manufacturing employment was 16.0% in 2000 and had fallen to 11.9% by 2017. Every county in Pennsylvania experienced a decline in manufacturing employment, although reliance on that sector differs considerably across the state. The loss of manufacturing jobs is frequently mentioned as one of the causes of white working-class anxiety.

More state residents had a bachelor's degree or higher in 2018 (30.1%) than in 2000 (22.4%). Only five counties, Allegheny, Bucks, Centre, Chester, and Montgomery, show college attainment among more than 40% of adults.

The state is a bit more diverse than it was at the turn of the century: 84.1% of the population identified as white alone in 2000 compared to 77.3% white alone today. Still, most counties in the state are overwhelmingly white.

These social and economic changes have produced clear divides between the state's rural communities and its urban and suburban areas. These divergent geographic realities in part underlie the emergent political trends that have made the state increasingly competitive.

Changes to the Pennsylvania Electorate in the Twenty-first Century

Pennsylvania voters normally cast a larger share of their votes, about two percentage points more on average since 1960, for Democratic presidential candidates compared to the nation as a whole, although this advantage has steadily declined since 2004.[14] Donald Trump's performance in Pennsylvania in 2016 narrowly exceeded his performance nationally. One revealing feature of Pennsylvania elections during this time is that the Democratic presidential candidates have carried fewer of the state's 67 counties, despite winning eleven of the fifteen presidential elections. From 1960 to 2016, Democrats won an average of 18.6 counties; from 2000 to 2016 they won an average of 14.6 counties (Cook 2020).

Voter Registration

The geographic distribution of Pennsylvania's registered voters and their corresponding electoral preferences have changed noticeably, and in some cases profoundly, during the first twenty years of the twenty-first century. Democratic registration has grown from 3.5 million to 4.05 million, or 15.3%. Republican registration has grown from 3.1 million to 3.2 million, or 5.2%. The Democrats' registration advantage by 2018 was 819,573 voters. The largest counties have a larger share of registered Democrats, and the smaller counties almost invariably have fewer registered Democrats. These changes seem to reflect pronounced geographic and demographic patterns—Democratic growth is in the southeast, while the southwest shows the greatest Democratic loss.

Although these changes are regional, they also reflect the uneven economic growth associated with population density and proximity to dense urban metro areas (Kolko 2019). Simply put, the rate of economic growth has diverged for urban and rural counties. Sizable Democratic defections have occurred in the large fringe metro outside of Pittsburgh, while sizable Democratic gains are seen in the large fringe metro outside of Philadelphia. Virtually every small metro, micropolitan, and noncore county has seen Democratic defections and increasingly large Republican registration advantages.[15]

The change in registration by urban-rural classification appears in Table 1.2. Most of the Democrats' statewide voter registration advantage comes from the state's two large central metros; Philadelphia and Allegheny Coun-

TABLE 1.2 VOTER REGISTRATION BY URBAN-RURAL CLASSIFICATION, PENNSYLVANIA 1998 AND 2018

County Classification	Democratic Registration 2018	Republican Registration 2018	Total Registration 2018	Democratic Registration 1998	Republican Registration 1998	Total Registration 1998
Large central metro	1,340,367	376,003	1,970,091	1,246,994	444,872	1,821,717
Large fringe metro	1,128,646	1,040,494	2,542,553	876,382	1,054,957	2,165,750
Medium metro	1,016,429	989,347	2,365,964	815,859	865,171	1,868,231
Small metro	267,451	353,844	73,436	238,154	288,904	589,305
Micropolitan	218,714	330,360	626,753	244,333	298,415	585,378
Noncore	80,540	142,526	253,250	93,248	119,980	228,441

Source: Compiled and created by the authors using data downloaded from the Pennsylvania Department of State. Available at https://www.dos.pa.gov/VotingElections/OtherServices
Events/VotingElectionStatistics/Pages/VotingElectionStatistics.aspx.

ty provide a 964,364-vote Democratic advantage, while the three smallest county categories give Republicans a 260,025-vote advantage. The state's battlefield is in the large fringe and medium metros, where neither party has a sizable advantage: Democrats had 2,145,075 voters and Republicans had 2,029,841 voters.

Voting Patterns

Voters' preferences follow the aforementioned voter registration patterns. Many counties, particularly in the southwest, demonstrate a linear and consistent trend away from Democratic presidential candidates in the state's presidential elections since 2000. Specifically, Beaver, Cambria, Fayette, Greene, Lawrence, and Washington Counties have shown a steady decline in the votes they provide Democratic candidates, moving from providing a majority of their votes to Democratic candidates to providing a majority of their votes for Republicans. Prior to 2000, Beaver, Fayette, Greene, and Washington Counties were among the top ten most Democratic counties in the state (Treadway 2005).

Compared to Al Gore in 2000, Hillary Clinton in 2016 had no real advantage in vote share in the large central metros, while she lost a large number of votes in the next two largest metro categories.[16] A defining feature of the 2016 presidential election in Pennsylvania was the way that voter turnout and the expected performance of the major-party candidates changed compared to prior elections. In 2016, according to Yost, Redman, and Thompson (2017), "counties with more working-class voters turned out in greater numbers and gave less support to Democratic candidates than in previous elections, while areas that should have been supportive of Democrats had lower turnout and offered little change in support." The counties that President Trump won in 2016 represented about 47% of voters, and Hillary Clinton won only one-third of the vote in those counties.

Figure 1.1 provides a direct comparison of Clinton and Gore vote share by county. Viewing Hillary Clinton's county vote share in relation to Al Gore's county vote share confirms the Democrats' sizable loss of support in the large fringe metros of southwestern Pennsylvania during the first part of this century and underscores a lack of significant gains elsewhere to offset those losses.

Comparing changes in the returns for Governor Tom Wolf and U.S. Senator Bob Casey in their past two elections helps further clarify how voting patterns are changing at the county level. A third of the state's counties gave Governor Wolf a smaller share of the vote in 2018 than in his 2014 campaign, with double-digit declines in rural counties and strong gains in a half dozen

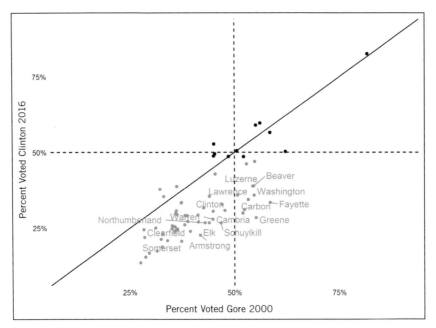

Figure 1.1 Change in Democratic vote, 2000 and 2016 presidential elections. The diagonal line represents no change in vote share; counties below the line gave a smaller share of their vote to Hillary Clinton compared to Al Gore. The labeled counties had a decline of 15% or more in their Democratic vote share. Black dots are counties won by Hillary Clinton in 2016. (Compiled and created by the authors using data downloaded from the Pennsylvania Department of State.)

suburban counties (Yost and Redman, in press). Senator Casey saw declines in counties located in northeastern Pennsylvania, and his greatest gains were, like those of Governor Wolf, in suburban counties. The changes in these two races show how the state has reorganized itself in the Trump era (Figure 1.2): The northeast seems to be moving away from Democrats and the southeast seems to be moving toward them.

The Realignment of Partisanship and Ideology

The data on party registration and voting over the past twenty years show how voting patterns in the state have changed. There are numerous reasons for these changing preferences, but no political change has been more consequential to state politics than the sorting of the state's voters into more ideologically consistent partisans. Figure 1.3 shows how the ideological composition of partisans has changed among Pennsylvania's registered voters

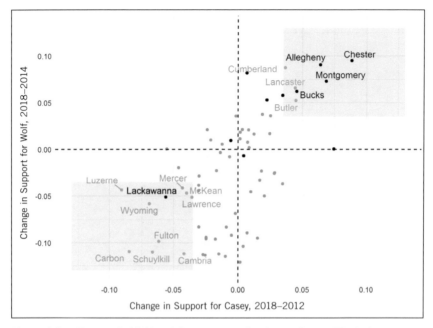

Figure 1.2 Changes in Wolf and Casey county-level vote shares. Black dots are counties won by Hillary Clinton in 2016. The gray boxes show counties where vote shares increased or declined by more than 3.5 points for both candidates. (Compiled and created by the authors using data downloaded from the Pennsylvania Department of State.)

between 2000 and 2018. Liberals are now more likely to identify as Democratic than they were in 2000, while conservatives are even more likely to identify as Republican today than in the past. This partisan realignment in Pennsylvania is consistent with patterns identified nationally and in other states (Abramowitz 2018).

This chapter has highlighted the central questions of our study, defined *nationalization*, and provided an overview of the scholarly literature. In addition, it has explained how the case studies are structured and why we situated them in Pennsylvania. Chapter 2 provides a statewide overview of the level of nationalization in presidential, congressional, and state legislative races. This aggregate-level analysis not only presents a context for our case studies but also establishes baseline measures of nationalization in Pennsylvania. The case study chapters that follow allow for an in-depth analysis of how nationalization played out in individual congressional and state legislative races. The concluding chapter ties together the aggregate-level analysis from Chapter 2 and the individual-level case studies. Because our understanding of nationalization's role in down-ballot races is limited, this work is large-

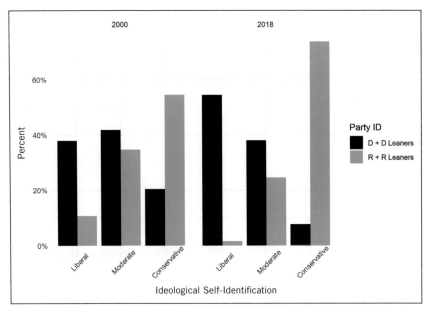

Figure 1.3 Ideological self-identification and party identification of Pennsylvania voters, 2000 and 2018. (Compiled and created by authors from October 2000 Keystone Poll, Millersville University, and October 2018 Franklin & Marshall College Poll.)

ly exploratory in nature; our goal is to produce generalizable conclusions that can be tested empirically in future work.

NOTES

1. We should note that we do not consider the role of the media in this review because we are interested in actors who make decisions that are explicitly political. For scholarship that examines nationalization and the media, see Hopkins (2018, Chapter 9) and Moskowitz (2021).

2. Quite a few years earlier, in a review of Austin Ranney's *The Doctrine of Responsible Party Government*, Schattschneider (1954) had noted the "nationalization of party alignments since 1932" (153).

3. See Stokes's (1973) comment on Katz's analysis and Katz's reply (1973b).

4. Although the view that members of Congress had become less vulnerable in the 1960s and 1970s was widely held, there were those who challenged that conclusion (see, for example, Jacobson [1987]; see also Ansolabehere, Brady, and Fiorina [1992] in response to Jacobson).

5. See Gimpel (1999) for a response to Renner's analysis.

6. For a complete treatment of the APSA's report, see Chapter 1 of Rosenfeld (2018).

7. The distinction between party reform and party renewal can be found in Conley (2013), among others.

8. Gavin (2012) argues that the GOP's renewal efforts of the 1970s had roots as far back as the New Deal era, when the party initiated institutional changes in response to devastating losses in the 1930s.

9. See also Azari (2016), who has described the present era as one of "weak parties and strong partisanship."

10. There are a number of studies of nationalized campaigning in the comparative politics literature. To give just one example, Hijino and Ishima (2021) coin the term *cross-level electoral appeals* (or CLEAs) and identify factors that lead to more frequent CLEAs in Japanese local elections.

11. Schoenberger's (1969) study of Republican House candidates' decisions to endorse Barry Goldwater in 1964 examined only the effects of those decisions and not the factors that influenced them in the first place.

12. See, for example, the FiveThirtyEight forecast that showed Pennsylvania as the key tipping-point state (available at https://projects.fivethirtyeight.com/2020-election -forecast/) and this analysis from the *Washington Post* (available at https://www.washing tonpost.com/politics/2020/11/01/here-are-states-which-have-been-most-likely-deliver -presidency/).

13. The state's population was 12,281,054 in 2000 (Table DP-1) and 12,790,505 in 2017 according to the 2013–2017 ACS 5-Year Population Estimates (Table S0501).

14. Source: https://uselectionatlas.org/RESULTS/, accessed October 31, 2019.

15. We use the definitions and names found in D. D. Ingram and S. J. Franco, 2014, "2013 NCHS Urban-Rural Classification Scheme for Counties," *Vital Health Statistics* (Series 2, Data Evaluation and Methods Research), 166:1–73.

16. We compare 2000 to 2016 because neither race included an incumbent.

REFERENCES

Abramowitz, Alan I. 2018. *The Great Alignment: Race, Party Transformation, and the Rise of Donald Trump*. New Haven, CT: Yale University Press.

Abramowitz, Alan I., and Steven Webster. 2016. "The Rise of Negative Partisanship and the Nationalization of U.S. Elections in the 21st Century." *Electoral Studies* 41:12–22. Available at https://doi.org/10.1016/j.electstud.2015.11.001.

Aldrich, John H. 1995. *Why Parties? The Origin and Transformation of Political Parties in America*. Chicago: University of Chicago Press.

Alford, John R., and John R. Hibbing. 1981. "Increased Incumbency Advantage in the House." *Journal of Politics* 43:1042–61. Available at https://www.journals.uchicago.edu /doi/abs/10.2307/2130188?journalCode=jop

Ansolabehere, Stephen, David Brady, and Morris Fiorina. 1992. "The Vanishing Marginals and Electoral Responsiveness." *British Journal of Political Science* 22:21–38.

APSA Committee on Political Parties. 1950. *Toward a More Responsible Two-Party System: A Report of the Committee on Political Parties of the American Political Science Association*. New York: Rinehart.

Azari, Julia. 2016. "Weak Parties and Strong Partisanship Are a Bad Combination." *Vox*, November 3, 2016. Available at https://www.vox.com/mischiefs-of-faction/2016/11/3 /13512362/weak-parties-strong-partisanship-bad-combination.

Bartels, Larry M. 1998. "Electoral Continuity and Change, 1868–1996." *Electoral Studies* 17:275–300.

———. 2000. "Partisanship and Voting Behavior, 1952–1996." *American Journal of Political Science* 44:35–50.

Bibby, John F. 1979. "Political Parties and Federalism: The Republican National Committee Involvement in Gubernatorial and Legislative Elections." *Publius* 9:229–36.

———. 1986. "Political Party Trends in 1985: The Continuing but Constrained Advance of the National Party." *Publius* 16:79–91.

Bibby, John F., James L. Gibson, Cornelius P. Cotter, and Robert J. Huckshorn. 1983. "Trends in Party Organizational Strength, 1960–1980." *International Political Science Review* 4:21–27.

Bone, Hugh A. 1958. *Party Committees and National Politics.* Seattle: University of Washington Press.

Born, Richard. 2008. "National Forces and the U.S. House Vote, 1980–2004: The Uncertain Progress of Nationalization." *Congress and the Presidency* 35:87–103.

Brady, David W., Robert D'Onofrio, and Morris P. Fiorina. 2000. "The Nationalization of Electoral Forces Revisited." In *Continuity and Change in House Elections,* edited by David W. Brady, John F. Cogan, and Morris P. Fiorina, 130–48. Palo Alto, CA: Stanford University Press.

Broder, David S. 1971. *The Party's Over: The Failure of Politics in America.* New York: Harper & Row.

Burnham, Walter Dean. 1970. *Critical Elections and the Mainsprings of American Politics.* New York: W. W. Norton.

Caramani, Daniele. 2004. *The Nationalization of Politics: The Formation of National Electorates and Party Systems in Western Europe.* New York: Cambridge University Press.

Carson, Jamie L., Joel Sievert, and Ryan D. Williamson. 2020. "Nationalization and the Incumbency Advantage." *Political Research Quarterly* 73:156–68.

Caughey, Devin, James Dunham, and Christopher Warshaw. 2018. "The Ideological Nationalization of Partisan Subconstituencies in the American States." *Public Choice* 176:133–51.

Chhibber, Pradeep K., and Ken Kollman. 2004. *The Formation of National Party Systems: Federalism and Party Competition in Canada, Great Britain, India, and the United States.* Princeton, NJ: Princeton University Press.

Claggett, William, William Flanigan, and Nancy Zingale. 1984. "Nationalization of the American Electorate." *American Political Science Review* 78:77–91.

Cohen, Marty, David Karol, Hans Noel, and John Zaller. 2008. *The Party Decides: Presidential Nominations Before and After Reform.* Chicago: University of Chicago Press.

———. 2016. "Party Versus Faction in the Reformed Presidential Nominating System." *PS: Political Science and Politics* 49:701–8.

Conley, Brian M. 2013. "The Politics of party Renewal: The 'Service Party' and the Origins of the Post-Goldwater Republican Right." *Studies in American Political Development* 27:51–67.

Conway, M. Margaret. 1983. "Republican Political Party Nationalization, Campaign Activities, and Their Implications for the Party System." *Publius* 13:1–17.

Cook, Rhodes. 2020. "Pennsylvania." *Sabato's Crystal Ball,* July. Accessed June 29, 2020. Available at http://centerforpolitics.org/crystalball/articles/states-of-play-pennsylvania.html.

Cotter, Cornelius P., and John F. Bibby. 1980. "Institutional Development of Parties and the Thesis of Party Decline." *Political Science Quarterly* 95:1–27.

Cotter, Cornelius P., James L. Gibson, John F. Bibby, and Robert J. Huckshorn. 1989. *Party Organizations in American Politics.* Pittsburgh: University of Pittsburgh Press.

Cotter, Cornelius P., and Bernard C. Hennessy. 1964. *Politics Without Power: The National Party Committees.* New York: Atherton Press.

Crotty, William J., and Gary Jacobson. 1980. *American Parties in Decline*. Boston: Little, Brown.

David, Paul T. 1956. "The Changing Party Pattern." *Antioch Review* 16:333–50.

Epstein, Leon D. 1982. "Party Confederations and Political Nationalization." *Publius* 12: 67–102.

Erikson, Robert S. 1971. "The Advantage of Incumbency in Congressional Elections." *Polity* 3:395–405.

———. 1972. "Malapportionment, Gerrymandering, and Party Fortunes in Congressional Elections." *American Political Science Review* 65:1234–45.

———. 2017. "The Congressional Incumbency Advantage over Sixty Years: Measurement, Trends, and Implications." In *Governing in a Polarized Age: Elections, Parties, and Political Representation in America*, edited by Alan S. Gerber and Eric Schickler, 65–89. New York: Cambridge University Press.

Ferejohn, John A. 1977. "On the Decline of Competition in Congressional Elections." *American Political Science Review* 71:166–76.

Fiorina, Morris P. 2017. *Unstable Majorities: Polarization, Party Sorting and Political Stalemate*. Stanford, CA: Hoover Institution Press.

Gavin, Daniel J. 2012. "The Transformation of Political Institutions: Investments in Institutional Resources and Gradual Change in the National Party Committees." *Studies in American Political Development* 26:50–70.

Gibson, James L., Cornelius P. Cotter, John F. Bibby, and Robert J. Huckshorn. 1983. "Assessing Party Organizational Strength." *American Journal of Political Science* 27:193–222.

———. 1985. "Whither the Local Parties?: A Cross-Sectional and Longitudinal Analysis of the Strength of Party Organizations." *American Journal of Political Science* 29:139–60.

Gimpel, James G. 1996. *National Elections and the Autonomy of American State Party Systems*. Pittsburgh: University of Pittsburgh Press.

———. 1999. "Contemplating Congruence in State Electoral Systems." *American Politics Quarterly* 27:133–40.

Green, Donald P., Bradly Palmquist, and Eric Schickler. 2002. *Partisan Hearts and Minds*. New Haven, CT: Yale University Press.

Herrnson, Paul S. 1988. *Party Campaigning in the 1980s*. Cambridge, MA: Harvard University Press.

———. 1996. "National Party Organizations at the Century's End." In *The Parties Respond: Changes in American Parties and Campaigns*, 3rd ed., edited by L. Sandy Maisel, 50–82. Boulder, CO: Westview Press.

Hetherington, Marc J. 2001. "Resurgent Mass Partisanship: The Role of Elite Polarization." *American Political Science Review* 95:619–31.

Hicken, Allen, and Heather Stoll. 2011. "Presidents and Parties: How Presidential Elections Shape Coordination in Legislative Elections." *Comparative Political Studies* 44:854–83.

Hijino, Ken Victor Leonard, and Hideo Ishima. 2021. "Multi-Level Muddling: Candidate Strategies to 'Nationalize' Local Elections." *Electoral Studies* 70:102281.

Hitlin, Robert A., and John S. Jackson III. 1979. "Change and Reform in the Democratic Party." *Polity* 11:617–33.

Holliday, Derek. 2020. *Nationalized Elections, Localized Campaigns: Evidence from Televised U.S. Debates*. Los Angeles: UCLA Department of Political Science.

Hopkins, Daniel J. 2018. *The Increasingly United States: How and Why American Political Behavior Nationalized*. Chicago: University of Chicago Press.

Hopkins, Daniel J., Eric Schickler, and David L. Azizi. 2020. "From Many Divides, One? The Polarization and Nationalization of American State Party Platforms, 1918–2017." Unpublished manuscript, accessed January 27, 2021. Available at https://papers.ssrn.com/sol3/papers.cfm?abstract_id=3772946.

Huckshorn, Robert J., James L. Gibson, Cornelius P. Cotter, and John F. Bibby. 1986. "Party Integration and Party Organizational Strength." *Journal of Politics* 48:976–91.

Ingram, D. D., and S. J. Franco. 2014. "2013 NCHS Urban-Rural Classification Scheme for Counties." *Vital Health Statistics*. Series 2, Data Evaluation and Methods Research. 166:1–73.

Jackson, John S., III, and Robert A. Hitlin. 1981. "The Nationalization of the Democratic Party." *Western Political Quarterly* 34:270–86.

Jacobson, Gary C. 1987. "The Marginals Never Vanished: Incumbency and Competition in Elections to the U.S. House of Representatives, 1952–82." *American Journal of Political Science* 31:126–41.

———. 2013. "How the Economy and Partisanship Shaped the 2012 Presidential and Congressional Elections." *Political Science Quarterly* 128:1–38.

———. 2015a. "It's Nothing Personal: The Decline of the Incumbency Advantage in US House Elections." *Journal of Politics* 77:861–73.

———. 2015b. "Barack Obama and the Nationalization of Electoral Politics in 2012." *Electoral Studies* 40:471–81.

———. 2015c. "Obama and Nationalized Electoral Politics in the 2014 Midterm." *Political Science Quarterly* 130:1–25.

———. 2017. "The Triumph of Polarized Partisanship in 2016: Donald Trump's Improbable Victory." *Political Science Quarterly* 132:9–41.

———. 2019. "Extreme Referendum: Donald Trump and the 2018 Midterm Elections." *Political Science Quarterly* 134:9–38.

Jones, Mark P., and Scott Mainwaring. 2003. "The Nationalization of Parties and Party Systems: An Empirical Measure and an Application to the Americas." *Party Politics* 9:139–66.

Kamarck, Elaine. 2021. "5 Lessons from Election Night 2021." *Brookings*, November 3, 2021. Accessed November 15, 2021. Available at https://www.brookings.edu/blog/fixgov/2021/11/03/5-lessons-from-election-night-2021/.

Kasuya, Yuko, and Johannes Moenius. 2008. "The Nationalization of Party Systems: Conceptual Issues and Alternative District-Focused Measures." *Electoral Studies* 27:126–35.

Katz, Richard S. 1973a. "The Attribution of Variance in Electoral Returns: An Alternative Measurement Technique." *American Political Science Review* 67:817–31.

———. 1973b. "Rejoinder to 'Comment' by Donald E. Stokes." *American Political Science Review* 67:832–34.

Kawato, Sadafumi. 1987. "Nationalization and Partisan Realignment in Congressional Elections." *American Political Science Review* 81:1235–50.

Key, V. O., Jr. 1958. *Politics, Parties, and Pressure Groups*, 4th ed. New York: Thomas Y. Crowell Company.

Knotts, H. Gibbs, and Jordan M. Ragusa. 2016. "The Nationalization of Special Elections for the U.S. House of Representations." *Journal of Elections, Public Opinion and Parties* 26:22–39.

Kolko, Jed. 2019. "Red and Blue Economies Are Heading in Sharply Different Directions." *New York Times*, November 13, 2019. Available at https://www.nytimes.com/2019/11/13/upshot/red-blue-diverging-economies.html.

Kuriwaki, Shiro. 2020. "Ticket Splitting in a Nationalized Era." Unpublished manuscript, accessed November 6, 2020. Available at https://osf.io/preprints/socarxiv/bvgz3/.

Ladd, Everett Carll. 1978. *Where Have All the Voters Gone? The Fracturing of America's Political Parties.* New York: W. W. Norton.

Lago, Ignacio, and José Ramón Montero. 2014. "Defining and Measuring Party System Nationalization." *European Political Science Review* 6:191–211.

Liu, Huchen, and Gary C. Jacobson. 2018. "Republican Candidates' Positions on Donald Trump in the 2016 Congressional Elections: Strategies and Consequences." *Presidential Studies Quarterly* 48:49–71.

Longley, Charles. 1980. "Party Reform and Party Nationalization: The Case of the Democrats." In *The Party Symbol: Readings on Political Parties*, edited by William Crotty, 359–78. San Francisco: W. H. Freeman.

Mayhew, David R. 1974. "Congressional Elections: The Case of the Vanishing Marginals." *Polity* 6:295–317.

Morgenstern, Scott. 2017. *Are Politics Local? The Two Dimensions of Party Nationalization around the World.* New York: Cambridge University Press.

Morgenstern, Scott, Stephen M. Swindle, and Andrea Castagnola. 2009. "Party Nationalization and Institutions." *Journal of Politics* 71:1322–41.

Moskowitz, Daniel J. 2021. "Local News, Information, and the Nationalization of U.S. Elections." *American Political Science Review* 115:114–29.

Nelson, Candice J. 1978–1979. "The Effect of Incumbency on Voting in Congressional Elections, 1964–1974." *Political Science Quarterly* 93:665–78.

Nie, Norman H., Sidney Verba, and John R. Petrocik. 1976. *The Changing American Voter.* Cambridge, MA: Harvard University Press.

Paddock, Joel. 1990. "Ideological Integration in Democratic Party Platforms, 1956–1980." *American Review of Politics* 11:125–36.

———. 1991. "Extent of Nationalization of Republican Policy Positions in the Post-New Deal Era." *Social Science Quarterly* 72:163–71.

Renner, Tari. 1999. "Electoral Congruence and the Autonomy of American State Party Systems." *American Politics Quarterly* 27:122–32.

Rogers, Steven. 2016. "National Forces in State Legislative Elections." *Annals of the American Academy of Political and Social Science* 667:207–25.

Rosenfeld, Sam. 2018. *The Polarizers: Postwar Architects of Our Partisan Era.* Chicago: University of Chicago Press.

Schattschneider, E. E. 1942. *Party Government.* New York: Rinehart & Company.

———. 1954. "Review of *The Doctrine of Responsible Party Government: Its Origins and Present State* by Austin Ranney." *The Annals of the American Academy of Political and Social Science* 295:152–53.

———. 1956. "United States: The Functional Approach to Party Government." In *Modern Political Parties: Approaches to Comparative Politics*, edited by Sigmund Neumann, 194–215. Chicago: University of Chicago Press.

———. 1960. *The Semi-Sovereign People: A Realist's View of Democracy in America.* New York: Holt, Rinehart, and Winston.

Schlesinger, Joseph A. 1985. "The New American Political Party." *American Political Science Review* 79:1152–69.

Schlozman, Daniel, and Sam Rosenfeld. 2019. "The Hollow Parties." In *Can America Govern Itself?*, edited by Frances Lee and Nolan McCarty, 120–51. New York: Cambridge University Press.

Schoenberger, Robert A. 1969. "Campaign Strategy and Party Loyalty: The Electoral Relevance of Candidate Decision-Making in the 1964 Congressional Elections." *American Political Science Review* 63:515–20.

Shafer, Byron E. 1983. *Quiet Revolution: The Struggle for the Democratic Party and the Shaping of Post-Reform Politics.* New York: Russell Sage Foundation.

Sievert, Joel, and Seth C. McKee. 2019. "Nationalization in U.S. Senate and Gubernatorial Elections." *American Politics Research* 47:1055–80.

Stokes, Donald E. 1965. "A Variance Components Model of Political Effects." In *Mathematical Applications in Political Science,* edited by John M. Claunch, 61–85. Dallas: Arnold Foundation, Southern Methodist University.

———. 1967. "Parties and the Nationalization of Electoral Forces." In *The American Party System: Stages of Political Development,* edited by William N. Chambers and Walter D. Burnham, 182–202. New York: Oxford University Press.

———. 1973. "Comment: On the Measurement of Electoral Dynamics." *American Political Science Review* 67:829–31.

Treadway, Jack. 2005. *Elections in Pennsylvania: A Century of Partisan Conflict in the Keystone State.* University Park: Pennsylvania State University Press.

Trounstine, Jessica. 2018. "Political Schizophrenics? Factors Affecting Aggregate Partisan Choice at the Local Versus National Level." *American Politics Research* 46:26–46.

Vertz, Laura L., John P. Frendreis, and James L. Gibson. 1987. "Nationalization of the Electorate in the United States." *American Political Science Review* 81:961–66.

Wattenberg, Martin P. 1984. *The Decline of American Political Parties, 1952–1980.* Cambridge, MA: Harvard University Press.

———. 1991. *The Rise of Candidate-Centered Politics: Presidential Elections of the 1980s.* Cambridge, MA: Harvard University Press.

Yost, Berwood. 2003. "Disappearing Democrats: Rethinking Partisanship within Pennsylvania's Electorate." *Commonwealth* 12:77–86.

Yost, Berwood, and Jacqueline Redman. In press. "The 2018 Pennsylvania Mid-Term Election: No Escaping Trump." *COMMONWEALTH: A Journal of Political Science.*

Yost, Berwood, Jacqueline Redman, and Scottie Thompson. 2017. "The 2016 Pennsylvania Presidential and US Senate Elections: Breaking Pennsylvania's Electoral Habits." *COMMONWEALTH: A Journal of Political Science* 19 (2): 3–26.

Zingher, Joshua N., and Jesse Richman. 2019. "Polarization and the Nationalization of State Legislative Elections." *American Politics Research* 47:1036–54.

2

Overview of the Pennsylvania Races in 2020

Stephen K. Medvic, Matthew M. Schousen,
and Berwood A. Yost

I f there were increasing doubts early in the twenty-first century that Pennsylvania remained a battleground state, those doubts were assuaged in 2016. Prior to that year, the Democratic candidate for president had won six straight contests in Pennsylvania. Donald Trump's narrow victory against Hillary Clinton renewed the state's status as one of the most crucial swing states in the country.

Recent congressional elections have also been hotly contested, and the delegation evenly divided, although until court-drawn district maps were imposed prior to the 2018 midterms, Republican gerrymandering gave the GOP an edge in these races. State legislative districts remain gerrymandered and, thus, Republicans have an advantage in state house and senate races. Nevertheless, Democratic control of the legislature has been a distinct possibility in the last few election cycles.

At all levels of government, Pennsylvania is among the most competitive states in the country. This chapter examines the 2020 campaigns at the presidential, congressional, and state legislative levels to provide an aggregate analysis of the outcomes and to provide context for the case studies that follow. For each level of election, we draw on available public opinion data as well as campaign spending data and advertising data to help understand party fortunes in these races. Of particular focus are the campaign themes and strategies the candidates appear to have employed. The chapter concludes with a preliminary assessment of evidence for and against claims of nationalization.

The Presidential Campaign

The 2020 presidential campaign in Pennsylvania was likely to be every bit as competitive as the 2016 campaign had been. As he reminded voters in the Commonwealth at every opportunity, Joe Biden was born in Scranton. Having represented a neighboring state in the U.S. Senate for thirty-six years, he was well known, and generally well liked, in Pennsylvania.

For his part, President Trump had the advantage of running as the incumbent. Although unpopular with voters in the cities and suburbs of the state, his support in more rural areas seemed to have grown during his four years in office. And while the economy had been quite strong for three of those years, COVID-19, and Trump's handling of it, hindered the president's ability to claim an unqualified success for his first term.

Pennsylvania voters were dissatisfied with the direction of both the state and the nation as the parties and campaigns waged the fall campaign. Two in five (43%) state voters felt the state was "headed in the right direction," which was well below the high of 57% the prior fall.[1] Voters listed COVID-19 (27%) as the most important problem facing the state, with concerns about the economy (including unemployment, personal finances, and business retention) being the second most common concern (21%). The only other issue listed as a problem by more than one in ten registered voters in Pennsylvania was concern about government and politicians (16%).

More of the state's registered voters had an unfavorable (57%) than favorable (42%) opinion of President Trump at the end of October 2020, while more voters had a favorable (52%) than unfavorable (47%) opinion of Joe Biden. About two in five (42%) voters thought President Trump was doing an "excellent" or "good" job as president, which was consistent with his ratings in Pennsylvania throughout his term of office. President Trump's job approval ratings were strongly associated with party and ideology: A majority of Republicans (83%) rated the president's performance positively, while few Democrats (8%) or independents (30%) did so; conservatives (83%) were much more likely than moderates (29%) or liberals (2%) to give the president a positive job approval rating. The president's approval rating for his management of the coronavirus outbreak was lower (33%) than his overall job approval rating.

Throughout the campaign, President Trump held an advantage on economic issues, but Mr. Biden held an advantage over the president on all other characteristics tested, most notably on issues in dealing with the coronavirus (see Table 2.1).

Perhaps the most notable feature of public opinion during the campaign was the energy created by President Trump's candidacy. This energy motivated voters from both parties: Four in five (78%) of those planning to vote

TABLE 2.1 PERCEPTIONS OF PRESIDENTIAL CANDIDATE ISSUE STRENGTHS, PENNSYLVANIA 2020

Which Candidate . . .		Trump	Biden	Neither	Don't Know
Is most prepared to handle the economy?	Oct. 2020	48%	45%	4%	3%
	Sep. 2020	48%	46%	4%	2%
	Aug. 2020	48%	44%	4%	3%
Will better handle the job of commander in chief of the military?	Oct. 2020	42%	51%	5%	3%
	Sep. 2020	41%	53%	5%	2%
	Aug. 2020	43%	47%	5%	5%
Has the best plan to handle the coronavirus?	Oct. 2020	31%	53%	12%	5%
	Sep. 2020	31%	50%	14%	5%
	Aug. 2020	30%	49%	15%	6%
Will better manage issues related to race?	Oct. 2020	34%	53%	9%	5%
	Sep. 2020	32%	54%	9%	6%
Will do a better of keeping communities safe?	Oct. 2020	42%	47%	6%	4%
	Sep. 2020	43%	48%	6%	3%

Source: 2020 Franklin & Marshall College Polls.
Note: The question asked was, "Regardless of how you plan to vote, which presidential candidate do you think is best described by each of the following statements?"

for the president said they were voting for him, not against Joe Biden. More than half (54%) of Biden's supporters said they were voting against President Trump, not for Biden. It seemed likely that the outcome in Pennsylvania would hinge largely on evaluations of the president, both good and bad.

Joe Biden's monthly polling averages in Pennsylvania were relatively stable throughout the fall, while the president's vote share indicated a slow rise. Monthly averages were Biden 50% to Trump 43% in July; Biden 49% to Trump 44% in August; Biden 50% to Trump 44% in September; Biden 50% to Trump 45% in October; and Biden 50% to Trump 46% in November (Figure 2.1). The monthly polling average and the general trend in the polls themselves suggested that President Trump was slowly closing Joe Biden's preelection lead as the campaign approached Election Day and that approximately 5% of voters were still undecided on Election Day itself.

The candidates and their campaigns were extremely active in Pennsylvania. According to one source, there were more campaign events in Pennsylvania (forty-seven) than in any other state, meaning more than one-fifth (22%) of all campaign events occurred in the Commonwealth (National Popular Vote n.d.). The campaigns and their allied party organizations and advocacy groups also spent huge sums of money on advertising. According

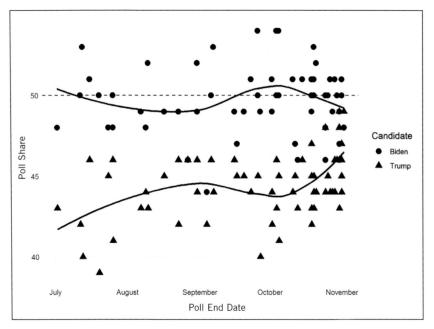

Figure 2.1 Pennsylvania presidential polls, 2020. (Created by the authors using data downloaded from RealClearPolitics. n.d. Accessed January 5, 2021. Available at https://www.realclearpolitics.com/epolls/2020/president/pa/pennsylvania_trump_vs_biden -6861.html.)

to the advertising tracking firm AdImpact, advertising in the presidential campaign accounted for three-quarters of all media spending in the state and exceeded $222.8 million from July through November.[2] Groups spending more than $1 million are listed in Table 2.2.

Presidential ads focused on the coronavirus (17%), jobs (10%), the economy (9%), and health care (8%). There were, of course, party differences in terms of the issues emphasized in ads. COVID-19 was mentioned in nearly one-quarter of all Democratic ads. Among the other issues emphasized by Biden and his allies were health care (9%), character (9%), the economy (9%), and jobs (6%). Republican ads barely mentioned COVID and instead highlighted jobs (15%), taxes (10%), the economy (9%), health care (7%), and Medicare (6%). Law and order also garnered considerable attention in Republican ads, including mentions of crime (7%), law enforcement (6%), defunding the police (4%), and riots (4%).

While most of these ads were national in scope, quite a few were tailored to a local audience. In fact, of the top fifty presidential campaign ads that ran in Pennsylvania, based on gross ratings points, a quarter of them (thirteen) made some mention of Pennsylvania either orally or in text on the screen.[3]

TABLE 2.2 GROUPS SPENDING MORE THAN $1 MILLION ON ADVERTISING IN THE PA PRESIDENTIAL CAMPAIGN, 2020

Group	Affiliation	Total Spending
America First Action	R	$28,856,369
Future Forward	D	$28,100,279
American Bridge 21st Century	D	$19,082,283
Priorities USA Action	D	$6,868,708
Democratic National Committee	D	$5,888,411
Restoration PAC	R	$4,752,880
Unite the Country	D	$4,443,830
Club for Growth Action	R	$2,760,033
NRA Victory Fund	R	$2,476,890
DNC/Biden	D	$2,085,239
RNC/Trump	R	$1,803,540
The Lincoln Project	D (anti-Trump Rs)	$1,600,068

Source: AdImpact; calculations by authors.

Often, any reference to Pennsylvania was subtle. In one ad for Biden, called "We Deserve Better" from American Bridge 21st Century, "Janie" from "Westmoreland County, PA" declares—in a distinctly western Pennsylvania accent—that Biden "would just be good. And that sounds so simple, but it's so powerful."

Pennsylvania's role as an energy-producing state garnered considerable attention among the ads with the greatest reach. The two ads with the most gross ratings points both focused on fracking in Pennsylvania (and both were sponsored by the pro-Trump super PAC America First Action). In one ad, entitled "November," a "third-generation oil and gas" worker speaks directly to the camera, saying, "When Joe Biden says he'd eliminate fracking, he's talking about my job; he's talking about our future." The screen then displays a single sentence, in white lettering on a black background: "Joe Biden's fracking ban would kill up to 600,000 Pennsylvania jobs."

The campaign clearly engaged a large portion of the electorate. Turnout among the voter-eligible population was 71%, which was 4.5 points higher than the voter-eligible turnout nationally.[4] Turnout for 2020 was the highest in the state since the 1936 presidential election (73.2% among the voting age population in 1936 [Treadway 2005]). A total of 6.9 million votes were cast in the presidential race in the state, and Joe Biden won 50.0% to Donald Trump's 48.8%. Biden's share of the vote in Pennsylvania was about one point lower than his national vote share.[5]

TABLE 2.3 STATEWIDE VOTE TOTALS FOR DEMOCRATIC CANDIDATES, 2020

Office	2020 Total Votes Cast	2020 Total Democratic Votes	Democratic Share	Roll-Off	Roll-Off (%)
President	6,915,283	3,458,229	0.500	—	—
Attorney general	6,806,596	3,461,472	0.509	108,687	0.016
Representative in Congress	6,779,307	3,346,712	0.494	135,976	0.020
State treasurer	6,761,806	3,239,331	0.479	153,477	0.022
Auditor general	6,751,657	3,129,131	0.463	163,626	0.024
Representative in the General Assembly	6,479,713	3,011,043	0.465	435,570	0.067

Source: Calculations by authors from official Pennsylvania state returns data. Accessed January 23, 2021. Available at https://electionreturns.pa.gov/ReportCenter/Reports.

The Democratic win in the presidential race did not translate into widespread success for other Democratic candidates in the state. Democrats won a majority share of the votes cast in only two races: the presidential race and the state row office of attorney general. Republicans won a larger share of the vote for the other two row offices, auditor general and treasurer, as well as for the U.S. Congress and the Pennsylvania State House (see Table 2.3). Nearly 2% fewer voters cast a ballot in congressional races, and almost 7% fewer voters cast a ballot in state house races than in the presidential race.[6]

The Congressional Races

The 2020 congressional elections in Pennsylvania were held in districts whose boundaries were drawn by the state Supreme Court in advance of the 2018 midterm elections. The "remedial plan" the court imposed was intended to correct for what it found to be the "clearly, plainly, and palpably" unconstitutional plan enacted by the legislature following the 2011 round of redistricting (Medvic and Yost 2020, 30). While Republicans held a 13–5 advantage in congressional seats from Pennsylvania prior to the remedial plan, the parties each took nine seats in the 2018 elections.

All eighteen incumbents ran for reelection in 2020. The *Cook Political Report* (2020) identified six of the eighteen races as at least somewhat competitive. The most competitive race (a "Republican Toss Up") was anticipated to be in the Tenth Congressional District, where Scott Perry was the incumbent. Brian Fitzpatrick (First District) was in a "Lean Republican" seat while

Matt Cartwright's (Eighth District) race was deemed a "Lean Democratic" seat. Finally, Republican Mike Kelly (Sixteenth District) and Democrats Susan Wild (Seventh District) and Connor Lamb (Seventeenth District) were in districts that were "likely" to be held by their parties but were by no means "safe."

Although polling in specific races was sparse, Democrats appeared to hold a slight advantage in the generic congressional ballot preference test. Democratic candidates held a roughly 50% to 44% advantage heading into the election, although enough voters remained undecided to sway the outcome to either side.[7] Of course, a generic statewide lead does not translate directly, or uniformly, to individual districts. As a result, Democrats were not likely to enjoy a significant advantage in the most competitive races in the state.

If spending is a measure of how competitive a race is, then three of the congressional races in Pennsylvania were hotly contested in 2020. As Table 2.4 indicates, both candidates in the First, Tenth, and Seventeenth Congressional Districts spent more than $2 million. In two of the other three races that the *Cook Political Report* deemed competitive, the incumbent—but not the challenger—raised at least that much. In the Sixteenth Congressional

TABLE 2.4 2020 PA CONGRESSIONAL CANDIDATES WHO SPENT AT LEAST $2 MILLION

District/Candidate	Amount Spent
First Congressional District	
Brian Fitzpatrick (R)*	$4,272,135
Christina Finello (D)	$2,339,748
Seventh Congressional District	
Susan Wild (D)*	$4,528,267
Eighth Congressional District	
Matt Cartwright (D)*	$4,144,070
Tenth Congressional District	
Scott Perry (R)*	$3,839,197
Eugene DePasquale (D)	$4,526,684
Seventeenth Congressional District	
Conor Lamb (D)*	$3,448,850
Sean Parnell (R)	$3,732,399

Source: Center for Responsive Politics. "Pennsylvania Congressional Races, 2020." OpenSecrets.org. Accessed March 8, 2021. Available at https://www.opensecrets.org/races/election?id=PA.
* Incumbent candidate.

District, Mike Kelly raised more than $2 million but spent just $1.3 million in his successful campaign.

Nearly $42 million was spent on advertising in congressional races, an amount that constituted about 14% of advertising spending in the state in 2020. More than half of that money (about 52%) was spent by party committees (including super PACs attached to the Hill committees) and outside groups. Table 2.5 reports advertising spending by parties and outside groups in the 2020 congressional elections. Aside from the parties and their super PACs, no group was active in more than two races, and only one, the Club for Growth, spent more than $1 million on advertising.

TABLE 2.5 ADVERTISING SPENDING IN THE PA CONGRESSIONAL CAMPAIGNS, 2020

Group	Affiliation	Total Spending
House Majority PAC (DCCC) (3)	D	$5,783,465
Congressional Leadership Fund (NRCC) (3)	R	$5,507,673
NRCC (2)*	R	$2,262,723
Club For Growth Action (2)	R	$1,850,030
DCCC (3)**	D	$1,634,044
Jobs For Our Future PAC (1)	R	$898,575
Defending Main Street Super PAC (1)	R	$730,159
House Freedom Action (1)	R	$508,356
Vote Vets (1)	D	$497,985
Republican Jewish Coalition Victory Fund (1)	R	$494,433
House Majority Forward (2)	D	$484,782
Future Progress PAC (1)	D	$373,301
UA Union Plumbers and Pipefitters Vote! PAC (1)	D	$368,100
AFSCME (1)	D	$294,715
American Action Network (1)	R	$229,000
With Honor Fund/Action (2)	Nonpartisan	$214,948
Special Operations for America (1)	R	$119,281
Keep Pennsylvania Great (1)	R	$118,186
Conservative Leadership Alliance (1)	R	$21,014
The Conservative Caucus (1)	R	$10,520

Source: AdImpact; calculations by authors.
Notes: Advertisers listed spent a minimum of $10,000. Numbers in parentheses are the number of races in which the group was active.
* Spent an additional $629,692 in coordination with House candidates.
** Spent an additional $1,974,881 in coordination with House candidates.

Perhaps not surprisingly, congressional campaign advertising focused on health care (14%) and the coronavirus (12%). Considerable attention was also given to taxes (6%), "defund the police" (6%), and jobs (5%). Democrats placed most of their emphasis on health care (22%), followed by COVID (14%). Among the other issues (or names) mentioned frequently in Democratic ads were jobs (7%), special interests (6%), and Donald Trump (6%). For Republicans, "defund the police" and taxes (11% each) were mentioned most, followed by COVID (9%), Nancy Pelosi (8%), character (7%), and crime (7%).

Ads containing nationalized messages often linked a congressional opponent to an unpopular national figure like Donald Trump or Nancy Pelosi. They focused exclusively on issues that are part of a national debate, like whether preexisting medical conditions should be protected in health care plans or whether police forces should be "defunded." A typical ad from Republican groups sounded like one from the Congressional Leadership Fund attacking Christina Finello, the Democratic candidate in the First Congressional District. In the ad, entitled "Can't Trust Her," the narrator says that Finello is "supported by the same radicals that want to defund our local police, causing vandalism and crime to rise in our neighborhoods, leading to schools and parks that are less safe by cutting crucial prevention programs and eliminating the officers in our communities who protect our most vulnerable." For her part, Finello ran several ads linking her opponent, incumbent Republican Brian Fitzpatrick, to Donald Trump and his attempts to defund Planned Parenthood and end protections for preexisting conditions.

Nevertheless, plenty of ads were local in nature, emphasizing either the individual traits, or life story, of a candidate or an issue that is specific to a given area. An ad for incumbent Republican Mike Kelly in the Sixteenth Congressional District focused entirely on a former drug addict and the second chance in life that Kelly gave him by hiring him to work at Kelly's car dealership. In the Tenth Congressional District, a Club for Growth ad entitled "Serves Himself" was devoted solely to attacking Democrat Eugene DePasquale for his ties to an allegedly corrupt Philadelphia union leader whom DePasquale had appointed to the Delaware River Port Authority.

Despite all the advertising, no Pennsylvania congressional district changed party in 2020, nor did any incumbents lose. Republicans had a slight advantage in total votes cast—50.6% to 49.4%—but this obscures the fact that only three races were decided by fewer than 5 points: the Seventh, Eighth, and Seventeenth (see Table 2.6). The average margin of victory in the state's congressional districts in 2020 was 27.7 points. Looking at only the congressional races in the state, one would likely conclude that 2020 was a status quo election year.

TABLE 2.6 CONGRESSIONAL ELECTION OUTCOMES IN PENNSYLVANIA

District	Democratic Candidate	D % of Vote	Republican Candidate	R % of Vote	Margin
01	Christina Finello	43.4	**Brian Fitzpatrick***	56.6	13.2
02	**Brendan Boyle***	72.5	David Torres	27.5	45.0
03	**Dwight Evans***	91.0	Michael Harvey	9.0	82.0
04	**Madeleine Dean***	59.5	Kathy Barnette	40.5	19.0
05	**Mary Gay Scanlon***	64.7	Dasha Pruett	35.3	29.4
06	**Christina Houlahan***	56.1	John Emmons	44.0	12.1
07	**Susan Wild***	51.9	Lisa Scheller	48.1	3.8
08	**Matt Cartwright***	51.8	James Bognet	48.2	3.6
09	Gary Wegman	33.7	**Dan Meuser***	66.3	32.6
10	Eugene DePasquale	46.7	**Scott Perry***	53.3	6.6
11	Sarah Hammond	36.9	**Lloyd Smucker***	63.1	26.2
12	Lee Griffin	29.2	**Fred Keller***	70.8	41.6
13	Raymond Rowley	26.5	**John Joyce***	73.5	47.0
14	William Marx	35.3	**Guy Reschenthaler***	64.7	29.4
15	Robert Williams	26.5	**Glenn Thompson***	73.5	47.0
16	Kristy Gnibus	40.7	**George Kelly***	59.3	18.6
17	**Conor Lamb***	51.2	Richard Parnell	48.9	2.3
18	**Michael Doyle***	69.3	Luke Negron	30.8	38.5

Source: Calculations by authors. Official Pennsylvania State Returns data. Accessed January 23, 2021.
Available at https://electionreturns.pa.gov/ReportCenter/Reports.
Note: Incumbents identified by asterisks; winners shown in bold.

It is notable that only sixteen congressional districts in the United States voted for a representative in Congress from a party different from the presidential candidate that won the district, and two of those seats are in Pennsylvania. Representative Brian Fitzpatrick (PA-1 R) won his seat by thirteen points, while Joe Biden carried the First Congressional District by six points; Representative Matt Cartwright (PA-8 D) won his seat by four points, while Donald Trump won the Eighth District by four points (Coleman 2021).

The State Legislative Races

Although Pennsylvania often votes Democratic in presidential elections, over the last several decades the General Assembly has consistently rested in Republican hands. Since 1992, the state senate has been in Republican control in all but one election cycle, with the lone exception occurring in

1992–1993 when both parties held twenty-five seats. In the state house, the Republicans have controlled the chamber in all but three cycles (1992–1993, 2006–2007, and 2008–2009).

However, the Democrats' significant gains in 2018 (eleven seats in the state house and five in the state senate), along with polling data suggesting that Biden could easily win the state, gave Democrats hope that they might win control of one or both chambers in 2020. They needed to pick up only five senate seats and nine house seats to take control of both chambers. Most political commentators, though, did not like the Democrats' chances. The *Cook Political Report* consistently rated both state legislative chambers as "lean Republican," and most state political reporters shared the view expressed by local NPR reporter Katie Meyer of affiliate WHYY: "Just because [a flip in both chambers is] in the realm of possibility, though, doesn't mean the legislature will have a dramatic shift" (Meyer 2020).

In the house, although all 203 seats were up for reelection, Ballotpedia identified only thirty-two vulnerable seats (nineteen Republicans and thirteen Democrats). If the Democrats were to win all nineteen vulnerable Republican seats but lose the thirteen vulnerable Democrats, they would pick up only six seats and still fall short of control. A similar problem existed in the senate, where twenty-five of the fifty senate seats were up for election in 2020. The Democrats needed to pick up five seats to win control of the chamber, but Ballotpedia identified only four vulnerable seats (three Republican and one Democrat).

A second problem for the Democrats was the limited number of open seats, exacerbated by the fact that most of these open seats tended to be in safe districts. In 2020 the house had only twenty-one open seats, while the senate had only four. Of the twenty-one open house seats (eleven Republican and ten Democratic), the party that held the seat before the election retained control of the seat nineteen times (each party lost one seat). On the senate side, both parties successfully defended their two open seats. If either party wanted to win a large number of seats, they would have to unseat safe incumbents—a tough task in any election cycle.

In a year that shattered many political fundraising records, the Pennsylvania state legislative races were no exception. The total amount of money raised by outside groups, parties, and candidates for 2020 state house and senate campaigns reached almost $70 million. Democratic candidates and their supporters in the state house led the way, raising $33 million, while their Republican counterparts raised only $11 million. In state senate races, Republican candidates and their supporters outraised Democrats by $2 million ($13 million to $11 million).[8] Our study, however, is particularly concerned with how campaigns used those funds to communicate to voters. For all state legislative races combined, campaign advertising on the airwaves, according to AdImpact, topped $30 million ($16 million in house races and $14.5 million in senate races). In senate races, media spending was about equal between the parties, but in the house the Democrats heavily outspent the Republicans.

Based on AdImpact data, most of the ads for state house campaigns were purchased by the candidates themselves (46%). The parties were responsible for 34% of ad spending, followed by outside groups at 20%. What is most surprising is that the Democrats outspent the Republicans three to one ($13.5 to $4 million), and overall incumbents were actually outspent by challengers (59% to 41%). For the Democrats, challengers spent more than incumbents (73%), while on the Republican side incumbents did most of the spending (60%).

In terms of outside groups, only two nonparty connected groups were active in house races, and once again the Democrats outspent the Republicans (see Table 2.7). In this case, the pro-Democratic group, PA Fund for Change, spent nearly $4 million on ads, while the pro-Republican group, Commonwealth Leaders Fund, spent just under half a million dollars. Democratic Party committees also outspent their Republican counterparts.

On the senate side, the vast majority of the $14 million spent on advertising came from the candidates themselves (84%), while 11% came from parties and 5% from outside groups. Surprisingly, challengers significantly outspent incumbents (62% to 38%). These spending data seem to suggest that Democratic challengers and those funding them believed that this was the year to unseat Republican incumbents. Of the $6.2 million spent by Democratic candidates, 91% was spent by challengers. On the Republican side, challengers were responsible for only 31% of $5.9 million in spending. Overall spending on campaign advertising was basically equal, with Republicans spending $7 million and Democrats $7.5 million.

Also, surprisingly, outside groups did not spend heavily in the 2020 general election (see Table 2.7). Overall, they represented only 5% of total spending, buying ads in only six of the twenty-five races (the 9th, 13th, 15th, 37th, 45th, and 49th Districts). Spending was roughly equal on both sides. The Commonwealth Leaders Fund spent $50,000 to $60,000 in three races (the 13th, 15th, and 37th Districts) and the Pennsylvania Chamber of Business and Industry between $92,000 and $150,000 in five races (the 9th, 13th, 15th, 45th, and 49th Districts). On the Democratic side, the Pennsylvania Fund for Change led the way, spending over $1 million in senate races.

Contrary to what one might expect in a highly polarized political environment, state legislative races were not carbon copies or scaled-down versions of the presidential campaigns. State legislative candidates tended to run their own campaigns, focusing on issues that could link them to their constituents and their communities. But while the candidates definitely

TABLE 2.7 MEDIA SPENDING IN THE PA STATE LEGISLATIVE
CAMPAIGNS, 2020

Group		Affiliation	Total Spending
Pennsylvania Fund for Change		D	$4,869,633
	House		$3,705,863
	Senate		$1,163,760
PA House Democratic Campaign Committee (HDCC)*		D	$3,374,271
Commonwealth Leaders Fund		R	$624,591
	House		$465,693
	Senate		$158,898
PA Democratic Legislative Campaign Committee (DLCC)		D	$600,146
	House		$429,462
	Senate		$170,684
PA Chamber of Business and Industry**		R	$564,334
Republican State Leadership Committee (RSLC)**		R	$309,806
PA House Republican Campaign Committee (HRCC)†		R	$80,000
PA House Republican Campaign Committee (HRCC)*		R	$40,489

Source: AdImpact; calculations by authors.
* Spent in coordination with candidates.
** Spent entirely on senate candidates.
† Spent entirely in House District 119.

tended to focus on local issues and personal characteristics, our analysis of campaign advertising suggests that they also managed to blend in nationalized issues. The most common issues in state house races were taxes (18%), coronavirus (15%), education (10%), and small business support (7%). In senate races, the most common issues were taxes (24%), education (13%), health care (10%), and character (10%). Democrats emphasized taxes (12%), COVID (17%), education (11%), and small business (9%). For their part, Republicans focused on taxes (29%), COVID (11%), and "defund the police" (11%), as well as character, education, and jobs (each mentioned in 8% of ads).

While candidates occasionally managed to weave nationalized issues—like health care and "defunding the police"—into their campaign messages, the central part of most messaging seemed to be the connection between the candidates and their local communities. An ad for state senator Jim Brewster (state senate District 45) is typical: "Here in western Pennsylvania we do things our way, and Senator Jim Brewster is working hard to protect our way of life. Jim is a sportsman, a grandfather and one of us. Our first responders are standing with Jim. And so are the steelworkers, mineworkers, Teamsters and teachers. Out here we know Jim, and we know he's got our back, so let's keep Senator Jim Brewster working for us."

Rather than tying themselves to Democratic or Republican party positions, or claiming to support their presidential candidate's positions, many candidates situated these issues within a local context. In fact, state house and senate candidates rarely mentioned national figures and rarely tried to tie their opponents to their presidential candidates. In terms of campaign advertising for state legislative races, President Trump's name appeared in only one race (state senate District 49). The challenger, Julie Slomski, aired two ads in which she claimed that the Republican incumbent stood with Trump 100% of the time. Neither Biden nor any other national Democrat was mentioned in any state house or senate ad, although Biden's name did make a cameo in two ads. In one, the camera pans to a front yard that sports a Biden sign, along with signs for the Democratic U.S. House and state legislature candidates. In the other, the Democratic candidate is talking with supporters and one of the supporters is wearing a mask with Biden's name on it. Other than these few examples, national figures played no role on the airwaves in state legislative campaigns.

When the dust settled, the commentators' skepticism was borne out. Not only were the Democrats unable to pick up a senate seat (they broke even) but the Republicans actually gained four house seats. All the spending by Democratic candidates, parties, and outside groups, all the campaigning, and all the advertising did little to change the balance of power in Harrisburg. How could this be, in an election cycle featuring a highly controversial and polarizing presidential incumbent, a weak economy, and a once-in-a-century pandemic? Unfortunately for the Democrats, many of the elements necessary for a wave election were not present. In the end, with too few open seats, too few vulnerable incumbents, and a highly polarized political climate, the Democrats could not take advantage of a political environment that, on paper, seemed to favor them.

The voting results confirm the limited number of competitive races. Using 55% or less of the vote as a measure of a competitive race, only four senate races and twenty-eight house races were competitive. In other words, in 175 of the 203 house races, the winner earned more than 55% of the vote. In the senate, twenty-one of the twenty-five winners garnered more than 55%. In the senate, 90% of incumbents won reelection (nineteen of twenty-one), and in the house 98% retained their seats (175 of 178). In open-seat races, the party that held the seat before the election retained control of the seat 90% of the time in the house (nineteen of twenty-one) and 100% of the time in the senate (four of four). The aggregate data seem to suggest that incumbency and party were critical factors in determining the outcome in state legislative races.

Evidence for and against Nationalization

The nationalization of politics implies that voters make their choices up and down the ballot based on their partisan and ideological assessments of national issues. Evidence from polls conducted during the fall suggest that roughly half of all voters "strongly agreed," and well over 80% agreed at least "somewhat," that the candidates they prefer in congressional and state house and state senate elections align with the views of the candidate they choose for president (Table 2.8).

The nationalization hypothesis is demonstrated by a strong correlation in county-level voting patterns for different offices (Hopkins 2018). As Figure 2.2 shows, county-level vote returns in Pennsylvania for 2020 fit this indicator of nationalization; there are strong correlations between presidential vote share and congressional vote ($r = 0.987$), state senate vote ($r = 0.950$), and state house vote ($r = 0.881$).

Postelection interviews showed that most voters reported straight party voting in 2020. Nearly nine in ten supporters of both Trump (87%) and Biden (87%) said they supported candidates from the same party in other state and

TABLE 2.8 AGREEMENT THAT U.S. HOUSE AND STATE HOUSE AND STATE SENATE CANDIDATES SHOULD REPRESENT PRESIDENTIAL CANDIDATES' VIEWS

	October 2020		September 2020	
	U.S. House $n = 260$	State House and State Senate $n = 298$	U.S. House $n = 343$	State House and State Senate $n = 282$
Strongly agree	57%	47%	50%	53%
Somewhat agree	29%	44%	36%	30%
Somewhat disagree	11%	7%	6%	12%
Strongly disagree	1%	0%	6%	2%
Do not know	2%	3%	2%	2%

Source: 2020 Franklin & Marshall College Polls.
Notes: The question asked was, "Do you agree or disagree with the following statement: It is important to me that the candidates I support in [U.S. House/state house and state senate] elections think about issues and problems in the same ways as the candidate I support for president." The use of "U.S. House" or "State House and Senate" was randomly assigned.

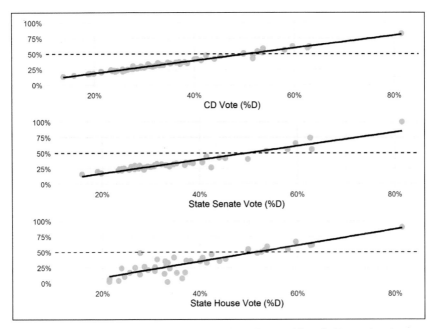

Figure 2.2 County-level Democratic vote share for president in Pennsylvania compared to congressional, state house, and state senate vote share. (Compiled and created by the authors using data downloaded from the Pennsylvania Department of State.)

local elections. These postelection interviews found that 41% of voters voted straight Republican, 42% of voters voted straight Democrat, and the balance, about one in six voters, split their tickets. This level of partisan consistency is high and aligned with national findings that show an increase in partisan consistency in recent elections (Abramowitz 2018). But it should be noted that a long-term view of partisan consistency, based on analysis of split-ticket voting in Pennsylvania, suggests that ticketsplitting was virtually unknown prior to 1948, after which it gradually increased into the 1990s (Treadway 2005).

To this point, the data on voting behavior we have presented suggests that the 2020 elections in Pennsylvania were quite nationalized. But evidence of nationalized campaign messaging is less abundant.

The claim that elections are nationalized implies that at least some political actors are expressing consistent, nationalized messages delivered within the context of multiple campaigns. Beyond the respective party campaign committees, advertising data does not support the notion that outside groups make message appeals across multiple campaigns, and there is virtually no evidence of coordinated spending by groups in presidential, congressional, and state races.

In all of the advertising we tracked in fall 2020, there were only a few organizations that advertised in more than one race. Specifically,

- AFSCME spent money in a single congressional district (PA-8) as well as the presidential campaign.
- Club for Growth Action ran ads in two congressional districts (PA-8 and PA-10) and the presidential campaign.
- Gun Owners of America spent minimally in PA-10 ($636) and a bit more in PA-17 ($5,733).
- Local Voices ran a small amount of advertising ($5,000) in state senate District 49 and in the presidential race ($12,300).
- The Pennsylvania Chamber of Business and Industry ran ads in five state senate Districts (9, 13, 15, 45, and 49).
- The Conservative Caucus spent in PA-10 ($10,520) and, minimally, in the presidential race ($2,630).

Notwithstanding the various party committees that spend money in multiple campaigns, there is very little spending by noncandidate groups that might link various races to a singular message. This is particularly true with respect to spending by outside groups in races at different levels of government. Only four groups spent money in more than one type of race, and three of those were active only in federal races for president and Congress.

Of course, spending by party committees could well be aligned in order to produce consistent messaging across campaigns and in races at all levels of government. The case studies in the chapters that follow will explore that possibility. It may also be the case that nonpartisan issue advertising serves that purpose. For instance, AARP ran advertising about COVID-19 throughout 2020, which could undoubtedly cue a nationalized topic in a way that has implications across campaigns and levels of government. Nevertheless, it is apparently rare for a single entity to spend money in multiple races, up and down the ballot, pushing a consistent theme in all those contests.

To determine the level of nationalization in congressional and state legislative campaign messages, we coded all ads on a scale of 1 to 5, with 5 being entirely nationalized and 1 being not at all nationalized (see the Appendix to this chapter for the coding rubric used). This coding shows that nationalization scores differ for the congressional and state house races (see Figure 2.3).

Congressional races had an average nationalization score of 3.5 for all ads. That average score suggests an almost equal balance of national and local messages, shading just a bit toward the nationalization end of the scale. Of course, some races were more nationalized than others (see Table 2.9). On the one hand, the contests in both PA-1 and PA-8 had an average score of 4.3, indicating a fairly high level of nationalization. Ads in PA-10, PA-16,

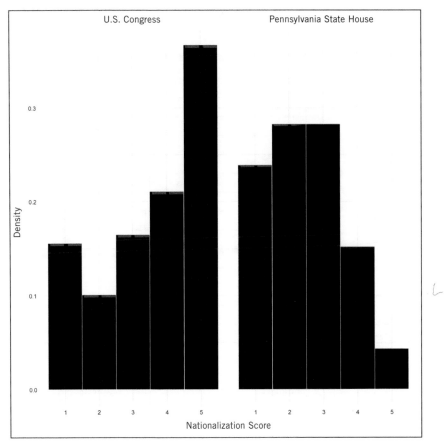

Figure 2.3 Density plot of nationalization scores for 2020 election advertising in Pennsylvania congressional (left-hand panel) and state house (right-hand panel) races. (Compiled and created by the authors.)

and PA-17, on the other hand, either were balanced between national and local messages or were decidedly local in their emphasis (with average scores of 3.0, 2.3, and 3.3, respectively).

State house races had an average nationalization score of 2.5 for all ads. This suggests relatively little nationalization of messages, although it should be noted that the ads are not entirely localized. As in the congressional races, some races were more nationalized than others. With a score of 4.1, the most nationalized of all state house races was the contest in the 105th District, which will be discussed in Chapter 6 on the Tenth Congressional District. Several districts, such as the 170th District, had messaging that balanced national appeals and more localized ones, but most races had scores on the localized end of the scale (see Table 2.10).

TABLE 2.9 NATIONALIZATION RATINGS FOR CONGRESSIONAL CAMPAIGN
ADVERTISING BY RACE

Race	Party	Nationalization Score	Number of Spots	Ads
PA CD-01	D	4.4	1,793	7
PA CD-01	R	4.2	1,977	8
PA CD-04	R	3.2	42	3
PA CD-05	D	1.3	25	1
PA CD-07	D	4.2	2,550	6
PA CD-07	R	2.6	1,301	5
PA CD-08	D	4.3	6,412	14
PA CD-08	R	· 4.2	2,572	11
PA CD-10	D	3.3	7,323	20
PA CD-10	R	2.7	4,299	16
PA CD-13	D	2.3	7	1
PA CD-16	D	1.7	502	1
PA CD-16	R	2.6	247	3
PA CD-17	D	4.0	1,251	7
PA CD-17	R	2.5	1,692	6
Totals	D candidates	3.8	19,863	57
	R candidates	3.2	12,130	52

Source: AdImpact; calculations by authors.
Note: Districts in bold are races included in the subsequent case studies.

Looking in the aggregate at races at each of three levels, as is done in this
chapter, does not show the level of campaign nationalization that might be
expected based on existing scholarship. The presidential race, while obviously national in scope, did contain localized messages. Congressional
contests straddled the divide between national and local. Because members of
Congress deal with national issues, those issues were the focus of many of
the appeals made by, and on behalf of, candidates. But U.S. House members
also represent local districts, and thus campaign ads often attempt to tie
these candidates to the district or to present the candidates as "one of us."
Finally, state legislative campaigns are heavily localized. National issues undoubtedly find their way into candidates' messages, but the bulk of the messaging consists of local appeals based on parochial issues or candidate traits.
    Advertising by parties and outside groups tends to follow the lead of the
candidate they support. If a candidate makes nationalized appeals, so too
will the parties and outside groups; if messages are more local in nature, the
parties and outside groups will typically reinforce those messages. Further-

TABLE 2.10 NATIONALIZATION RATINGS FOR STATE HOUSE CAMPAIGN ADVERTISING BY RACE

Race	Party	Nationalization Score	Number of Spots	Ads
PA HD-18	D	2.3	28	1
PA HD-26	D	2.7	40	1
PA HD-28	D	1.5	154	2
PA HD-29	D	1.0	64	1
PA HD-30	D	2.7	400	2
PA HD-33	D	2.5	248	2
PA HD-33	R	1.7	296	2
PA HD-44	D	3.3	146	1
PA HD-72	D	3.5	236	2
PA HD-72	R	3.7	136	1
PA HD-87	R	1.0	57	1
PA HD-105	D	4.1	972	3
PA HD-105	R	4.0	133	2
PA HD-106	D	3.7	134	1
PA HD-106	R	1.0	256	3
PA HD-114	D	2.0	168	1
PA HD-114	R	2.7	14	1
PA HD-115	D	3.0	24	1
PA HD-116	D	1.7	136	1
PA HD-116	R	3.0	24	1
PA HD-118	D	1.2	74	2
PA HD-119	D	2.1	159	3
PA HD-119	R	1.3	46	1
PA HD-124	D	1.3	1	1
PA HD-131	D	1.7	142	2
PA HD-131	R	3.0	125	2
PA HD-138	D	2.7	77	1
PA HD-170	D	3.3	60	2
PA HD-170	R	3.0	73	1
PA HD-176	D	2.7	276	1
PA HD-178	D	2.0	68	1
Totals	D candidates	2.5	3,607	32
	R candidates	2.4	1,160	15

Source: AdImpact; calculations by authors.

Note: Districts in bold are races included in the subsequent case studies.

more, very few noncandidate groups spend money in races at different levels. And although we often think of parties as monolithic, the party committees stay entirely in their own lanes. That is, national committees spend in the presidential race, Hill committees spend in congressional races, and state party committees spend in state legislative races. This is not at all surprising, but it serves as a reminder that coordination up and down the ballot may not be as common as one might guess.

Of course, this analysis may be overlooking very specific ways in which campaigns at different levels coordinate with one another, and there may be some subtle ways in which campaigns are nationalized. They might, for example, make more national appeals in direct mail, or during debates, or on the stump. The case studies in the following chapters provide a "vertical analysis" of races at three levels within their congressional districts. As a result, the case studies can provide a more nuanced examination of the nationalization hypothesis.

APPENDIX—NATIONALIZATION CODING SCHEME

Each congressional and state legislative ad in our database was coded by all three authors on several variables. The only one we have utilized in this chapter is the level of nationalization of an ad's message. That variable was coded on a 5-point scale according to the amount of time within the ad devoted to nationalized issues. The coding scheme was as follows:

1 = Not at all nationalized
2 = Somewhat nationalized (from very little to less than half)
3 = 50/50 (about equally nationalized and not nationalized)
4 = Quite a bit nationalized (over half to almost all)
5 = Entirely nationalized

The following are examples of ads that were given scores of 5, 3, and 1, respectively:

Example 1: PA State House District 105
Ad Transcript "Our Future" (D)
I'm Brittney Rodas. And I'm running for state representative to fight for affordable and accessible health care for veterans like my dad. A living wage for workers like my mom and a future for families like mine and yours.

Level of Nationalization = 5
Every issue in the ad is part of the national debate and there is no mention of any local or state issues. The issues are health care for veterans and a living wage for workers and families.

Example 2: PA State House District 115
Ad Transcript "Fighting for Us" (D)
Representative Maureen Madden is fighting for us. When COVID-19 hit, she introduced legislation to protect frontline workers and keep families in their homes. She secured funding for laptops to help our children with remote learning. Madden called on Harrisburg to direct the $1 billion of remaining CARES funding to our small businesses. She worked across the aisle to improve health care choice and expand coverage. Reelect Maureen Madden in the 115th District.

Level of Nationalization = 3
This ad is a mix of nationalized issues and local or state-level concerns. The primary issue is COVID-19, which is a nationalized issue. The candidate also specifically mentions a piece of federal legislation (the CARES Act) and wants to improve health care choice and expand coverage (all nationalized issues). But the ad also spends equal time on legislation she worked on in Harrisburg and state-level efforts to fight COVID-19.

Example 3: PA State House District 106
Ad Transcript "Cover Up" (R)
Special interest groups are spending big to cover up Lindsay Drew's real record. Drew voted to raise property taxes, was taken to court for failing to pay her own taxes, and faced foreclosure for not paying her mortgage. Reject Lindsay Drew.

Level of Nationalization = 1
The ad does not mention a national issue but instead focuses on property taxes and candidate failings.

NOTES

1. Unless otherwise noted, the public opinion data presented in this chapter come from polls conducted during the fall campaign by Franklin & Marshall College. Franklin & Marshall College's Center for Opinion Research conducted four surveys during the fall campaign: July 20–26 ($n = 667$), August 17–23 ($n = 681$), September 14–20 ($n = 625$), and October 19–25 ($n = 558$). They also conducted postelection re-interviews in December 2020 with 1,092 respondents who had been interviewed during the fall campaign.

2. We contracted with AdImpact to use their ADMO creative and DELTA spending products. The AdImpact data identified 586 campaign spots that were aired over 250,000 times during the fall general election campaign in Pennsylvania.

3. *Gross ratings points* measure the exposure of an advertisement and are calculated as the percentage of the total potential audience for an ad multiplied by the average number of times each member of the target audience is likely to see the ad. Gross ratings points for campaign ads that aired in Pennsylvania in 2020 were provided by AdImpact.

4. Turnout figures from Michael P. McDonald, "2020 November General Election Turnout Rates," accessed February 10, 2021, available at http://www.electproject.org/2020g.

5. Election results from Dave Leip's "Atlas of U.S. Presidential Elections," accessed November 24, 2020, available at https://uselectionatlas.org/RESULTS/.

6. We do not discuss the state senate races here because only half of the state senate stood for reelection in 2020. Republican state senate candidates also won a majority share of votes cast in those races: 50.9% to 49.1%.

7. The share of the generic ballot preference was 50% D to 44% R in October, 47% D to 41% R in September, 45% D to 42% R in August, and 46% D to 42% R in July.

8. The state fundraising data were compiled by the authors using data downloaded from the Pennsylvania Department of State, accessed February 16, 2021, available at https://www.dos.pa.gov/VotingElections/CandidatesCommittees/CampaignFinance/Resources/Pages/FullCampaignFinanceExport.aspx. The 2020 data file was created by the Department of State on January 26, 2021. There were some apparent data entry errors in dates, but we did not remove any cases based on date because the state specifically noted that the file contained 2020 data.

REFERENCES

Abramowitz, Alan I. 2018. *The Great Alignment: Race, Party Transformation, and the Rise of Donald Trump.* New Haven, CT: Yale University Press.

Coleman, J. Miles. 2021. "2020's Crossover Districts." *Sabato's Crystal Ball*, February 4, 2021. Available at https://centerforpolitics.org/crystalball/articles/2020s-crossover-districts/.

Cook Political Report. 2020. "2020 House Race Ratings," November 2, 2020. Available at https://cookpolitical.com/ratings/house-race-ratings.

Hopkins, Daniel J. 2018. *The Increasingly United States: How and Why American Political Behavior Nationalized.* Chicago: University of Chicago Press.

Medvic, Stephen K., and Berwood Yost. 2020. "An Endangered Republican Incumbent Survives in the Suburbs: Fitzpatrick vs. Wallace in Pennsylvania's 1st Congressional District." In *Cases in Congressional Campaigns: Split Decision*, 3rd ed., edited by Randall E. Adkins and David A. Dulio, 30–48. New York: Routledge.

Meyer, Katie. 2020. "Here's How Democrats Could Flip the Pennsylvania Legislature." *WHYY News*, October 12, 2020. Available at whyy.org/articles/heres-how-democrats-could-flip-the-pennsylvania-legislature/.

National Popular Vote. n.d. "Map of General-Election Campaign Events and TV Ad Spending by 2020 Presidential Candidates." Accessed April 4, 2021. Available at https://www.nationalpopularvote.com/map-general-election-campaign-events-and-tv-ad-spending-2020-presidential-candidates.

Treadway, Jack M. 2005. *Elections in Pennsylvania: A Century of Partisan Conflict in the Keystone State.* University Park: Pennsylvania State University Press.

3

Campaigns in the First Congressional District

Fighting the Nationalized Campaign Currents
along the Delaware River

CHRISTOPHER BORICK

For decades, suburban Philadelphia has been heralded as one of the most crucial political regions in the country. As the most populous area in one of the nation's key swing states, the four "collar counties" around Pennsylvania's largest city have been identified as both crucial in determining electoral outcomes in the Keystone State and a bellwether for the direction of American politics (Frey and Texiara 2016). In 2020, the Philadelphia suburbs once again were in the national spotlight as Pennsylvania emerged as a premier swing state in the presidential race. Both President Trump and former vice president Biden targeted the region with their campaigns. In particular, Biden's prioritization of the region was evidenced in his selection of Philadelphia as his campaign headquarters and his repeated visits to the region (Otterbein and Caputo 2020). Trump, while concentrating more on other regions of the Commonwealth, invested substantial time and resources in the Philadelphia suburbs as he tried to squeeze votes out of the populous area (Sullivan 2020).

While the most national of elections was being hotly contested throughout the suburban Philadelphia region, competitive races were simultaneously occurring at the congressional and Pennsylvania state legislative district levels. Nowhere was this competition more evident than in Bucks County. In this bucolic county along the Delaware River, the last of southeastern Pennsylvania's Republican members of Congress fought for survival in a county that has increasingly moved away from the GOP in the twenty-first century. And in races for seats in the Pennsylvania General Assembly, Bucks

County was home to many of the Commonwealth's most competitive districts.

But as this chapter chronicles, for an area that is in the national spotlight and is considered a harbinger of national trends, suburban Philadelphia's most competitive congressional district and two of its most hotly contested state house races were notable for the very limited nationalization of the races that played out there in the fall of 2020. For if, as political scientist Morris Fiorina claims, "elections are nationalized, when people vote for the party, not the person," and "candidates of the party at different levels of government win and lose together," then the results in Pennsylvania's First Congressional District indicate limited evidence of this outcome (Fiorina 2016). In this chapter, the race in Pennsylvania's First Congressional District and the campaigns in the 143rd and 144th Pennsylvania State House Districts are examined, with a concentration on how three Republican candidates emerged victorious despite Donald Trump losing in their districts.

An Overview of the First Congressional District and the 143rd and 144th Pennsylvania State House Districts

In an age of hyper-gerrymandered congressional districts, where competitive balance between parties is rare, Pennsylvania's First Congressional District can be considered an outlier. This congressional district, which encompasses all of Bucks County and a sliver of neighboring Montgomery County, is striking for its balanced political characteristics. As with all Pennsylvania congressional districts, the First Congressional District is relatively new, with the Pennsylvania Supreme Court establishing the district in February 2018 as part of a ruling that found the previous congressional districting illegal (Gabriel and Bidgood 2018). As Table 3.1 shows, this highly competitive characteristic of the district is driven by a nearly even party registration distribution, with 43% of voters in the district registered as Democrats and 40% registered as Republican in 2020 (Pennsylvania Department of State 2020). If the district had been in place during the 2016 presidential election, Hillary Clinton would have carried it by just a 2-point margin. Given the tight 2016 presidential results, and the fairly even partisan balance among registered voters, it is not surprising that the *Cook Political Report* rated Pennsylvania's First Congressional District as a "Republican+1" district, placing it among the most competitive districts in the nation heading into the 2020 election (*Cook Political Report* 2017).

A glance at a color-coded map of congressional districts in southeastern Pennsylvania, with districts shaded in the traditional blue and red to signify

TABLE 3.1 DEMOGRAPHIC AND REGISTRATION CHARACTERISTICS OF PENNSYLVANIA'S 143RD AND 144TH STATE HOUSE DISTRICTS, FIRST CONGRESSIONAL DISTRICT, AND PENNSYLVANIA IN 2019

	PA 143rd State House District[a]	PA 144th State House District[b]	First Congressional District[c]	Pennsylvania[d]
Population density: people/square mile	380.5	1,057.3	1,117.4	286.1
Population white	92%	87%	82%	76%
Population black	1%	2%	4%	11%
Population Hispanic	3%	4%	6%	8%
Foreign-born	6.4%	8.4%	11%	7.0%
Median household income	$103,081	$98,634	$93,474	$63,463
Bachelor's degree or higher	51.8%	45.9%	42.6%	32.3%
Registered Democrat[e]	38.2%	37.6%	43.1%	46.5%
Registered Republican[e]	43.7%	45.3%	39.9%	39.0%
Registered none/other[e]	18.1%	16.9%	16.8%	14.5%

Sources:
(a) Compiled from U.S. Census Bureau. n.d. "Census Reporter: State House District 143, PA."
    Accessed April 4, 2021. Available at https://censusreporter.org/profiles/62000US42143-state-house
    -district-143-pa/.
(b) Compiled from U.S. Census Bureau. n.d. "Census Reporter: State House District 144, PA."
    Accessed April 4, 2021. Available at https://censusreporter.org/profiles/62000US42144-state-house
    -district-144-pa/.
(c) Compiled from U.S. Census Bureau. n.d. "Census Reporter: Congressional District 1, PA."
    Accessed April 4, 2021. Available at https://censusreporter.org/profiles/50000US4201-congressional
    -district-1-pa/.
(d) Compiled from U.S. Census Bureau. n.d. "Census Reporter: Pennsylvania." Accessed April 4, 2021.
    Available at https://censusreporter.org/profiles/04000US42-pennsylvania/.
(e) Compiled from Pennsylvania Department of State. n.d. "Voting and Election Statistics." Accessed April 4,
    2021. Available at https://www.dos.pa.gov/VotingElections/OtherServicesEvents/VotingElectionStatistics
    /Pages/VotingElectionStatistics.aspx.

party control, would show a deep blue sea with one "red island." That "red island" reflects the First Congressional District, and the seat held by Republican congressman Brian Fitzpatrick. Fitzpatrick first won the seat in 2016, after his brother Mike decided to not seek reelection after holding the seat (the former Eighth Congressional District) for much of the twenty-first century. Brian Fitzpatrick was able to narrowly win reelection in the 2018 midterm election, even as four southeastern Pennsylvania districts flipped from Republican control to Democrat control (Otterbein 2018).

While the First Congressional District, and its Bucks County core, are highly balanced in terms of partisan electoral politics, this is a relatively new condition. Historically, Bucks County was dominated by the GOP, with Republicans largely controlling local and state elections from the Civil War until early in the twenty-first century. This Republican dominance showed signs of erosion initially in presidential races, where Democratic candidates, after winning the county only three times between 1860 and 1988, carried Bucks County in every election from 1992 to 2016. Yet, while Democrats found success in Bucks County in presidential races, congressional, state, and local races in the county continued to be largely claimed by Republican candidates until the last fifteen years. Over this period, Democrats scored victories at the congressional level in 2006 and 2008, and picked up state legislative seats and county government offices on numerous occasions over the last decade.

These Democratic gains culminated in the two cycles before the 2020 election. In 2018, Bob Casey and Tom Wolf achieved dominating wins in Bucks County, helping Casey to easily win a third term in the U.S. Senate and Wolf to coast to reelection as governor. Then, in 2019, Democrats won control of the Bucks County Board of Commissioners and major row offices in the county for the first time in generations (Quann and Ellerly 2019). Yet even in these two positive election cycles for Democrats in Bucks County, Republicans scored some important victories, with Fitzpatrick surviving in 2018 and the Republicans holding a state house seat in a March 2020 special election in a fairly competitive district (McElwee 2020).

The Democratic gains in the First Congressional District, during the last decade in particular, appear to be strongly tied to the region's demographics. As with the other suburban Philadelphia congressional districts, the First Congressional District includes one of the wealthiest and highest-educated electorates in the Commonwealth. In 2019, the median income for households in the First Congressional District was about $93,500, placing it well above the state median household income of $63,500 (U.S. Census Bureau 2019). About 43% of adults in the First Congressional District have attained a four-year college degree, a mark well above the statewide level of 32%. With higher-educated voters increasingly moving away from the Republican Party at a national level, Bucks County has followed the trend, and the onetime Republican stronghold has become a highly competitive political region (Pew Research Center 2020).

Given the fairly even divide of registered voters among Democrats and Republicans in the First Congressional District, it may not be surprising that the makeup of the state legislative delegation from the district is also very balanced. In the lead-up to the 2020 general election, there were ten Pennsylvania State House districts and three Pennsylvania state senate districts located either completely or primarily within the First Congressional District. Of those ten Pennsylvania State House districts, six were held by Republicans and four by Democrats. Among the three senate districts primarily within the First Congressional District, Republicans held two seats and Democrats held one. Not only was partisan control of the state legislative districts fairly evenly distributed within the First Congressional District; many of the legislative districts were highly competitive in recent election cycles. Most notably, in the 2018 midterm elections, four of the ten Pennsylvania State House races within the First Congressional District were decided by less than 5%. Among those close races were two state house districts that are a primary focus of this chapter: PA-143 and PA-144.

In these two state house districts, situated in the less densely populated northern areas of Bucks County, the 2018 elections were decided by less than 2%, with one Republican and one Democrat claiming victories in races where there were no incumbents on the ballot. Despite a Republican registration advantage in the 143rd District (see Table 3.1), in the 2018 race the seat was claimed by Democrat Wendy Ullman, flipping this district from Republican to Democratic control (*Intelligencer* 2018). In the 144th District, where Republicans held a fairly substantial registration advantage (see Table 3.1), Republican Todd Polinchock emerged victorious, narrowly keeping the seat in GOP hands (Keeler 2018).

With the election outcomes in 2018 being extremely close in the First Congressional District, and both the 143rd and 144th State House Districts, the 2020 elections in these districts were certain to draw considerable attention from both parties. In essence, these districts were seen as winnable by Democrats and Republicans alike, and thus destined to be highly contested. Of course, these races would take place simultaneously with a presidential election that would also be contested heavily in this corner of the Keystone State. The confluence of competitive presidential, congressional, and state house races in the same region provides a very valuable opportunity to examine aspects of the nationalization of campaigns in contemporary American politics.

Scholarly research has shown that at the state level, elections have become more nationalized, with presidential and national politics exerting greater influence over down-ballot contests (Sievert and McKee 2019). While a number of reasons have been offered for this "nationalization" phenomenon, many recent studies have pointed to the rise of negative partisanship as a key factor (Abramowitz and Webster 2016). Negative partisanship suggests that as partisan identities have become more closely aligned with social, cultural, and ideological divisions in American society, party supporters—including leaning independents—have developed increasingly negative feelings about the opposing party and its candidates. This has led to dramatic increases in party loyalty and straight-ticket voting, a steep decline in the advantage of incumbency, and growing consistency between the results of presidential elections and the results of House, Senate, and even state legislative elections.

So, in an era of nationalized elections, how would the campaigns and candidates in the Bucks County races focused on in this chapter relate to the national races that they would share a ballot with? Would the candidates seek synergy with their party's presidential campaigns, or would they attempt to create distance that would help insulate their campaigns from any potential drag that the top of their tickets may cause? As noted earlier, Bucks County and its congressional districts have a history of ticket-splitting in the twenty-first century, making the region to some degree a counter to the nationalization dynamics that have been a defining feature of politics in the century. But with the polarization and presence of negative partisanship rising in the country as the 2020 elections neared, it was fair to ask: Would Bucks County and the First Congressional "island" retain their "outlier" status, or would they be washed over by a "nationalization" wave? The remainder of this chapter attempts to answer this question, and to offer insight into what happened in this key corner of the Commonwealth.

How the Campaigns Played: Locating Nationalization

This chapter has established that both the First Congressional District and the Pennsylvania house districts within the congressional district are notable for their very competitive nature and their history of fairly significant split-ticket voting. So how did the candidates and campaigns in these consummately competitive districts, in one of the nation's high-profile political regions, connect to the broader national races and issues that defined national politics in 2020? While the answers to this question are of course complex, one overarching conclusion is that the Republican candidates in these races overwhelmingly steered clear of the presidential race, and largely focused their campaigns on issues that can best be described as local and regional in nature. The Democratic candidates were more willing to connect to their presidential ticket, and more aggressive at linking their Republican opponents to the top of the Republican ticket. Let us look more deeply at how things played out in the congressional and state house races.

The First Congressional District Race

Like many of his fellow Bucks County Republicans, Brian Fitzpatrick rarely identifies as a GOP official, instead heralding his independence as a member of Congress. On his official congressional website home page, above a picture of George Washington crossing the Delaware after departing from a

Bucks County shoreline, are the words "Brian Fitzpatrick: Our Independent Voice" (Brian Fitzpatrick Congressman Official Website 2020). One aspect of Fitzpatrick's "independence" is his relationship with President Trump. From the earliest stages of Trump's ascension in Republican politics in 2015, Fitzpatrick's relationship with Trump could best be described as uneasy. In the 2016 campaign, Fitzpatrick kept a distance from his party's presidential nominee, ultimately stating that he did not vote for Trump, instead casting a write-in vote for Mike Pence (Muschick 2020).

As may be expected, Fitzpatrick's reticence to support Trump in the 2016 campaign drew the ire of many of the forty-fifth president's ardent and passionate supporters, both in and out of the First Congressional District. This ire was only exacerbated by Fitzpatrick's mixed support for Trump's agenda. Fitzpatrick voted with President Trump less often than any GOP House member, aligning with the president only about 33% of the time during the 116th Congress (FiveThirtyEight 2021). The second-term congressman also was one of only four Republicans to formally condemn Trump in July 2019 for his racially tinged attacks on four Democratic congresswomen (Hirschfeld 2019).

Unlike his fellow Republican House members from Pennsylvania, who heralded their support for Trump, Fitzpatrick regularly touted his bipartisanship as a defining characteristic of his tenure in Washington. He had co-sponsored legislation extending federal contributions to children's health insurance with Democratic congresswoman Susan Wild of the neighboring Seventh Congressional District, and he had joined Democrats in supporting the right of workers to remotely unionize during the COVID-19 pandemic (Meyer 2020a).

Fitzpatrick's strained relationship with President Trump, and the elevation of his bipartisanship efforts in Congress, led to regular claims that he was a Republican in name only, or "RINO" (Deane 2020). The dissatisfaction with Fitzpatrick among the president's supporters culminated with a Republican primary challenge in 2020. In the 2020 Republican primary, Fitzpatrick faced Andy Meehan, an avid supporter of President Trump. Meehan, who labeled Fitzpatrick as "Fake Fitz," claimed that unlike "disloyal" Fitzpatrick he would always be faithful to Trump (Plott 2020). In one of his campaign videos, Meehan refers to Fitzpatrick as "Pelosi's pawn," in a bid to link Fitzpatrick to the polarizing Democratic Speaker of the House (Meehan for Congress 2020).

Given the fairly acrimonious relationship between Fitzpatrick and Trump, and Meehan's expressed loyalty to the president, a key question during the campaign involved possible intervention in the race by Trump. While there was no love lost between the congressman and the White House, a number of factors acted to keep Trump on the sidelines in the race. Most importantly, while regularly breaking with Trump on congressional votes, Fitzpatrick did support Trump on the one vote that mattered most: impeachment. Despite highly critical comments regarding Trump's intervention in Ukrainian matters that led to the 2020 impeachment, Fitzpatrick voted against the impeachment articles (Itkowitz 2019). This vote apparently helped to prevent any Trump intervention on the part of Meehan, as a senior White House official who requested anonymity told the *New York Times*: "Sure, he may have gone against him on a number of issues, but he had, after all, voted against impeachment" (Plott 2020).

In the end, Fitzpatrick cruised to victory in the June 2, 2020, primary, beating Meehan by 36 points, 63.3% to 36.7% (Ballotpedia 2020). The local Bucks County Republican Party rallied around Fitzpatrick, with the local GOP chairwoman citing his "commitment to individual liberty and freedom" and commending his "common sense approach to dealing with issues in Congress" (Plott 2020). While Fitzpatrick's vote against impeachment may have helped him to secure party support, and ultimately his Republican primary victory, it also connected him to a president whose standing in his district was certainly not stellar. Democrats in the district of course took notice.

Even before Fitzpatrick's vote against impeachment, Democrats had targeted Fitzpatrick's seat as a potential pickup. In the 2018 midterm, Fitzpatrick survived a major challenge, beating Democratic nominee Scott Wallace by less than 3%. The general consensus was that while Fitzpatrick ran a solid campaign, the Democratic nominee was not a strong candidate and had run a very weak campaign. Dave Wasserman, U.S. House editor of the *Cook Political Report*, said Wallace was perhaps the "worst" Democratic contender in the election cycle (Otterbein 2018). Given the closeness of the 2018 race, and the general consensus that Wallace was a weak candidate, Democrats were optimistic that the 2020 cycle would add the First Congressional District to their growing southeastern Pennsylvania success in congressional races.

In the 2020 Democratic primary in the First Congressional District, Christine Finello easily beat Skyler Hurwitz (77.5% to 22.5%) to claim her party's nomination. Unlike Scott Wallace, who was regularly criticized for spending much of his life outside the district, Finello grew up in Bucks County, and she was raising her family in Ivyland, where she served on the borough council. The Democratic Party's optimism for Finello's candidacy was apparent, as the Democratic Congressional Campaign Committee (DCCC) added her to their "Red to Blue Top-Tier Candidate Program," providing her with added organizational and fundraising support in the race (Solfield 2020a).

Given President Trump's increasing struggles among higher-educated, upper-income suburban voters nationally, it was not unexpected for Finello to make linking Trump and Fitzpatrick a central tenet of her First Congressional District campaign (Siders 2020). While Fitzpatrick's uneasy relationship with Trump made it somewhat challenging to paint the congressman as an acolyte of the president, there were certainly opportunities to make the linkage to voters. Fitzpatrick's vote against impeachment stood out as the most visible support for Trump, but his overall voting record over the course of the Trump administration provided opportunities to cast the Republican incumbent as a backer of the president's agenda. Most notably, during the first two years of the Trump presidency, Fitzpatrick voted with the White House's position 84% of the time, and over the course of the Trump presidency he aligned with the administration on 62% of votes (FiveThirtyEight 2021). Thus, Fitzpatrick's fairly substantial alignment with Trump's positions on legislative matters became the cornerstone of Finello's attempts to nationalize the race.

Almost from the start of the general election campaign, Finello attempted to establish the Trump/Fitzpatrick link and erode Fitzpatrick's "independent" claims and persona. A prime example was an October 6, 2020, tweet, where Finello wrote, "Brian Fitzpatrick pretends he is independent, but the NRCC and Republican SuperPacs pumped $8 million into his 2018 campaign. When the Trump GOP needs him, they know he's always a reliable vote" (Finello 2020a).

With polls showing health care among the most salient issues for voters in the election cycle, and also showing high disapproval rates for Trump's handling of this policy area, Finello saw opportunities to connect Fitzpatrick to Trump on this issue (Burns and Martin 2020). In a September 2020 television ad from the Finello campaign, Fitzpatrick's past votes on health-related matters were framed as votes for the Trump agenda (see Figure 3.1). The voice-over in the TV spot declares, "Four years of Donald Trump's agenda, bailouts for big corporations, working to end protections for pre-existing conditions, and stripping away healthcare in the middle of a pandemic. One Congressman refused to speak up." The ad continues: "Brian Fitzpatrick voted with Trump when it mattered most" (Cole 2020a).

Finello's attempts to link Fitzpatrick to Trump implicitly acknowledged that Fitzpatrick was not completely tied to the president. Instead, Finello's campaign attempted to make the case that on the biggest of issues (e.g., im-

Figure 3.1 Christine Finello ad linking Brian Fitzpatrick to the Trump agenda. (Christine Finello for Congress: https://www.youtube.com/watch?v=PlgUkc8ByGo.)

peachment, health care), when it mattered most, Fitzpatrick was there for Trump. The real and significant differences between Trump and Fitzpatrick made Finello's efforts to nationalize Fitzpatrick's candidacy significantly more difficult than if she could simply claim Fitzpatrick was all in. In essence, she embraced a "nationalized light" strategy that reflected the reality of an opponent who never fully opened himself up to nationalized linkages.

While clearly trying to nationalize the First Congressional District race by tying Fitzpatrick to Trump, Finello also selectively linked herself to the Biden/Harris campaign. Polls had shown Biden performing exceedingly well throughout suburban Philadelphia during the general election, and connecting to Biden thus provided the Finello team with potential synergy (Muhlenberg College Institute of Public Opinion 2020a). Finello campaigned with Biden during the former vice president's "drive-in" campaign rally in Bristol on October 24, 2020. During the rally Biden pointed toward Finello and said, "I'm looking forward to serving with you, kid. You've got the grit, toughness and smarts to get this done." Biden continued, "She's going to fight like hell for the people of Bucks County, the hard-working folks" (Solfield 2020b). Notably, a few days later at President Trump's campaign event in Upper Makefield Township on Halloween, Congressman Fitzpatrick was absent from the stage (DiMattia and Callahan 2020). These campaign events were certainly symbolic representations of how the congressional candidates sought to connect, or distance, themselves from their party's national standard bearers.

After securing the Republican nomination in June, Fitzpatrick turned his attention to Finello. While Finello worked hard to link Fitzpatrick to Trump, there is no evidence that Fitzpatrick sought to tie his opponent to the top of the Democratic ticket. Instead, the Fitzpatrick campaign's main focus regarding Finello was to link her to the "Defund the Police" movement and support for illegal immigrants. Throughout the fall campaign, Republicans nationally were seizing on a "law and order" message, and the "Defund the Police" efforts had become a go-to trope (Jamerson and Bykowitz 2020). In one of the Fitzpatrick campaign's major television ads (see Figure 3.2), the narrator states, "Christina Finello wants to defund our police, release dangerous criminals from prison because of coronavirus, and give illegal immigrants stimulus checks, while American families struggle." The ad ends with the narrator saying, "Christina Finello, too extreme for our community" (Cole 2020b).

Throughout the campaign, Finello appeared on the defensive to the efforts to align her with the "Defund the Police" movement, expending considerable effort to counter the attacks. This late August tweet from Finello was indicative of her attempts to balance the need for reform while distancing herself from the defund efforts, as she states, "I oppose defunding the police. I've worked with law enforcement to lead de-escalating trainings, and

Figure 3.2 Brian Fitzpatrick ad linking Christine Finello to the "Defund the Police" movement. (Brian Fitzpatrick for Congress: https://host2.adimpact .com/admo/viewer/3095344.)

I know we need more resources for community-based policing programs to ensure we keep everyone in our community safe" (Finello 2020b). Late October unrest in Philadelphia after the police shooting of Walter Wallace Jr., a mentally ill black man, led to the deployment of the National Guard, which elevated law-and-order issues in the election cycle and caused unease among Democrats.

As Fitzpatrick attempted to build a narrative that Finello was too extreme for the district, his campaign worked hard to portray him as the "most bipartisan" and "independent" member of the U.S. House of Representatives. Fitzpatrick went to great lengths to distance himself from the Trump administration's efforts to repeal the Affordable Care Act (ACA, also known as "Obamacare"). In fact, he overtly used his vote against the repeal of the ACA to demonstrate his difference from Trump.

While many Republicans in the House, including the eight other Republicans in the Pennsylvania House delegation, heralded their support and working relationship with Trump, Fitzpatrick made his bipartisan record the cornerstone for the campaign narrative he was building. Instead of publicizing an endorsement from Trump, Fitzpatrick regularly cited a Georgetown University and Lugar Center rating that identified him as the most bipartisan member of the House (Lugar Center 2020). Fitzpatrick also commonly cited his membership, and cochair position, in the bipartisan Problem Solvers Caucus. When describing his work with the Problem Solvers, Fitzpatrick said, "We reject the demands for ideological purity. I believe in coming to the center. That's the way life works. That's the way we think government should work" (Kelly 2020).

Fitzpatrick's efforts to establish a healthy distance from Trump, and Finello's efforts to distance herself from the more radical aspects of the progressive movement, were both tested during the first congressional debate in the district on October 8, 2020. Fitzpatrick's and Finello's attempts to use nationalization as a means of undermining their opponents were obvious. Fitzpatrick found regular opportunities to reinforce his campaign's effort to paint Finello as part of a radical Democratic agenda to undermine law enforcement and formalize open borders. At a particularly confrontational point in the debate, Fitzpatrick told Finello, "I haven't seen you once stand up for our police officers in Bucks County. Not once. I haven't seen you condemn the riots forcefully at all" (Bambino 2020). Finello used a question regarding the federal government's response to the COVID-19 pandemic to tie Fitzpatrick to Trump, stating, "Donald Trump played down the severity of this virus and so has my Republican opponent. There's been countless instances of my opponent and his people going around without masks, and we can't have that" (Bambino 2020). The attempt to draw Fitzpatrick and Trump together on the pandemic response was likely born out of the broad desire by Finello to link her opponent to the president, but more particularly to tie Fitzpatrick to Trump's COVID-19 response, which polls showed was viewed highly unfavorably by voters (Muhlenberg College Institute of Public Opinion 2020b).

The 143rd State House District Race

Like the First Congressional District that engulfs it, Pennsylvania's 143rd State House District reflects the changing nature of politics in the southeastern corner of the state. When the district in the historically Republican areas of northern Bucks County flipped to a Democrat in 2018, it was considered just another sign of the decline of the GOP in suburban Philadelphia. But the 2018 race was extremely close, and that cycle was extraordinarily strong for Democrats, thus giving Republicans optimism that with the right candidate and campaign strategy, they could flip the seat back.

First-term Democratic representative Wendy Ullman won her seat in 2018 in a contest for an open seat. The district had been held by Republican Marguerite Quinn since the district was established in 2012, with Quinn winning easily in the races throughout the decade. In 2018 Quinn opted to run for a state senate seat, leaving the 143rd open. With the political winds at her back, in a district that was edging Democratic, Ullman beat her Republican opponent Joe Flood by 1.7%, becoming the first Democrat to represent this area of central and northern Bucks County since the 1980s (*Intelligencer* 2018).

In a district that leaned Republican, Ullman's campaign selectively toggled between nationalized and localized communication strategies. Throughout the race, Ullman did attempt to draw connections between her campaign and the Biden/Harris ticket, but generally she avoided trying to link her opponent to President Trump. During the Democratic convention in August 2020, Ullman offered Facebook posts and tweets celebrating the choice of Kamala Harris as Joe Biden's running mate. In October, Ullman tweeted that she was honored to receive the endorsement of Biden. Ullman also periodically pitched her candidacy as part of a broader Democratic ticket, such as in a mid-October Facebook post that read, "It's time to start getting out the vote for Wendy and the rest of the Democratic ticket!" The few mentions of President Trump were related to election matters, including an August tweet denouncing Trump's actions with the U.S. Post Office (Ullman 2020).

Ullman did bring national politics into her campaign communications, often denouncing the severe partisanship in Washington, DC. Her campaign website noted that Ullman stands opposed to the hyperpartisan politics that dominates national politics, and that her record is one of pragmatic efforts. Ullman also made the Republicans' efforts to repeal and replace the ACA a central focus of her messaging, and she linked this law to other related policy matters. For example, in a September 29th post on her campaign's Facebook page, Ullman stressed that the ACA was more essential than ever during the COVID-19 pandemic, and if it had fallen to Republican efforts to repeal, millions of Americans would be left without health insurance. Ullman's campaign website also linked the ACA as essential to the protection of women's health in the United States, including in the area of reproductive rights.

While Ullman did not aggressively try to link her Republican opponent Shelby Labs to President Trump, her campaign selectively pushed Lab's connection to the Republican Party. The most notable example was an October Facebook post calling out Labs for receiving 80% of her campaign funds from the Republican Party. Ullman's campaign mailings also linked Labs to Republican money and control, painting her as the chosen candidate of GOP leaders and interests.

Labs, a Bucks County native and political newcomer, had secured the GOP nomination when she won the June 2020 Republican primary in a race where she ran unopposed. After becoming the Republican nominee, Labs structured a campaign that appears to be hyperlocalized. Her campaign website's overview of her candidacy exemplifies a framing that is devoid of nationalization. In her introduction to voters, Labs focuses on three broad areas: her roots in the local community, her commitment to preserving the local environment, and a list of issues she is committed to working on that were framed very generally (Labs 2020b). In this pitch, Labs leads with her family's 200-year history in Bucks County and her work and volunteering efforts in Central and Upper Bucks County. Notably, the issue that the campaign highlights and prioritizes on its website is environmental protection. The environment is at best a secondary level issue for Republicans nationally, and certainly not the type of issue a GOP nominee would prioritize if trying to nationalize their campaign (Ridge 2020).

The Labs campaign made scant reference to other Republican candidates, or to the GOP in general. Not once, on either the official campaign website or the campaign Facebook page, did Labs identify as a Republican. Given the campaign's reticence to even identify with the Republican Party, it is not surprising to find that Labs completely avoided public references to President Trump. While avoiding mention of the Republican Party and President Trump, Labs highlighted her desire to represent the district as an independent voice and to embrace bipartisanship. In her official candidate statement to the *Bucks County Courier Times,* Labs reinforces themes that were consistently present throughout her campaign. She writes, "I'm running for State Representative because our community needs an independent voice in Harrisburg that works on behalf of our community. Partisan division is destroying our society. Hatred on both sides of the aisle is no longer confined to Washington, D.C. We are seeing it in Harrisburg and even here in Bucks County. As a society, we need to bring back civility and respect to political discourse" (Labs 2020a).

Labs rarely engaged in direct criticisms of Ullman, but in one notable exchange in October she attempted to tie her opponent to "Democrat Party bosses." In response to an Ullman campaign mailing that had tied Labs to special interests and GOP leaders, Labs posted a short video on her campaign Facebook page stating that Ullman "refused to fully fund our public schools to please party bosses," and that "this is why I'm running, because we deserve better" (Labs 2020c).

In all, the 143rd State House District race was about as localized as one might imagine for a state government office in 2020. The review of the Labs campaign in particular identified a striking absence of connections to national politics, and particularly to the presidential race that was being fought alongside the legislative contest. Ullman made some modest efforts to align with her party's national ticket, and she highlighted national laws that impacted issues, such as health care, that she prioritized, but she never really went hard on making Labs a proxy for Trump. The campaigns made some late back-and-forth charges regarding their opponent's connections to their respective parties, but the charges were limited and were not in the least defining characteristics of the race.

The 144th State House District Race

As with its neighboring district the 143rd, the Pennsylvania 144th State House District is a once solid Republican stronghold that had been trending Democrat in recent years. For much of the last decade, long-time Republican incumbent Katharine Watson ran unopposed in the 144th before opting not to run for reelection in 2018. In that 2018 race, Republican Todd Polinchock defeated his Democratic opponent Meredith Bock by a narrow 51% to 49% margin. The tight 2018 race certainly gave Democrats optimism for the 2020 cycle, with the state party targeting the district as a priority (Swing Left 2020).

Gary Spillane, who secured the 2020 Democratic nomination, running unopposed in the June primary, received endorsements from all major Democratic elected officials in the Commonwealth, and eventually from Joe Biden and Kamala Harris (Spillane 2020a). In addition to endorsements, Spillane received robust campaign contributions from the state party, with over half a million dollars contributed to his campaign by the state Democratic Party and the Democratic House Campaign Committee (Transparency USA 2020) Clearly, Democrats were invested in flipping this seat, as it was the type of suburban Philadelphia district where they had found increasing success over the last decade, and had almost flipped two years earlier.

Like Spillane, Polinchock won his party's primary without opposition, and drew interest from his state party leaders. Republicans in Harrisburg, interested in maintaining the narrow GOP advantage in the Pennsylvania State House, needed to protect a number of vulnerable seats. More specifically, after the 2018 election the Republican advantage in the 203-seat State House had fallen to only nine seats. Given the location of the 144th District, and the 2018 results, Polinchock appeared to be one of the more endangered Republican incumbents (Meyer 2020b).

Spillane, like both Ullman and Finello, attempted to publicly align with the Biden/Harris ticket. In a mid-October Twitter posting, Spillane tweeted, "As Joe Biden has said over and over, winning back the White House is just the beginning. If we want to reclaim the soul of America and secure a brighter future for us all, we must win up and down the ballot. Together we will 'Build Back Better' in Bucks" (Spillane 2020b). Spillane's incorporation of the Biden "Build Back Better" campaign slogan was certainly a signal of alignment with the national campaign. Notably, his Republican opponent Todd Polinchock stayed clear of any "Make America Great Again" or "Keep America Great" references throughout the course of the campaign.

After winning his primary, Spillane used his campaign communications to regularly tie his candidacy to broader Democratic Party national policy priorities. As with Wendy Ullman's campaign, protection of the Affordable Care Act was prioritized on his campaign website and was listed first on his Issues page (Gary Spillane for State Representative 2020). Spillane was also very active in promoting LGBTQ concerns and policies throughout the campaign; LGBTQ rights was listed as a top priority on his website, and he regularly used social media platforms to address this issue. One significant example was a Facebook post on the eve of Election Day, where Spillane appeared in a video with his daughter and her wife, with the caption for the video reading, "Tomorrow is Election Day and it is the wedding anniversary of my daughter Nora and her wife Jen. They are a wonderful example of the power of love and the strength of our community. So, let's celebrate democracy and the right to marry the one you love" (Gary Spillane for State Representative 2020).

Spillane also actively campaigned with other Pennsylvania Democrats, including Governor Wolf, who joined Spillane on the campaign trail on October 31st (Spillane 2020c) The campaign event with Wolf is particularly notable, given that Wolf had become the face of Pennsylvania's COVID-19 response, and by the fall had seen his public standing diminished in relation to the prepandemic period when his job approval ratings had been fairly high (Stefano 2020). Hitting the trail with Wolf only days before the election seemingly carried considerable risk for Spillane, but it may have been recognition that his fate may be tied to getting Democratic voters out, an area where Wolf may have still been an asset.

While Spillane was fairly willing to connect his campaign with national- and state-level Democrats, and to national-level issues such as the ACA and LGBTQ rights, his opponent Todd Polinchock followed a playbook that other Bucks County Republicans were turning to. The first-term Republican state representative from Warrington Township almost totally avoided mentioning President Trump and the presidential race in general. Like Fitzpatrick and Labs, Polinchock rarely, if ever, publicly described himself as "Republican Todd Polinchock." Instead, his campaign communications describe him as a pragmatic legislator who looks for solutions to the problems facing his constituents (Todd Polinchock Campaign Website 2020).

Also like Fitzpatrick and Labs, Polinchock stressed his work on environmental issues, noting that he was the first Republican in the Pennsylvania State House to support House Bill (HB) 1425, which called for 100% renewable energy in the state by 2050, and that he had also worked on a "Clean Water Surcharge" bill, with Democratic Governor Tom Wolf thanking him for his efforts (Quann 2020). To cite both the support of a Democratic governor and a strong environmental protection record is certainly not part of the national Republican playbook, but in Bucks County such an approach was not unusual in 2020. The 144th State House District race may have been the only campaign in the state where both candidates acknowledged some support from Governor Wolf.

Polinchock made bipartisanship a cornerstone of his campaign, regularly citing his work "across the aisle" in Harrisburg. His choice as a defining issue for his campaign—veterans affairs—may also be the most bipartisan of any issue in contemporary American politics (Steinhauer 2018). As a Naval Academy graduate and U.S. Navy veteran, Polinchock focused much of his campaign effort on matters and policies related to military veterans. A review of his social media posts during the campaign indicates that no other issue approached veteran affairs as an expressed priority. Polinchock regularly discussed events that would honor or support veterans, including the most prominent event on his fall calendar: an October 9th "Veterans Drive Thru Expo" (PA State Representative Todd Polinchock Facebook Page 2020). Notably, this event on the homestretch of the campaign was organized through Polinchock's legislative office, not through his campaign. Focusing on veterans made the event largely immune from possible claims of incumbent privilege, and it helped reinforce Polinchock's standing as being above the partisan rancor that is common in Washington and Harrisburg.

Overall, the race in the 144th District took on many of the dynamics of the Bucks County races examined earlier in the chapter. Polinchock largely avoided entanglement with the presidential race, and he stayed focused on largely bipartisan issues that posed little risk of attaching him to the liabilities of the Republican Party brand. Spillane, like both Finello and Ullman, was more willing to connect his campaign to national politics, including alignment with the Biden/Harris ticket. As the campaigns drew to a close, the different strategies employed by the Democrat and Republican slates of candidates would provide an interesting test of the various approaches employed.

The Results: An Antinationalized Enclave

In the end, did the results in the First Congressional District and the Bucks County, Pennsylvania, state house district align with expectations of nationalized elections? Certainly, the performance of the presidential candidates in these races was not dramatically different from the results of the congressional and state house candidates of their party. However, in each of the three races examined, Republican candidates emerged victorious in districts that President Trump failed to carry. Most notably, Brian Fitzpatrick outperformed Trump by 8.9 points, cruising to a 13-point victory over Christine Finello in a district that Trump lost by over 4 points. Both Shelby Labs in the 143rd and Todd Polinchock in the 144th also outperformed Trump by over 5 points on their way to fairly comfortable victories in their legislative districts. The comparisons between the presidential and congressional/state house districts can be seen in Table 3.2.

While it is difficult to determine what impact the Fitzpatrick, Labs, and Polinchock campaigns had on the divergent outcomes between their races, and on the presidential race in their district, there were certainly commonalities among the strategies that these Republicans employed. First, they consistently avoided identifying as Republican. A comprehensive examination of their campaign communication, including websites, social media posts, and campaign ads, indicates almost no mention of the GOP. Second, unless forced by their opponents or the press, these Republican candidates steered clear of mentions of the presidential race, and in particular President Trump. They seemed to take the risk that the upside of being distant from the pres-

TABLE 3.2 COMPARISON OF 2020 PRESIDENTIAL ELECTION RESULTS WITH FIRST CONGRESSIONAL DISTRICT AND BUCKS COUNTY, PENNSYLVANIA, 143RD AND 144TH STATE HOUSE DISTRICT RESULTS

First Congressional District	Trump (R)	Fitzpatrick (R)	Difference		Biden (D)	Finello (D)	Difference
	47.3%	56.6%	Fitzpatrick +8.9		51.6%	43.4%	Finello −8.2

PA 143rd State House District	Trump (R)	Labs (R)	Difference		Biden (D)	Ullman (D)	Difference
	45.8%	51.5%	Labs +5.7		52.8%	48.5%	Ullman −4.3

PA 144th State House District	Trump (R)	Polinchock (R)	Difference		Biden (D)	Spillane (D)	Difference
	49%	55.5%	Polinchock +6.5		49.5%	45.5%	Spillane −4

Source: Bucks County Board of Elections. Available at https://www.buckscounty.org/docs/default-source /boe/boecertifiedreturnbyprecinctnov2020.pdf?sfvrsn=46fc0def_0.

ident's campaign offset any potential loss of support from the president's loyal followers. Third, the Republican candidates embraced issues that had broad appeal in Bucks County but low prominence in national Republican politics. In particular, Fitzpatrick, Labs, and Polinchock all identified environmental matters as one of their top priorities, separating themselves from the GOP's poor brand image on this issue (Sellers 2020). Fourth, the Republican candidates all heralded bipartisanship, and the need for pragmatic approaches to solve problems. Fitzpatrick and Polinchock trumpeted their bipartisan work in office, noting accomplishments they had reached along with Democrats, and Labs made her commitment to bipartisanship central in her messaging. Finally, while not necessarily a strategy, the candidates all maintained generally congenial and respectful public images, and emphasized their deep family roots in Bucks County. They were well matched with strategies that were focused on localizing their campaigns.

As for the Democratic candidates, was their ultimate failure the product of the strategies they employed? Once again, isolating campaign impacts on election outcomes is challenging, so any conclusion that the strategies employed were the cause of the defeats should be reached with caution. The decision by Finello, Ullman, and Spillane to publicly attach to the Biden campaign does not seem to be an obvious mistake. Biden carried all their districts, and there was no evidence that he was a drag on their election efforts. Their opponents' characteristics, which were discussed earlier, made it very difficult to nationalize the race by attaching the Republican candidates to Trump. Simply put, Fitzpatrick, Polinchock, and Labs were not easy to nationalize, and efforts to do so may have done more harm than good.

Part of the emerging 2020 election narrative is that while Trump failed, Republicans in other races had a generally positive cycle. However, in an overwhelming number of places where Trump failed, so too did his fellow Republicans. The nature of "red" and "blue" states and heavily gerrymandered legislative districts made the alignment of outcome the rule rather than the exception in 2020. Only in Maine did a senator win a state that her party's presidential candidate lost, with Republican Susan Collins carrying the state fairly convincingly despite Trump losing even more convincingly (Brewer 2020). And in just sixteen congressional districts in the country did voters support one party for president and another for Congress (Coleman 2021). In Pennsylvania, only Matt Cartwright in the Eighth Congressional District, and Fitzpatrick in the First Congressional District, carried districts that their party's presidential candidate did not. Notably, the difference between Fitzpatrick's and Trump's respective performance in the district was the second largest in the country, with only the New York Twenty-fourth Congressional District surpassing the margin in the Pennsylvania First Congressional District (Coleman 2021). Fitzpatrick carried many central and lower Bucks County municipalities that Biden won, while also outperforming Trump in the more rural and conservative townships in northern Bucks County that the president carried. Strikingly, there was not a single municipality in the First Congressional District where Trump outperformed Fitzpatrick.

Conclusion

For years Bucks County, and its congressional district, have drawn national attention for their ability to provide insight into broader national political trends. Indeed, in 2020, the election results in this high-profile region captured many of the broad national outcomes that would define this cycle. Biden beat Trump by a margin of 51.7% to 47.3% in Bucks County, which was incredibly close to the national results, where Biden defeated Trump by a 51.3% to 46.9% gap. Thus, Bucks County and the Pennsylvania First Congressional District have maintained their status as key bellwethers of American politics.

Republican candidates in the First Congressional District outperformed Trump, aligning with the conclusion that the GOP had a solid cycle, while Trump of course did not. While not all Republicans who outperformed Trump in their districts may have followed the intensely localized strategies that helped Bucks County Republicans score victories in 2020, the approaches they took appear impactful in this time and place. The Democratic candidates in these competitive state and congressional races were more likely than their Republican counterparts to nationalize their campaigns, and given the usual alignment of presidential and congressional election results, this approach seemed to be merited given Biden's ultimate performance.

The Republican success in these races may be seen as a roadmap for the GOP to remain competitive in an era where their national brand may be more of a liability than an asset in certain regions. Certainly, if the GOP is to win congressional and state house races in the growing Philadelphia suburbs, nationalized election strategies seem very ill suited. This is especially true if the Republican Party continues to move in the populist, nationalist direction that was fully ushered in during the Trump years. Fitzpatrick's ability to easily survive a primary challenge from a Trump acolyte in 2020 provides evidence that even among Republicans, there is significant recognition that one size may not fit all in electoral politics. In reflecting on his victory, Fitzpatrick noted that "We've always been a ticket-splitting district," and that "the overwhelming majority of people in our community are very pragmatic. They're independent thinkers like I am" (Mullaney 2020). So, while nationalization has made ticket-splitting an endangered species in American politics, there remains a habitat along the banks of the Delaware River where this practice continues to flourish.

REFERENCES

Abramowitz, Alan I., and Steven W. Webster. 2016. "The Rise of Negative Partisanship and the Nationalization of U.S. Elections in the 21st Century." *Electoral Studies*, 41:12–22.

Ballotpedia. 2020. "Pennsylvania's 1st Congressional District Election, 2020." Accessed June 2, 2020. Available at https://ballotpedia.org/Pennsylvania%27s_1st_Congressional _District_election,_2020.

Bambino, Samantha. 2020. "Fitzpatrick, Fanello Square off in Congressional Debate." *Lower Bucks Times*, October 8, 2020. Available at https://lowerbuckstimes.com/2020/10/08 /fitzpatrick-finello-square-off-in-congressional-debate/.

Brewer, Mark. 2020. "The Political Survival of Susan Collins." *FixGov Blog, The Brookings Institution*. Accessed December 22, 2020. Available at https://www.brookings.edu /blog/fixgov/2020/12/22/the-political-survival-of-susan-collins/.

Brian Fitzpatrick Congressman Official Website. 2020. "Legislative Work." Accessed March 30, 2021. Available at https://fitzpatrick.house.gov/legislative-work.

Burns, Alexander, and Jonathan Martin. 2020. "Voters Prefer Biden Over Trump on Almost All Major Issues, Poll Shows." *New York Times*, October 20, 2020. Available at https://www.nytimes.com/2020/10/20/us/politics/biden-trump-times-poll.html.

Cole, John. 2020a. "PA1: Finello Ad Links Fitzpatrick to Trump on Healthcare and Tax Reform." *PoliticsPA*, September 28, 2020. Available at https://www.politicspa.com/pa1 -finello-ad-links-fitzpatrick-to-trump-on-healthcare-and-tax-reform/95960/.

———. 2020b. "Fitzpatrick Ad Blasts Finello on Police, Crime and Immigration." *PoliticsPA*, September 16, 2020. Available at https://www.politicspa.com/fitzpatrick-ad -blasts-finello-on-police-crime-and-immigration/95816/.

Coleman, Miles. 2021. "2020's Crossover Districts: Only a Handful of House Democrats and Republicans Represent Turf Won by the Other Party's Presidential Nominee." *Sabato's Crystal Ball,* February, 4, 2021. Accessed, March 23, 2021. Available at https://centerforpolitics.org/crystalball/articles/2020s-crossover-districts/.

Cook Political Report. 2017. "Partisan Voting Index Districts of the 115th Congress." Accessed December 5, 2020. Available at https://www.cookpolitical.com/file/Cook_Political_Report_Partisan_Voter_Index.6.pdf.

Deane, Leonard A. 2020. "Brian Fitzpatrick-Fitz a Republican/Democrat? Gone Underground?" *Patch,* May 31, 2020. Accessed March 23, 2021. Available at https://patch.com/pennsylvania/newhope-lambertville/brian-fitzpatrick-fitz-republican-democrat-gone-underground.

DiMattia, Anthony, and Marion Callahan. 2020. "President Donald Trump: 'Pennsylvania Will Save the American Dream.'" *Bucks County Courier Times,* October 31, 2020. Available at https://www.goerie.com/story/news/2020/10/31/donald-trump-visits-bucks-county-late-push-woo-pennsylvania-voters/6105418002/.

Finello, Christine (@FinelloforPA). 2020a. "Brian Fitzpatrick pretends he is independent." Twitter, October 6, 2020. Available at https://twitter.com/FinelloForPA/status/1313537800508264452.

———. 2020b. "I oppose defunding the police." Twitter, August 23, 2020. Available at https://twitter.com/FinelloForPA/status/1297720783733694471.

Fiorina, Morris P. 2016. "The Nationalization of Congressional Elections." The Hoover Institution (Stanford University). October 19, 2016. Available at https://www.hoover.org/research/nationalization-congressional-elections.

FiveThirtyEight. 2021. "Tracking Congress in the Age of Trump." Last modified January 13, 2021. Accessed March 16, 2021. Available at https://projects.fivethirtyeight.com/congress-trump-score/brian-fitzpatrick/.

Frey, William, and Ruy Teixaira. 2016. "The Political Geography of Pennsylvania: Not Another Rust Belt State." *The Brookings Policy Brief, April 2008.* Accessed April 3, 2021. Available at https://www.brookings.edu/wp-content/uploads/2016/06/04_political_demographics_frey_teixeira.pdf.

Gabriel, Trip, and Bidgood, Jess. 2018. "Court-Drawn Map in Pennsylvania May Lift Democrats' House Chances," *New York Times,* February 19, 2018. Available at https://www.nytimes.com/2018/02/19/us/pennsylvania-map.html.

Gary Spillane for State Representative. 2020. Campaign Website. Accessed March 7, 2021. Available at https://www.electgaryspillane.com/priorities.

Hirschfeld, Julie. 2019. "After Trump Accuses Four Democratic Congresswomen of Hating U.S., They Fire Back." *New York Times,* July 15, 2019. Available at https://www.nytimes.com/2019/07/15/us/politics/trump-go-back-tweet-racism.html.

Intelligencer. 2018. "Ullman Takes District in 143rd District Race," November 6, 2018. Accessed April 3, 2021. Available at https://www.theintell.com/news/20181106/ullman-takes-victory-in-143rd-district-race.

Itkowitz, Colby. 2019. "GOP Moderate Refuses to Defend Trump on Ukraine but Won't Back Impeachment." *Washington Post,* December 18, 2019. Available at https://www.washingtonpost.com/politics/gop-moderate-refuses-to-defend-trump-on-ukraine-but-wont-back-impeachment/2019/12/17/49b95c86-210d-11ea-86f3-3b5019d451db_story.html.

Jamerson, Joshua, and Julie Bykowitz. 2020. "Republicans Highlight Public Safety in Campaign Ads." *Wall Street Journal,* October 22, 2020. Available at https://www.wsj.com/articles/republicans-highlight-public-safety-in-campaign-ads-11603371565.

Keeler, Bob. 2018. "Election 2018: Polinchock Wins 144th District Seat." *Perkasie News Herald*, November 7, 2018. Available at https://www.thereporteronline.com/2018/11/06/election-2018-polinchock-wins-144th-district-seat/

Kelly, Mike. 2020. "So You Thought the Campaign and Election Were Ugly? Just Wait Until January." *NorthJersey.com*, November 20, 2020. Available at https://www.northjersey.com/story/news/columnists/mike-kelly/2020/11/20/problem-solvers-caucus-emerges-congress-evenly-divided-can-lead/3766626001/.

Labs, Shelby. 2020a. "Bringing Back Civility, Respect." *Bucks County Courier Times*, October 14, 2020. Available at https://www.buckscountycouriertimes.com/story/opinion/columns/your-voice/2020/10/14/labs-bringing-back-civility-respect-politics-harrisburg/3639423001/.

———. 2020b. Campaign Website. Accessed March 14, 2021. Available at http://shelbyforpa.com/?fbclid=IwAR3bfinzPl1tqT3eI9cmR4-lwQhwGzC9iHhsimEALQEXWWAikvD1cbdWeO0.

———. 2020c. "Setting the Record Straight." Shelby Labs for State Rep. Facebook, October 7, 2020, Video, 0:37. Available at https://www.facebook.com/ShelbyforPA/videos/954689215036348.

Lugar Center. 2020. "The Lugar Center and Georgetown University's McCourt School Unveil New Bipartisan Index Rankings for the First Year of the 116th Congress." Media Coverage, May 12, 2020. Available at https://www.thelugarcenter.org/newsroom-news-405.html.

McElwee, Charles. 2020. "Pennsylvania's Bucks County: Ultimate Suburban Bellwether." *Lincoln Journal Star*. Updated October 1, 2020. Available at https://journalstar.com/pennsylvania-s-bucks-county-ultimate-suburban-bellwether/article_0b3f0cf2-d168-5eb6-98c1-501aaab45e1b.html.

Meehan for Congress. 2020. "Andy Meehan. Against Us, Helping Them." YouTube Video. Filmed January 2, 2020. Available at https://www.youtube.com/watch?v=QCXjUI2H59k.

Meyer, Katie. 2020a. "In Bucks, U.S. Rep. Fitzpatrick Getting Challenged from the Right and Left." *WHYY News*, June 1, 2020. Available at https://whyy.org/articles/in-bucks-u-s-rep-fitzpatrick-getting-challenged-from-the-right-and-left/.

———. 2020b. "Here's How Democrats Can Flip the Pennsylvania Legislature." *WHYY News*, October 12, 2020. Available at https://whyy.org/articles/heres-how-democrats-could-flip-the-pennsylvania-legislature/.

Muhlenberg College Institute of Public Opinion. 2020a. "Final 2020 PA Presidential Election Poll." October 30, 2020. Available at https://www.muhlenberg.edu/aboutus/polling/politicselectionssurveys/archivedpolls/final2020paelectionsurvey/.

———. 2020b. "Muhlenberg College/Morning Call Pennsylvania 7th Congressional District Poll: September 2020." September 27, 2020. Available at https://www.muhlenberg.edu/aboutus/polling/politicselectionssurveys/archivedpolls/2020-pa7thdistrictpoll/.

Mullaney, J. D. 2020. "Why Fitzpatrick Beat Trump and Clobbered Finello in PA-1." *Bucks County Courier Times*, November 14, 2020. Available at https://www.buckscountycouriertimes.com/story/opinion/2020/11/14/brian-fitzpatrick-trump-christina-finello-bucks-county-2020/6259452002/.

Muschick, Paul. 2020. "Room for Moderates: Pennsylvania Race Shows Republicans Don't Have to Blindly Support Trump to Win." *Morning Call*, June 9, 2020. Available at https://www.mcall.com/opinion/mc-opi-rep-brian-fitzpatrick-2020-primary-muschick-20200609-w3zzw52nbveqje2hbv4t4kfcfu-story.html.

Otterbein, Holly. 2018. "How Brian Fitzpatrick Won in an 'Atrocious Political Environment' for Suburban Republicans." *Philadelphia Inquirer*, November 7, 2018. Available at https://www.inquirer.com/philly/news/politics/elections/pa-3rd-district-brian-fitzpatrick-suburban-republican-democrat-scott-wallace-election-20181107.html.

Otterbein, Holly, and Marc Caputo. 2020. "If Pennsylvania Goes, So Will Go the Country." *Politico*, November 1, 2020. Available at https://www.politico.com/news/2020/11/01/pennsylvania-trump-biden-campaign-433798.

PA State Representative Todd Polinchock Facebook Page. 2020. Accessed October 9, 2020. Available at https://www.facebook.com/RepPolinchock/events/?ref=page_internal.

Pennsylvania Department of State. 2020. "Voting and Election Statistics." *Voting and Elections*. Accessed January 17, 2021. Available at https://www.dos.pa.gov/VotingElections/OtherServicesEvents/VotingElectionStatistics/Pages/VotingElectionStatistics.aspx.

Pew Research Center. 2020. "Voters Rarely Switch Parties, but Recent Shifts Further Educational, Racial Divergence." August 4, 2020. Available at https://www.pewresearch.org/politics/2020/08/04/voters-rarely-switch-parties-but-recent-shifts-further-educational-racial-divergence/.

Plott, Elaina. 2020. "A Primary from the Right? Not in Trump's GOP." *New York Times*, January 28, 2020. Available at https://www.nytimes.com/2020/01/28/us/politics/pennsylvania-republicans-trump.html.

Quann, Peg. 2020. "Pennsylvania's 144th District: Polinchock Defeats Spillane for Reelection." *Bucks County Courier Times*, November 2, 2020. Available at https://www.buckscountycouriertimes.com/story/news/2020/11/02/pennsylvanias-144th-district-polinchock-spillane-economy/6045747002/.

Quann, Peg, and Chris Ellery. 2019. "Democrats Take Control of Bucks County Government." *Intelligencer*, November 5, 2019. Accessed April 4, 2021. Available at https://www.theintell.com/news/20191105/democrats-take-control-of-bucks-county-government.

Ridge, Tom. 2020. "My Fellow Conservatives Are Out of Touch on the Environment." *The Atlantic*, April 22, 2020. Available at https://www.theatlantic.com/ideas/archive/2020/04/environment-gop-out-touch/610333/.

Sellers, Christopher. 2020. "How Republicans Came to Embrace Anti-Environmentalism." *Vox*, June 7, 2020. Available at https://www.vox.com/2017/4/22/15377964/republicans-environmentalism.

Siders, David. 2020. "Donald Trump's Suburban Horror Show." *Politico*, June 24, 2020. Available at https://www.politico.com/news/2020/07/25/trumps-suburban-nightmare-376823.

Sievert, Joel, and Seth C. McKee. 2019. "Nationalization in U.S. Senate and Gubernatorial Elections." *American Politics Research* 47, no. 5: 1055–80.

Solfield, Tom. 2020a. "Poll Shows Congressman Fitzpatrick Leading Over Challenger Finello, Trump Behind Biden in First District." *LevittownNow.com*, July 17, 2020. Available at http://levittownnow.com/2020/07/17/poll-shows-congressman-fitzpatrick-leading-over-challenger-finello-trump-behind-biden-in-first-district/.

———. 2020b. "Joe Biden Makes Pitch from Bristol Twp.: 'The Stakes Have Never Been Higher.'" *LevittownNow.com*, October 24, 2020. Available at http://levittownnow.com/2020/10/24/joe-biden-makes-pitch-from-bristol-twp-the-stakes-have-never-been-higher/.

Spillane, Gary (@electspillane). 2020a. "As Vice President @JoeBiden has said over and over." Twitter, October 14, 2020. Available at https://twitter.com/electspillane/status/1316436160818937858.

———. 2020b. "What an honor to have @TomWolfPA here in Warrington." Twitter, October 31, 2020. Available at https://twitter.com/electspillane/status/1322665043788517376.

———. 2020c. "Let's Celebrate." Twitter, November 2, 2020. Available at https://twitter.com/electspillane/status/1323339915170586624.

———. 2020d. Campaign Website "Endorsements." Accessed March 23, 2021. Available at https://www.electgaryspillane.com/endorsements.

Stefano, Jennifer. 2020. "Could Pennsylvania's Democratic Governor Deliver Trump the Election?" *TheHill.com*, October 12, 2020. Available at https://thehill.com/opinion/campaign/520329-could-pennsylvanias-democratic-governor-deliver-trump-the-election.

Steinhauer, Jennifer. 2018. "Republicans and Democrats Unite on at Least One Issue: Oversight of the V.A." *New York Times*, December 10, 2018. Available at https://www.nytimes.com/2018/12/10/us/politics/veterans-affairs-congress.html.

Sullivan, Sean. 2020. "Democrats Grow More Anxious About Pennsylvania." *Washington Post*, November 1, 2020. Available at https://www.washingtonpost.com/politics/democrats-anxiety-pennsylvania/2020/10/31/10536746-1b19-11eb-aeec-b93bcc29a01b_story.html.

Swing Left. 2020. "Pennsylvania: Super State Strategy." Accessed February 22, 2021. Available at https://swingleft.org/p/pennsylvania.

Todd Polinchock Campaign Website. 2020. "Accomplishments." Re-Elect Todd Polinchock for State Rep. Accessed February 22, 2021. Available at https://www.toddpolinchock.com/accomplishments.

Transparency USA. 2020. "Gary Spillane." Candidates. Accessed January 15, 2022. Available at https://www.transparencyusa.org/pa/candidate/gary-spillane/donors.

Ullman, Wendy. 2020. Campaign Facebook Post, October 17, 2020. Accessed April 3, 2021. Available at https://www.facebook.com/wendyullman143/.

U.S. Census Bureau. 2019. "Congressional District 1, PA." *Census Reporter*. Available at https://censusreporter.org/profiles/50000US4201-congressional-district-1-pa/.

4

Campaigns in the Fourth Congressional District

Running in Philadelphia's Democratic Suburbs

J. Wesley Leckrone and Angela M. Corbo

Philadelphia and its suburbs were national news during the 2020 election as mail-in ballots were counted and the nation waited for Pennsylvania's final results. Democrats have dominated Philadelphia politics since the 1950s. However, the four surrounding "collar counties"—Bucks, Chester, Delaware, and Montgomery—have only recently shifted from Republican strongholds to solidly Democratic. Biden needed a strong Democratic turnout in southeastern Pennsylvania to win the state. Montgomery County, as the third largest county in the state with approximately 830,000 residents, is of particular importance for Democrats in statewide races. A postelection commentator argued that Montgomery County is becoming "a place where Democrats can expect smashing margins in statewide races to offset the party's struggles with white working-class voters elsewhere" (Terruso 2020). However, congressional and state legislative races in Montgomery County had different qualities than the presidential race. This chapter examines how candidates campaigned and interacted with voters in the Fourth Congressional District and the 150th and 154th State House Districts. The two state legislative seats are located in Montgomery County, as is the Fourth Congressional District, with the exception of a very small part in Berks County. These races took place in either Democratic-leaning or safe Democratic districts. Consequently, different strategies and messages were employed in contrast to the competitive statewide presidential race.

We interviewed a combination of local candidates, party officials, and campaign staff. The majority of the candidates focused on local issues or localized national issues. Some candidates coordinated efforts with the top-of-the-ticket or party-based organizations. In contrast to the other local races, candidates in the Fourth Congressional District connected more with the top-of-the-ticket and nationalized issues. The Dean campaign staff supported the Biden/Harris literature drop efforts. The Barnette campaign echoed the Trump platform messaging in speaking points and social media posts. They toed the party line and supported the president's policies, but not always his personality. Analysis showed that both candidates exhibited nationalized messaging, while making room for their own personal characteristics and stories to help form the narrative of their campaigns. Both candidates embraced nationalized themes that demonstrated their alliance with the party's values.

Southeastern Pennsylvania, which is a densely populated corridor of the Commonwealth, was predicted to have great influence in the national election outcome. Donald Trump identified Philadelphia as a problem region during the first presidential debate, saying "Bad things happen in Philadelphia." In contrast, the Biden family home in Greenville, Delaware, is only thirty-three miles from the city of Philadelphia. This proximity enables the Delawarean "Uncle Joe" persona to reach into the Philadelphia media outlets. This dichotomy fueled toxic partisanship and influenced the public narrative around the election's integrity.

This chapter captures the local and national campaign messaging within the southeastern corner of the Commonwealth. A brief history of the region provides a contextual understanding of the political landscape, and the candidate presentation-of-self descriptions follow.

Case Studies

Montgomery County is representative of metropolitan suburbs transitioning from Republican strongholds to areas that consistently elect Democratic politicians (Meyer and Briggs 2020). The three races covered in this chapter focus on districts with varying degrees of Democratic control that allow for an examination of different types of messaging from candidates from both political parties. The Fourth Congressional District is solidly Democratic. In 2020, however, Representative Madeleine Dean was running for reelection for the first time, a point at which elected officials are most vulnerable. She has quickly built a national profile owing to her position on the House Judiciary Committee during both impeachments of President Trump and her frequent appearances on cable news (Cochrane 2021). Her Republican opponent, Kathy Barnette, was one of thirty black GOP candidates running for U.S. House or Senate in the general election (Andrews 2020). How Barnette crafted her message as a black Republican running against a white progressive like Dean provides an interesting case study. Both candidates aligned themselves with nationalized messaging and remained loyal to the party's national agenda.

Democrats were successful in winning Montgomery County state house seats during the "Blue Wave" election of 2018. Their attempt to take control of the state house in 2020 was predicated on holding onto gains from two years before, including Joe Webster's seat in the 150th District. Democrats outnumbered Republicans by only 2.6% in this district, so a solid campaign from a female Republican like Beth Ann Bittner Mazza should have led to this being a competitive race. The question was whether the candidates would run on national party themes and try to win on turnout or would attempt to appeal to local issues and pull in swing voters. The 154th State House District seat was open, but with little chance of Republican victory. The district offered the opportunity to follow how Napoleon Nelson, a black man from Cheltenham, ran his campaign in the diverse district and how Kathleen Bowers defined herself as the Republican running in a relatively unwinnable race. In sum, the three races offer a mix of competitive and noncompetitive elections and a mix of racial and gender demographics.

The Fourth Congressional District

The Pennsylvania Supreme Court ordered the state's congressional map to be redrawn in 2018 because the map violated the state constitution's "free and equal elections" clause (Becker Kane 2019, 58–61). The entire state was gerrymandered, but critics were particularly critical of the way suburban Philadelphia was carved up to ensure Republican victories. Montgomery County was at the heart of this discussion since it was divided into five different house districts, with none of the incumbents living in the state's third most populous county (Lai and Navratil 2018). The redrawn congressional map created Pennsylvania's Fourth Congressional District, which encompasses most of Montgomery County and a small part of Berks County. Portions of Montgomery County are in the First and Fifth Congressional Districts, but 86% of the county's registered voters are consolidated in the Fourth.

The Pennsylvania Fourth Congressional District is affluent, educated, and less diverse than the state and nation as a whole. At $91,030, the district's 2019 median household income puts the Fourth Congressional District among the top 15% wealthiest in the United States (#53) and second in the Commonwealth after the First Congressional District (ProximityOne n.d.). Only 6% of its residents live below the poverty line, half the number for the state and nation. Affluence is also indicated by the price of its owner-occupied housing stock, which is 68% above the Commonwealth average. Residents in this district are highly educated, with almost half of them having a

TABLE 4.1 DEMOGRAPHIC CHARACTERISTICS OF PENNSYLVANIA'S 150TH AND 154TH STATE HOUSE DISTRICTS, FOURTH CONGRESSIONAL DISTRICT, PENNSYLVANIA, AND THE UNITED STATES IN 2019

	PA 150th State House District[a]	PA 154th State House District[b]	Fourth Congressional District[c]	Pennsylvania[d]	United States[d]
Population	67,642	61,297	730,701	12,801,989	328,231,337
Population density: people/square mile	1,634.7	3,752.1	1,532.1	286.1	92.9[e]
Population white	75%	61%	80%	76%	60%
Population black	9%	25%	10%	11%	12%
Population Hispanic	5%	5%	6%	8%	18%
Foreign-born	11.3%	9.8%	9.6%	7.0%	13.7%
Median household income	$107,381	$92,490	$91,030	$63,463	$65,712
Below poverty line	4.0%	7.5%	6.4%	12.0%	12.3%
Median value of owner-occupied housing units	$330,600	$305,700	$323,500	$192,600	$240,500
Bachelor's degree or higher	48.4%	57.3%	48.5%	32.3%	33.1%

Sources:
(a) Compiled from U.S. Census Bureau. n.d. "Census Reporter: State House District 150, PA." Accessed January 4, 2021. Available at https://censusreporter.org/profiles/62000US42150-state-house-district -150-pa/.
(b) Compiled from U.S. Census Bureau. n.d. "Census Reporter: State House District 154, PA." Accessed January 4, 2021. Available at https://censusreporter.org/profiles/62000US42154-state-house-district -154-pa/.
(c) Compiled from U.S. Census Bureau. n.d. "Census Reporter: Congressional District 4, PA." Accessed January 4, 2021. Available at https://censusreporter.org/profiles/50000US4204-congressional-district -4-pa/.
(d) Compiled from U.S. Census Bureau. n.d. "Census Reporter: Pennsylvania." Accessed December 30, 2020. Available at https://censusreporter.org/profiles/04000US42-pennsylvania/.
(e) Duffin, Erin. 2020. "Population Density of the United States from 1790 to 2019 in Residents Per Square Mile of Land Area." *Statista*, February 12, 2020. Available at https://www.statista.com/statistics/183475 /united-states-population-density/.

TABLE 4.2 VOTER REGISTRATION STATISTICS BY PARTY

2020 General Election Registration	Total	Democratic	% D	Republican	% R	No Affiliation/ Other	% NA/O
Fourth Congressional District	535,351	261,543	48.9	190,380	35.6	83,428	15.6
150th State House District	58,613	25,041	42.7	23,500	40.1	10,072	17.2
154th State House District	47,978	32,917	68.6	9,101	19.0	5,960	12.4

Source: Compiled from Pennsylvania Department of State. n.d. "Voting and Election Statistics." Accessed November 1, 2020. Available at https://www.dos.pa.gov/VotingElections/OtherServicesEvents/Voting ElectionStatistics/Pages/VotingElectionStatistics.aspx.

bachelor's degree or higher. Demographically, the Fourth Congressional District is comparable to the state, but it is whiter and has fewer Hispanics and fewer foreign-born residents than the nation as a whole (Table 4.1).

Major election forecasters consider the Fourth Congressional District a solid or safe Democratic seat (Ballotpedia n.d.b). The *Cook Political Report* (n.d.) ranks the district as D+7 in its Partisan Voting Index, with Hillary Clinton winning the 2016 presidential vote with 57.9% and Barack Obama receiving 56.1% of the vote in 2012. Among registered voters in the district, Democrats lead Republicans 48.9% to 35.6%, with 15.6% nonaffiliated or registered with another party. In 2018, former Democratic state representative Madeleine Dean won the redrawn Fourth Congressional District over Republican Dan David, 63.5% to 36.5% (see Table 4.2).

The 150th State House District

The 150th State House District is located in south central Montgomery County, abutting Chester County. The district transitions from suburban to exurban as you travel further west from Philadelphia and the county seat of Norristown. The 150th is very affluent, with median household incomes 69.2% higher than Pennsylvania and 18% higher than the Fourth Congressional District. Its poverty level is one-third the rate for the state and the nation. The racial and ethnic composition is comparable to the Fourth District and Pennsylvania, with a slightly higher proportion of foreign-born residents.

Like many areas of suburban Philadelphia, the 150th District has become more Democratic over the last decade. In 2011, Republicans held a plurality of voters there and a 6.6% registration advantage. By October 2020, Democrats had a 2.4% edge among registered voters. The seat had been held by a Republican since seat numbers were assigned to districts in 1969. As recently as 2014, incumbent Republican Mike Vereb won the seat with 64% of the vote. He retired and was replaced by Republican Michael Corr, who won election in 2016 but declined to run again in 2018. Democrat Joseph Webster won the open seat that year with 56% of the vote.

The 154th State House District

The 154th State House District is located in southeastern Montgomery County and abuts northwestern and northern Philadelphia. Median household income is comparable with the Fourth Congressional District, but is 45.7% higher than Pennsylvania as a whole. At 7.5%, the poverty rate is slightly higher than that of the Fourth Congressional District, but well below state and national levels. The 154th is more diverse than either the Fourth District or Pennsylvania as a whole, due to 25% of the population being black. Of the district's total population, 57% have a bachelor's degree or higher—outpacing the state and the nation by about 25%, and 9% higher than the Fourth Congressional District.

The 154th District is overwhelming Democratic, with the party holding an almost 50% voter registration advantage over Republicans. Over the last decade the district has become 5.1% more Democratic, with similar increases in its three constituent townships. The 154th was reliably Republican until 1992, when Larry Curry flipped the seat en route to serving ten terms in the state house. After Curry's retirement, Democrat Steve McCarter was elected to four terms, each time with at least 74% of the vote. McCarter's retirement after the 2020 legislative session set up an open race for the seat.

Campaign Nationalization?

Campaigns are *nationalized* when candidates focus on issues representing broad-based partisan cleavages from across the country. If the campaign is so generic that it could be run in any district around the country, it is nationalized. Campaigns are *localized* when geographically specific issues and personal characteristics dominate the discourse. The contests in the Fourth Congressional District all displayed some national themes, primarily because it was a presidential election year. However, the further down-ballot the race, the less the nationalization. Democrats functioned as a much more cohesive unit than Republicans over 2020 with an anti-Trump message stressing that change would come not only by replacing the incumbent president, but by getting Democrats in power throughout the political system. There was cooperation on the Republican side, but the down-ballot Republican candidates crafted their own campaign messages that emphasized some of Trump's policy ideas while not fully embracing the man.

This section of the chapter analyzes the candidates' presentation of their image and issue stances obtained through their websites, social media, commercials and advertisements, targeted mailings, public appearances, debates, and interviews with candidates, campaign officials, and party leaders.[1] We assessed the electronic communications for nationalized and localized content. Social media content frequently promotes local campaign events and focuses on local issues. As such, the state house district candidates presented predominately localized content. The Fourth Congressional District candidates demonstrated loyalty to the party and connected their posts to nationally aligned party issues.

The Presidential Election

Pennsylvania was heavily targeted by both the Biden and Trump campaigns. As the largest media market in the state, metropolitan Philadelphia was of particular importance for getting messaging out. None of the candidates made a campaign appearance within the confines of the Fourth Congressional District. However, there were nine appearances that got media coverage to some or all of the district (Ruthhart and Berlin 2020). The campaigns focused on different constituencies: Biden and Harris made six stops in Philadelphia and one in Bucks County, while Trump and Pence campaigned in the suburbs and exurbs with two stops in Berks County and one in Bucks County. In campaign stops and print and media advertising, both Biden and Trump referenced the importance of Pennsylvania. However, very little of either candidate's messaging focused specifically on issues unique to southeastern Pennsylvania or to the Fourth District in particular.

Thematically the Biden campaign established nationalized messages with three core issues: getting out the vote, Biden's ability to address major policy issues and divisions in American society, and stopping Donald Trump. The campaign ran 107 television ads in the Fourth Congressional District media market. Addressing the COVID-19 pandemic accounted for 37% of the commercials, with negative ads about Trump's inaction and positive commercials about Biden's plans. The economy and jobs (18%), health care (15%), discussion of Biden's good character and Trump's lack of integrity (15%), and encouraging people to vote (12%) were other predominant themes in commercials. The same themes emerged on targeted mailings promoting Biden. "Make a Plan" to vote was the most common theme. "Be one of the first to move our country forward" and "Thousands of your friends and neighbors will be voting in this election. Join them and vote" were typical of the

"Get Out The Vote" (GOTV) slogans. Some of the mailers were Pennsylvania-specific because they highlighted the state's unique process of mail-in voting. However, the content and issues were generic and did not address any parochial issues related to the Fourth Congressional District.

Thematically the Trump campaign focused on economic growth during his presidency, painting the Democrats as radical leftists, and attacking Biden's character. The Trump campaign ran fifty-six different television ads in the Fourth District media market. They focused on three primary nationalized themes. Positive ads touted Trump's handing of the economy and jobs (25%), with some focusing on the economy strengthening during the pandemic. Negative ads sought to portray Biden as a threat to Medicare (30%) and to tie the former vice president to crime and rioting in major cities and the "Defund the Police" movement (23%). Targeted mailers from the Trump campaign and its nonaffiliated super PAC America First Action contrasted the president's plans to move the economy forward during the pandemic with the claim that Biden and Democrats were "surrendering to the virus." Slogans such as "America can't hide from the coronavirus" and "President Donald Trump is building the world's greatest economy again!" were used to portray a president who was restoring normality by supporting the re-opening of businesses and schools.

Trump localized the attacks in a speech in Reading, in Berks County, on October 31, 2020, where he used Philadelphia as an example of a radical antipolice city and claimed that it had been "ransacked by violent mobs and Biden supporters" (Rev.com 2020). Finally, campaign literature attacked Biden as a racist and a cheater. Mailers with pictures of black males, and even a quote from Maya Angelou, aimed to dissuade people from voting for Biden because of his support for mass incarceration, his opposition to school busing, his "racist comments," and the claim that he is "taking Black voters for granted." Across all the mailers, Biden was visualized and described as old, "out of it," and "weak." Like Biden's messaging, the content of the Trump campaign messaging related to national issues, including the candidate's ability to serve. There was little acknowledgment of local issues other than that Pennsylvania was a key swing state.

Pennsylvania Fourth Congressional District

Incumbent Madeleine Dean was reelected to serve as U.S. congresswoman representing Pennsylvania's Fourth District. Dean's communication strategy centered around her "important role in DC" and her knowledge (and service) to the Fourth Congressional District. During her first term in office, Dean cosponsored over 400 pieces of legislation, including a bipartisan bill providing mental health resources to first responders. She also played important roles on the House Judiciary Committee and the House Financial Services Committee. Throughout her time in Congress and on the campaign trail she was a vehement opponent of Trump and his abrasive brand of politics. She also railed against Republican political posturing on judiciary appointments, particularly the decision to fill the U.S. Supreme Court seat left empty by the death of Justice Ruth Bader Ginsburg prior to the election. The promotion of Dean's experience and record naturally favored nationalized messaging.

After only two years in office, Madeleine Dean ran with the confidence of a ten-term incumbent. This confidence was driven by the demographics of the district as well as her familiarity with the area after serving as a state representative. It also had to do with her quick rise to prominence within the House and in the media. She had become a national presence in one term, and she had leveraged this by supporting other congressional and state legislative candidates in southeastern Pennsylvania. Numerous local party and campaign officials noted that her profile in Washington, D.C., and her constituent service produced a satisfactory body of work that became the hallmark of her campaign message. An official with her campaign stated that Dean's mindset was that "if a representative does their job correctly there is no real need to campaign." This was certainly the case as she ran no television commercials, and one of her final major public events before the election was billed as a constituent town hall drive-in rather than a campaign event (Office of Representative Madeleine Dean 2020). Her focus on casework for residents of her district is among the best in Congress. Dean's commitment to her Catholic faith and her support for social justice issues both guide her service philosophy for her constituents (Panaritis 2019). Throughout the election, however, issue advocacy emerged as the most fundamental form of Dean's constituent service. COVID relief, education, addressing racism, environmental protection, health care, and "holding President Trump accountable" were among the top issues of her campaign. This issue advocacy, combined with her emerging prominence as a Democratic voice in the House, served significantly to nationalize her campaign. As one Democratic official noted, she ran as a "big time Democrat" focused on defeating Trump. While Dean was not as hyperbolic as some candidates, the issues she campaigned on could have been used by almost any suburban Democrat running for reelection in a moderately safe district. In sum, Dean's campaign was mostly nationalized, with aspects of localization related to her constituent work.

Dean received over eighty endorsements from organizations, elected officials, and labor groups. Notable endorsements came from former officials including president Barack Obama, vice president Joe Biden, governor Edward G. Rendell, and mayor Michael Nutter. Dean also received endorsements from well-established organizations such as Giffords Courage to Fight Gun Violence, EMILY's List, Women's Leadership Initiative, Sierra Club, American Nurses Association, and Pennsylvania AFL-CIO. The campaign collaborated with Back To Blue PA, Turn PA Blue, and the Montgomery County Democratic Party, according to her campaign staff. These endorsements provided nationalized support for her candidacy.

Kathy Barnette ran as a Republican against incumbent Madeleine Dean. She relied heavily on her personal narrative to connect to the voters, while at the same time arguing that Dean was an out-of-touch rich woman whose politics were too extreme for the Fourth Congressional District. She defined herself with traditional Republican characteristics in her Instagram profile: "God. Family. Country . . . and in that order. Veteran. Political Commentator. Homeschooling momma." The website KathyBarnetteforCongress.com outlined Barnette's conservative stands on safety, education, health care, taxes and spending, local control, energy, and infrastructure. The core of her philosophy is that government should "give a hand-up, not a hand-out to those who are marginalized." She combined this message with a charismatic personality. Local party leaders said her message of an independent person who spoke her mind was refreshing and was effective at swaying voters when they heard her. One said, "I wish everyone in the country could hear her speak."

Race was the primary tool used to build Barnette's campaign persona. The theme of racial injustice was a nationalized issue during the 2020 election. Barnette's campaign connected the personal and political regarding race in America. According to her campaign website, Barnette "grew up on a pig farm" in Alabama. She tells the story of poverty, race, and service. She is a proud U.S. Armed Forces Reserve officer who lived the American dream of pursuing her undergraduate and graduate education. She achieved professional success as a corporate finance professional, adjunct professor, political commentator, and author. Her messaging conveys her patriotism and dedication to the country, and her belief that "my story represents all that is good about this country" (Tierney 2020). Key to this narrative was the claim that "No one told me I was a victim" so she worked hard and achieved. She claimed that being a black conservative woman made her an independent thinker who would make a good representative. At a Virtual BYOB talk, she stated that "white progressive liberals are using the color of my skin and the history of the U.S. to get power" through "cancel culture" (Kathy Barnette 4 USA 2020). Barnette placed Dean at the forefront of these white progressives. Numerous times she chided Dean on her statement that she had walked over the Edmund Pettus Bridge twice with John Lewis as a signal of her understanding of racism and civil rights. However, Barnette argued that white progressives, who knew nothing about being black, teamed up with "black gatekeepers" to convince blacks that they were oppressed victims. This made them a key constituency of the Democratic Party, which in Barnette's estimation had done nothing for them. On the other hand, she believed that the white Republican establishment did not believe in her because she was a black woman conservative. She sought to create an aura that although no one supported her, she remained determined.

Kathy Barnette ran on her unique story, which contrasted with Madeleine Dean's life. However, many of the themes of her campaign were similar to those of the national GOP and Trump. Barnette defined herself as an outsider, a black Republican who was not accepted by the national GOP or by other blacks. She claimed that she was someone her critics believed should not "exist": a poor black girl who achieved the American dream. In her view, this background allowed her to remain independent of the political class and make thoughtful decisions in the best interest of her potential constituents, especially those of color. Dean, on the other hand, was portrayed in commercials as being a wealthy white woman who had spent a privileged life in wealthy Montgomery County, who profited from her husband's business that imported bicycles from "sweatshops" in China, and who was in hock to big business because of their PAC contributions to her campaigns. A Barnette radio commercial questioned how a person with a million-dollar home and a beach house in Cape May could understand real people. In sum, Dean's out-of-touch wealthy lifestyle led her to progressive solutions that adversely affected the middle and working classes. Barnette argued that her life experiences made her more prepared to serve in Congress because she had a larger worldview than her opponent.

Barnette also tried to lump Dean in with the national Democratic Party. She claimed that Dean "has demonstrated how out of touch she is with our district by voting 95% of the time in line with 'the squad,' these far-left legislators" (Dom Giordano Program 2020). Dean was also portrayed as one of the Democrats who wanted to defund the police by cutting $600 million from the Health and Economic Recovery Omnibus Emergency Solutions (HEROES) bill in an effort to lower the pandemic relief measure's price tag to mollify Republicans (Schultz 2020).[2] These and other examples reflected the nationalized agenda, with generalized Republican talking points on issues such as Black Lives Matter, the COVID shutdown's effects on the Trump economy, holding China accountable for unfair trading practices, and the prolife cause. Barnette's strategy of contrasting her life story with Dean's helped focus her campaign on the specifics of the Fourth Congressional District. On the other hand, she tried to associate Dean with progressive Democrats across the country whose ideology was "not even socialism any more—more like Communism—like Marxism" (Kathy Barnette 4 USA 2020). Postelection, her website and social media turned away from these issues and had a theme similar to President Trump's Twitter feed. She questioned the "fraudulent" election process and COVID protocols with the vaccine and social distancing restrictions. Barnette remarked, "The media DOES NOT get to declare a winner. Democrats, with their lying and scheming selves, DO NOT get to declare a winner" (KathyBarnetteCongressPA04 Facebook December 4, 2020). Barnette combined this type of Trumpian rhetoric about Democrats with her own unique story and criticism of Dean. Consequently, the Barnette campaign can be described as equally national and local.

Pennsylvania House of Representatives District 150

Democratic state representative Joe Webster was first elected to the House in 2018. Webster earned a bachelor's degree from the U.S. Air Force Academy, a master's degrees from Wright State University and the U.S. Naval War College, and a Ph.D. in Public Policy from George Washington University. He worked in the Pentagon for twenty years, including on September 11, 2001. In the months that followed, Webster served abroad in thirty-two different countries. Webster entered the business world in 2004. He also founded a nonprofit organization, Convergence Music.

Webster's campaign slogan was "Service—Equity—Progress." He used his military and business experiences, combined with his education, to portray himself as the type of person who can get things done in Harrisburg without theatrics and self-promotion. Webster's legislative priorities, according to his campaign website, include providing quality education; protecting the Commonwealth's natural resources and environment; combating gun violence; providing access to affordable healthcare in order to promote a healthy workforce; election reform; property taxes; and enhanced economic growth. Webster's campaign staff stated that he was not able "to get as much done" in Harrisburg as he had planned because he was not a member of the dominant party. He used that as a tool to promote his campaign, arguing that Democrats needed to take control of the state legislature so that they could end Republican-caused gridlock and accomplish policy goals. For example, on June 8, 2020, he argued on Facebook that "there are at least 19 bills that have been introduced over the past 6 months addressing issues like use of force, police accountability, data systems, and NOT ONE has had a vote in the House of Representatives."

Locally, Webster focused on hunger in the community. A JoeWebsterPA Facebook post on July 7, 2020, highlighted the "Meals for 150" community effort to distribute food to families in need on Tuesdays and Thursdays. Another primary campaign theme was equity for all. However, after the deaths of George Floyd, Breonna Taylor, Ahmaud Arbery, and other people of color ignited the national Black Lives Matter (BLM) movement, Webster focused significant energy on equity for the black community. He strongly condemned Montgomery County commissioner Joe Gale's verbal attack on the BLM movement. Gale referred to BLM as a "terrorist organization." Webster's June 4, 2020, Facebook post stated, "For decades Black Americans have been the victims of hate, discrimination, and police brutality. To say anything else is insensitive and historically inaccurate." Webster made a national issue local as he attended community events supporting racial justice, including a June 15th event sponsored by local students.

Webster and other Democratic candidates, including Madeleine Dean, Joanna McClinton, and Brian Sims, attended virtual events and some pandemic-friendly in-person events during the campaign season. According to Webster's campaign manager, the campaign canvased for the Biden/Harris ticket. While the Democratic candidates coordinated campaigning efforts, they were free to develop their own messaging.

Webster received endorsements from VoteVets.org, Sierra Club, PASNAP (Pennsylvania Association of Staff Nurses and Allied Professionals), PSEA/PACE (Political Action Committee for Education), the Humane Society, and congresswoman (and 2020 candidate) Madeleine Dean, to highlight a few.

Webster ran an almost entirely localized campaign based on the strength of his résumé, arguing that he was the right person to represent the district in Harrisburg because he had the "experience to get the job done." His campaign actively promoted his involvement in local food drives to help those who suffered economic harm during the pandemic. Additionally, even though the 150th District is affluent, Webster pushed for a more equitable state school funding formula because there were several poorer school districts among his constituency. He also focused heavily on a more generic message of "moving Pennsylvania forward." This was predicated on Democrats winning control of the General Assembly and changing the Republican leadership that he claimed would not address state problems. Webster's campaign highlighted fairly generic Democratic issues: gerrymandering, education, infrastructure, economic development, health care and sick leave, equality, and the minimum wage. However, the focus was on how these issues could be addressed at the state level if he were reelected and the Democrats could take control of the legislature. This optimism was summed up in a campaign video where he stated, "I think we're on the cusp of a new day in Pennsylvania."

First-time political candidate but long-time community activist Beth Ann Bittner Mazza saw an opportunity to serve her community through elected office. Like Webster, she ran an almost entirely local campaign. Bittner Mazza is a resident of Lower Providence Township and the mother of three grown sons. She publishes *Lower Providence Living*, a monthly magazine for residents in and around the township. Prior to her run for state representative, Bittner Mazza worked in Montgomery County in a variety of professional roles, including community relations coordinator for the Audubon Branch of the Philadelphia Freedom Valley YMCA, deputy director of the Montgomery County Division of Emergency Medical Services, and membership ambassador for MidAtlantic Employers' Association.

Bittner Mazza's campaign slogan, "People Over Politics," was designed to show a nonpartisan approach to her potential governing style. She argued that "Instead of focusing on partisan political agenda, my priorities are the same as yours" (Bittner Mazza Website, 2020). Bittner Mazza believed that uniting people based on shared values is more important than focusing on differences. "As I meet more and more people in our community, we all seem to agree that we must bring civility, kindness and mutual respect back to state government" (Bittner Mazza Website, 2020). She focused her campaign on shared interests within the local community.

Food insecurity was a top priority for Bittner Mazza. She talked about her commitment to working with community groups to distribute meals to children and families. Her Facebook posts mention the Montgomery County Anti-Hunger Network, Fill-a-Truck Food Drive, Lower Providence Food Donations, and Fish-for-Free. One source shared that Bittner Mazza deserves credit for organizing the Fill-a-Truck Food Drive program while her opponent Joe Webster benefited from promoting that event and other anti-hunger resources highlighted by Bittner Mazza on his social media platforms. Bittner Mazza also ran as an advocate for education, families, youth, and building a healthy community.

Bittner Mazza campaigned with fellow Republicans during the election season. She promoted events for congressional candidate Kathy Barnette and for Stacy Garrity's bid for Pennsylvania treasurer. She received the unanimous endorsement of the Pennsylvania State Troopers Association. In an interview, Bittner Mazza said she focused her campaign on local issues to help address the need for resource allocation in her district.

Beth Ann Bittner Mazza found herself in a district that was only about 2% more Democratic than Republican, and she was facing a first-term incumbent. Interviews showed that her strategy was to position herself as a local citizen with deep ties to the community and as a Republican who would represent the 150th District on its own terms, not necessarily in the style of the national GOP. There was a conscious effort to keep the campaign local to help attract independents and moderate Democrats. Speaking at an in-person "Coffee with Kathy" Barnette event on October 23, 2020, Bittner Mazza stressed that the importance of Republican candidates telling their personal stories in order to win in Democratic Montgomery County. Her story focused on being a mother, a small-business owner, someone experienced in emergency medical services, a known advocate within the local community, and someone who believes in the American Dream. She claimed those life experiences gave her the qualifications to help provide the services the local community needed and to help craft a safe but business-friendly COVID-19 response. The only mention of Trump at that event was that her son had a MAGA hat. Overall, her campaign was almost entirely localized.

Pennsylvania House of Representatives District 154

Kathleen (Kathy) Garry Bowers is a lifelong resident of Glenside, Pennsylvania, and a graduate of Cheltenham High School. She raised three daughters as a single mother and was the sole supporter of their educational pursuits. Bowers received her associate's degree in business administration from the Lansdale School of Business in 2009. She is a state-licensed insurance producer.

She presents herself as a member of the community who will fight for her neighbors. Her website features this quote: "It is time to replace career politicians with one of us." Bowers championed issues that are important to parents, including improved safety at local pools and in schools. In these endeavors, she challenged the Cheltenham Township commissioner and the Cheltenham Township school board to address problems affecting local families. Her campaign materials highlight her advocacy for single parents and her fight against "antiquated" child support and divorce laws.

Bowers aligned herself with local constituents rather than a political party. She identifies as an Independent on Kathy4PA.com, although she won the Republican primary for Pennsylvania House District 154. Her website states that "Kathy represents all of us. She is an independent candidate who will fight for what is right for our community." This did not always ingratiate her with fellow Republicans. Local Facebook communities attract a range of responses that can sometimes lead to a heated exchange among members. The KathyForPA page on Facebook did not identify her political affiliation. Republican supporters criticized Bowers for not being transparent. One commenter stated, "As someone who stands behind Donald Trump, I could never support you" (October 15, 2020).

Sources said that Bowers did not get the support of the Republican Party in this race. The Bowers campaign was also at a disadvantage because she relied on a grassroots approach to meeting constituents. Her previous canvasing consisted of attending local meetings and knocking on doors. The in-person outreach was important for Bowers, as she is in a predominantly Democratic district.

Kathy Bowers ran an entirely localized campaign in a district that was difficult for a Republican. Her personal story—of someone who had grown up in the district and was a single mother of three who had been through hardships—shaped the issues of her campaign. She argued that she knew the problems that people in the 154th District faced and wanted to be a representative to help the community. Her issue advocacy in debates and on social media had little to do with mainstream Republican rhetoric. She focused on helping "vulnerable people" and fellow single parents, on issues like child support and divorce laws, and on building economic opportunities and better educational and vocational opportunities. During her closing statement in the 154th District debate she stated, "I'm the Republican candidate, but I'm not in Washington, I am local." Her Democratic opponent countered that "I wish the top of this ticket sounded more like Kathy Bowers." Bowers ran as an independent voice in the community. However, during the debate she did argue that as a Republican she would be in the majority in the state house, therefore having more influence over policy than a Democrat would.

Napoleon Nelson became the Democratic nominee for District 154 after a crowded and competitive primary race. Nelson graduated from the Massachusetts Institute of Technology with a bachelor of science degree and from the Wharton School of the University of Pennsylvania with a master of business administration degree. He is a finance professional who has worked for Vanguard, Campbell Soup Company, and SEI Investments. He currently serves on the board of trustees for Montgomery County Community College.

Nelson's website and social media accounts reached a broad audience that reflected his constituents' need for diversity. Nelson promised to continue the prominent level of constituent service provided by former representative McCarter. At a 154th Legislative District Candidate Forum he said he was in politics to "fight for all of you within our community." His core issues included funding equity for education, addressing racism, and creating a fair tax system. Nelson argued that communities could be rebuilt if Harrisburg would address these areas with progressive policies.

He showed awareness of local needs facing his voters during the pandemic and time of social injustice. Nelson's messaging encouraged constituents to vote during the 2020 election. His campaign recognized the sociolinguistic needs of members within his district. His campaign reached out to Asian Americans and Pacific Islanders, whereas other campaigns did not invest the time with these demographic groups. His social media also provided translated instructions for his Spanish-speaking, Chinese, Korean, and Vietnamese voters.

Residents of the 154th District are diverse in culture, religion, lifestyle, and beliefs. Nelson's posts and tweets foster a sense of diversity and inclusion. He acknowledged holidays such as Diwali, Dussehra, Chuseok, Ramadan, Yom Kippur, and World Braille Day, in addition to more widely recognized holidays such as Christmas, Hanukkah, and Kwanzaa. His communication plan reflected the richness of diversity within his district.

Nelson's social media accounts were intentional and administered professionally. He followed the nationalized "Blue Wave" momentum without compromising his local agenda. His posts were frequent, but at the same time the content was timely and informative. On his social media platforms, followers could watch an interactive media countdown called "The Blue Wave is coming in." Many of his social media photos have the Biden/Harris logo in the frame. He greeted Jill Biden during her visit to Jenkintown on October 9, 2020. He met with former presidential candidate Andrew Yang to inspire the Asian American voters in his district. Nelson supported and connected with Madeleine Dean, commissioner Valerie Arkoosh, and attorney general Josh Shapiro. Nelson also shared content from President Biden, former president Barak Obama, Michelle Obama, Governor Wolf, Connie Chung, and other prominent figures. He also connected with former and long-serving (1972–2014) Democratic leader Shirley Curry on Election Day.

Nelson received the support and endorsement of congresswoman Madeleine Dean, Suburban Realtors Alliance, SEIU PA State Council, PSEA-PACE, Philadelphia Federation of Teachers, Association of Pennsylvania State College and University Faculties, the Pennsylvania AFL-CIO, Conservation Voters of PA, and PA Working Families, to name a few.

Napoleon Nelson's campaign provided an interesting contrast, because the large Democratic majority in the 154th District virtually ensured his victory in the general election. This freed him up to focus more on GOTV to help the entire ticket. The campaign focused on the people who did not vote regularly, particularly in the African American and Asian American/Pacific Island demographic groups. Being an African American, he thought he might be able to appeal to these constituencies and get them to vote even if they were not enthused by the top of the ticket. The Nelson campaign strategy can be summed up by two quotes from his website's call for volunteers. The first paragraph begins, "All politics are local and who we send to Harrisburg matters." The next paragraph starts, "If we want to get Trump out of office, we need to start right here in our neighborhood" (Napoleonfor154 n.d.). His campaign focused on electing Democrats at all levels in order to foster change and make a more equitable society. He stressed issues that were part of the national party platform, but he always localized them to reflect his future constituents or the state of Pennsylvania. For example, in his debate with Bowers, he regularly addressed issues of inequity that could be addressed by state action. Education was an issue that could be addressed by equitable funding, the pandemic exposed gaps in social services that needed to be addressed, redistricting should require that prisoners are counted in the districts they live in to provide representation for poorer areas, and so on. In sum, the Nelson campaign was mostly localized, with some nationalization.

Campaign Coordination and Party Collaboration

Interviews with officials from both parties show a very different approach to campaign coordination. In the Fourth Congressional District, and Montgomery County in particular, Democrats running for all offices worked together, with a similar message: that every vote mattered and that change would occur only if Democrats were elected across the board. Republicans provided some coordination but were not nearly as unified, because those candidates were running individualized campaigns with varying degrees of allegiance to the national GOP and President Trump.

Democrats focused on GOTV operations. Montgomery County Democrats knew that the key to a Biden win in Pennsylvania was to run up the vote tally in Philadelphia and its suburbs. Consequently, candidates at all levels focused on voter turnout even if they came from safe districts like the Fourth Congressional District and the 154th State House District. It was votes from these Democratic-rich areas that would help Biden keep pace with Trump in the rural areas of Pennsylvania. According to our sources, weekly calls were held between Biden, Dean, and the Democratic state house candidates to synchronize campaigning. At various times the Dean campaign worked with the Nelson and Webster campaigns on phone-banking. Local parties worked with the campaigns to coordinate literature drops. The Montgomery County Democratic Committee copromoted Biden and local candidates with a customized graphic.

Election reform in 2019 led the party to unite around two common GOTV themes: how to cast a vote, and the need to vote for every Democrat on the ballot. In a rare act of bipartisanship, Pennsylvania undertook its most significant election reform in decades the year before the presidential election. Democrats secured no-excuse absentee balloting and Republicans ended straight-ticket voting (Calvert 2019). The new process of mail-in balloting proved confusing to many people. The pandemic exacerbated the problem, since many people wanted to avoid in-person voting out of safety concerns. All of the Democratic candidates in this study joined with their local parties to educate people on how to apply for mail-in ballots, to keep them informed of when the ballots would arrive, to explain the process of correctly filling out the ballot, to let them know how to submit the ballots, and finally, to describe what to do if they wanted to vote in person after receiving a mail-in ballot. Democrats emphasized early mail-in voting to make their voices heard.

Second, Democrats were concerned that the demise of straight-ticket voting would result in ballot roll-off, leading to fewer votes for their candidates, particularly state row offices and state legislature. The coordinated message undertaken by all the campaigns was that real change would take place only if Democrats were elected to both federal and state offices. An official from the Dean campaign said that whenever they visited local Democratic meetings, they stressed that party leaders should "be sure to tell people to fill in all the bubbles." A Dean campaign email was more pointed: "The Republican path to success runs right through PA-4 and the surrounding communities. That means we have to be able to reach as many voters as possible and make sure they're voting Democratic up and down the ticket" (Mad4pa.com 2020). Nelson's campaign echoed the theme: "We have come a long way and poured so much time, talent and treasure into electing Democrats up and down this ticket" (Napoleonfor154.com 2020). In the words of one local Democratic leader, "Everyone is campaigning for everyone."

Republicans were not as tight-knit. The Montgomery County Republican Committee (MCRC) held bi-weekly virtual strategy meetings with the congressional and state legislative candidates, as well as doing phone-banking and door-knocking on behalf of the Trump campaign. However, there did not appear to be the same kind of coordination between the Trump campaign and the down-ballot Republicans as was seen on the Democratic side. Trump did not formally endorse Barnette (Ballotpedia n.d.a). However, a Barnette campaign official stated that the Trump campaign had been "very kind" to them by including a question about the Fourth Congressional District in one of their polls. In late September Erik Trump also tweeted a Barnette campaign video to his four-million-plus followers and stated, "What a powerful video by @Kathy4Truth in Pennsylvania CD-4! Kathy go get them! We are behind you 100%." Trump representatives and supporters showed up at her rallies, but she consistently walked a fine line by endorsing the ideas and policies of the president without latching herself directly onto the MAGA movement. Bowers and Bittner Mazza maintained an even greater distance from Trump.

There was cooperation for this study from the three candidates and from other Republicans running for office in Montgomery County. The Montgomery County Republican Women's Leadership (MCRWL), nested within MCRC, served as a forum for female candidates to consult with each other about strategy and messaging. They leveraged the retirement of state representative Marcy Toepel to hold a fundraiser for the female candidates on the Republican slate. Nine of the eighteen GOP candidates running for state legislature in Montgomery County were female, and seven of those candidates received funding from MCRWL. Kathleen Bowers received $1,150,

Beth Ann Bittner Mazza received $1,000, and $500 went toward Barnette's congressional race (Pennsylvania Department of State n.d.a; Transparency USA n.d.). The pandemic slowed down coordination and more active showcasing of the large group of Republican women running in Montgomery County. Barnette's campaign invited state legislative candidates to participate in events she held with their constituents.

Interviews highlighted that MCRC prioritized races it thought it could win, at the expense of turning out the GOP vote throughout the entire county. The MCRC was also plagued by factionalism. Following the national party, the committee did not place as much emphasis on early mail-in balloting. Consequently, they didn't provide the structure needed to unify the disparate campaigns in the county. MCRC's in-person Summer Picnic did unite various campaigns, as it included the PA GOP chair, the PA Trump Victory director, the three Republican statewide row office candidates, and Kathy Barnette (Montgomery County Republican Committee 2020).

National and state party organizations had a mixed level of support for the candidates. According to one Republican official, the National Republican Congressional Committee was "not helpful" to the Barnette campaign because they thought the district was unwinnable. Late in the campaign, there was an attempt to organize the thirty black Republicans running for Congress. However, it never coalesced and did not receive the support of national Republicans. At the state level, the Republican Party of Pennsylvania and the Pennsylvania House Republican Campaign Committee (HRCC) were more supportive through in-kind contributions. HRCC sent out postcards on behalf of Bittner Mazza ($606.21) and Bowers ($311.71). The state party did not provide services to Bowers, but it spent $39,672.20 for mailers on behalf of the Bittner Mazza campaign in October.[3] One local Republican official voiced disappointment with the HRCC, claiming the committee focused too much on retaining Todd Stephens's seat in the 151st District (Montgomery County) instead of helping Bittner Mazza.

A total of $82,804 was spent on independent expenditures in the Fourth Congressional District race, with $81,015 of it supporting Barnette and $1,514 going to Dean (ProPublica n.d.).[4] The group Black Americans to Re-Elect the President spent $76,600 on pro-Barnett radio ads. The group focuses on competing for the black vote based on Trump's platform (Baxter 2020; Black Americans to Re-Elect the President n.d.). About two-thirds of their expenditures were pro-Trump or anti-Biden. However, of the seven congressional races they targeted, only the two Georgia Senate seats received more financing than the Pennsylvania Fourth Congressional District (OpenSecrets.org n.d.). The remainder of Barnette's outside spending came from the National Right to Life Victory Fund and the Pennsylvania Prolife Federation PAC. The only independent expenditures over $250 for Dean were from Together We Thrive, a group that supports liberal Democrats, and the International Brotherhood of Electrical Workers Local 98, which spent $345 on Dean for Congress "Halloween goody bags." Less than $300 combined was spent on literature opposing the two candidates, with the Pennsylvania Prolife Federation PAC spending $159 opposing Dean and Planned Parenthood Votes spending $116 opposing Barnette. Both groups used the money on voter guide–related expenses.

Independent expenditures did not play a significant part in campaigns in the 150th or 154th State Legislative Districts. Joe Webster was the only candidate to receive support, with $3,149.46 spent by Pennsylvania Fund for Change on direct mail in the days before the general election (Pennsylvania Department of State n.d.). This group was active around the Commonwealth supporting Democrats in competitive state house districts. They raised over $7.2 million in 2020, gaining support from trial lawyers, the AFL-CIO, American Federation of State, County and Municipal Employees (AFSCME), and the National Education Association. More than half of the funding for Pennsylvania Fund for Change came from PA Alliance Action, a "dark money" group that supports progressive causes (Mahon and Seidman 2020; Mooney 2020).

Results

Democrats made a clean sweep of these districts during the 2020 general election. Biden defeated Trump 61.5% to 37.4% among the voters in the Fourth Congressional District (see Table 4.3). This compares to Hillary Clinton's 57.8% to Trump's 38.5% margin in 2016 (Nir 2020). In the other races, all three Democrats won comfortably, but with a smaller margin of victory than in 2018. Dean defeated Barnette 59.5% to 40.5%, with Dean polling almost 4% below 2018. Barnette won the Berks County portion of the Fourth District with 64.4% of the vote. However, Berks accounted for only 2.4% of the overall district vote, which was not enough to make up for Dean's strength in Montgomery County. Webster defeated Bittner Mazza 54.4% to 45.6% in the 150th District with Bittner Mazza receiving 1.5% more votes than her Republican counterpart in 2018. Finally, Nelson defeated Bowers 77% to 22.3% in the open-seat race for the 154th District. Bowers increased her vote by 7.8% over her total in 2018, when she lost to incumbent Stephen McCarter.

Trump received a smaller share of the vote than the other three Republican candidates embedded in the Fourth Congressional District, while Biden ran ahead of his Democratic counterparts. This is most likely due to ticket-splitting, particularly among anti-Trump Republicans who did not support the president but were willing to vote for down-ballot GOP candidates. Beyond that, there is very little evidence that individual voters distin-

TABLE 4.3 COMPARISON OF 2020 PRESIDENTIAL ELECTION RESULTS
WITH FOURTH CONGRESSIONAL DISTRICT AND MONTGOMERY COUNTY,
PENNSYLVANIA, 150TH AND 154TH STATE HOUSE DISTRICT RESULTS

Fourth Congressional District	Trump (R)	Barnette (R)	Difference		Biden (D)	Dean (D)	Difference
	37.4%	40.5%	Barnett +3.1		61.5%	59.5%	Dean −2.0
PA 150th State House District	Trump (R)	Bittner Mazza (R)	Difference		Biden (D)	Webster (D)	Difference
	41.5%	45.6%	Bittner Mazza +4.1		57.5%	54.4%	Webster −3.1
PA 154th State House District	Trump (R)	Bowers (R)	Difference		Biden (D)	Nelson (D)	Difference
	19.1%	22.3%	Bowers +3.1		80.2%	77.7%	Nelson −2.5

Sources: Compiled by authors from Montgomery County Board of Elections: Available at https://www
.montcopa.org/1652/Past-Election-Results; Pennsylvania Department of State: Available at
https://www.electionreturns.pa.gov/; *Daily Kos:* Available at https://www.dailykos.com/stories/2020/11
/19/1163009/-Daily-Kos-Elections-presidential-results-by-congressional-district-for-2020-2016-and-2012.
Note: Winning percentages are in bold italics.

guished between the presidential, congressional, and state house candidates
of their party. They voted for the tribe they supported.

Conclusion

There were no surprises in the case studies related to Pennsylvania's Fourth
Congressional District. Democrats composed a majority of voters in these
congressional and state legislative races and made a clean sweep of the elections, although by smaller margins than in 2018. While the contests in the
Fourth Congressional District all displayed some national themes, there was
less nationalization the further down-ballot the race. The congressional race
featured a rising star in the Democratic Party, Madeleine Dean, who emphasized her constituent work but largely ran on campaign themes popular
in Democratically dominated metropolitan suburbs. Her opponent, Kathy
Barnette, ran on her personal story and criticized Dean's personal narrative
while adhering closely to the agenda of the national Republican Party. The
state legislative races were largely personality-driven, with Democratic candidates focusing on how Democratic priorities could help their constituents,
while the GOP candidates took a cafeteria approach to Republican policy
positions and placed a strong emphasis on their relationship to their com-

munities. Although Black Lives Matter protests, calls for criminal justice reform, and the economic and social effects of COVID-19 were unavoidable issues in campaigns up and down the ballot, the focus of these races was mostly on the candidates and their résumés.

NOTES

1. The following websites and social media accounts were utilized for this research: Barnette: https://kathybarnetteforcongress.com, https://www.facebook.com/Kathy BarnetteCongressPA04, https://twitter.com/Kathy4Truth; Dean: https://www.mad 4pa.com, https://www.facebook.com/RepMadeleineDean, https://www.facebook.com /Mad4PA; Bittner Mazza: https://bethannforstaterep.com, https://www.facebook.com /BAforPA, https://twitter.com/beth_state; Webster: https://joewebsterpa.com, https:// www.facebook.com/JoeWebsterPA, https://twitter.com/joewebsterpa; Bowers: http:// kathy4pa.com, https://www.facebook.com/KathyForPA, https://twitter.com/Kathy4PA; Nelson: https://napoleonfor154.com, https://www.facebook.com/NapoleonFor154, https://www.linkedin.com/in/napoleon-nelson-1787623/, https://twitter.com/napoleon for154.

2. This claim was made by House GOP Whip Steve Scalise and made headlines on *Fox News*. Barnette ran an ad based on the claim.

3. According to campaign finance reports, the Bittner Mazza campaign donated $44,000 to the HRCC during the same month as the mailers were sent out.

4. ProPublica incorrectly reported that $95,407 was spent in independent expenditures in Pennsylvania's Fourth Congressional District. Their total incorrectly included expenditures on behalf of Representative Scott Perry, who represented the Fourth prior to redistricting in 2018.

REFERENCES

Andrews, Natalie. 2020. "GOP Hopes to Add Black Lawmakers to House." *Wall Street Journal*, October 28, 2020. Available at https://www.wsj.com/articles/gop-hopes-to -add-black-lawmakers-to-house-11603892455.

Ballotpedia. n.d.a. "Endorsements by Donald Trump." Accessed January 26, 2021. Available at https://ballotpedia.org/Endorsements_by_Donald_Trump.

———. n.d.b. "Pennsylvania's 4th Congressional District Election, 2020." Accessed January 14, 2021. Available at https://ballotpedia.org/Pennsylvania%27s_4th_Congressio nal_District_election,_2020.

Baxter, Holly. 2020. "'The Party of the Bushes and McCain Is Dead': Inside the Black Super PAC Raising Millions for Trump." *The Independent*, September 9, 2020. Available at https://www.independent.co.uk/news/world/americas/us-politics/vernon-robinson -super-pac-trump-black-americans-reelect-president-2020-election-b420765.html.

Becker Kane, Jenna. 2019. "Why State Supreme Court Elections Matter: Pennsylvania's 2015 Supreme Court Election and Redistricting in Pennsylvania." In *Pennsylvania Politics and Policy: A Commonwealth Reader, Volume 2*, edited by J. Wesley Leckrone and Michelle J. Atherton, 49–64. Philadelphia: Temple University Press.

Black Americans to Re-Elect the President. n.d. "About." Accessed January 21, 2021. Available at https://www.blackamericansmaga.org/.

Calvert, Scott. 2019. "Pennsylvania Overhauls Election Rules Ahead of 2020." *Wall Street Journal*, October 31, 2019. Available at https://www.wsj.com/articles/pennsylvania -overhauls-election-rules-ahead-of-2020-11572535865.

Cochrane, Emily. 2021. "Madeleine Dean: Impeachment Manager Brings Ethics Experience to Trial." *New York Times*, January 13, 2021. Accessed January 17, 2021. Available at https://www.nytimes.com/2021/01/13/us/politics/madeleine-dean-impeachment -manager.html.

Cook Political Report. n.d. "District PVI Map and List." Accessed January 14, 2021. Available at https://cookpolitical.com/pvi-map-and-district-list.

Dom Giordano Program. 2020. "Giordano: 'Meet Madeleine Dean's Worst Nightmare.'" *Talk Radio 1210 WPHT*, January 2, 2020. Available at https://www.radio.com/1210 wpht/articles/feature-article/giordano-meet-madeleine-deans-worst-nightmare.

Kathy Barnette 4 USA. 2020. "Virtual BYOB: Pre-Election Edition." YouTube Video. Filmed November 1, 2020. Available at https://www.youtube.com/watch?v=K4qgkxmY7wM.

Lai, Jonathan, and Liz Navratil. 2018. "Pa. Gerrymandering Case: State Supreme Court Releases New Congressional Map for 2018 Elections." *Philadelphia Inquirer*, February 19, 2018. Available at https://www.inquirer.com/philly/news/politics/pennsylvania-gerry mandering-supreme-court-map-congressional-districts-2018-elections-20180219.html.

Leigh, Harri. 2018. "Amid Affluence, Pockets of Poverty." *PBS39*, December 13, 2018. Available at https://www.wlvt.org/blogs/montgomery/poverty-deepening-in-pockets-of -montgomery-county/.

Mad4pa.com. 2020. "Re: scary news." Campaign email message to author, October 15, 2020.

Mahon, Ed, and Andrew Seidman. 2020. "Democrats Have Control of the Pa. State House within Their Reach." *Spotlight PA*, October 26, 2020. Available at https://www.spot lightpa.org/news/2020/10/pa-election-state-house-flip-democrats-republicans/.

Meyer, Katie, and Ryan Briggs. 2020. "Tracing Montco's Decades-Long Shift from GOP Stronghold to Boon for Biden." *WHYY News*, December 9, 2020. Available at https:// whyy.org/articles/tracing-montcos-decades-long-shift-from-gop-stronghold-to-boon -for-biden/.

Montgomery Count Republican Committee. 2020. "This Saturday-FREE MCRC Outdoor Summer Picnic." Email message to author, July 27, 2020.

Mooney, Kevin. 2020. "Teachers Unions and Trial Lawyers Help Fund Pennsylvania PAC Trying to Oust Republican State Legislators." *Washington Examiner*, October 20, 2020. Available at https://www.washingtonexaminer.com/opinion/teachers-unions-and-trial -lawyers-help-fund-pennsylvania-pac-trying-to-oust-republican-state-legislators.

Napoleonfor154.com. n.d. "Join Team Nelson." Accessed September 29, 2020. Available at https://napoleonfor154.com/join_team_napoleon.

———. 2020. "We Didn't Come This Far Just to Come This Far!" Email message to author, September 25, 2020.

Nir, David. 2020. "Daily Kos Elections' Presidential by Congressional District for 2020, 2016, and 2012." *Daily Kos*, November 19, 2020. Available at https://www.dailykos .com/stories/2012/11/19/1163009/-Daily-Kos-Elections-presidential-results-by-con gressional-district-for-the-2012-2008-elections.

Office of Representative Madeleine Dean. 2020. "Rep. Dean Hosts Drive-in Town Hall." Press release, October 21, 2020. Available at https://dean.house.gov/media/press-re leases/rep-dean-hosts-drive-town-hall.

OpenSecrets.org. n.d. "Black Americans to Re-Elect the President, Targeted Candidates, 2020 Cycle." Accessed January 21, 2021. Available at https://www.opensecrets.org /outsidespending/recips.php?cmte=C00668517&cycle=2020.

Panaritis, Maria. 2019. "U.S. Rep. Madeleine Dean Refuses to Say 'No' to People in Need, and It's Making All the Difference." *Philadelphia Inquirer*, December 5, 2019. Available at https://fusion.inquirer.com/news/columnists/congress-pa-madeleine-dean-con stituent-service-judiciary-committee-maria-panaritis-20191205.html.

Pennsylvania Department of State. n.d.a. "Campaign Finance Online Reporting." Accessed January 26, 2021. Available at https://www.campaignfinanceonline.pa.gov/pages/CF ReportSearch.aspx.

———. n.d.b. "Independent Expenditures List." Accessed February 7, 2021. Available at https://www.campaignfinanceonline.pa.gov/Pages/IndependentExpenditure.aspx.

ProPublica. n.d. "Election Databot, Independent Expenditures: Pennsylvania's 4th House Race—2020 Cycle." Accessed January 21, 2021. Available at https://projects.propublica .org/itemizer/independent_expenditures/2020/pa/house/4#cd3e8db01db5f08f322e2 a479da5a50b795ab59b.

ProximityOne. n.d. "Congressional District Analysis and Insights." Accessed December 30, 2020. Available at http://proximityone.com/cd.htm.

Rev.com. 2020. "Donald Trump Rally Speech Transcript Reading, PA October 31." November 1, 2020. Available at https://www.rev.com/blog/transcripts/donald-trump-rally -speech-transcript-reading-pa-october-31.

Ruthhart, Bill, and Jonathon Berlin. 2020. "Campaign Trail Tracker: Where Trump, Biden and Their Running Mates Have Traveled in Presidential Race's Final Weeks." *Chicago Tribune*, November 5, 2020. Available at https://www.chicagotribune.com/politics/ct -viz-presidential-campaign-trail-tracker-20200917-edspdit2incbfnopchjaelp3uu-html story.html.

Schultz, Marissa. 2020. "House Democrats' New Coronavirus Relief Bill Eliminates $600M for Policing: 'It's Shameful.'" *Fox News*, September 30, 2020. Available at https://www .foxnews.com/politics/house-democrats-new-coronavirus-relief-bill-eliminates-600m -for-policing.

Terruso, Julia. 2020. "The 2020 Election Established Montgomery County as a Powerful Democratic Stronghold in Pennsylvania." *Philadelphia Inquirer*, December 16, 2020. Available at https://www.inquirer.com/politics/election/montgomery-county-penn sylvania-biden-trump-democrats-20201216.html.

Tierney, Kevin. 2020. "Video: 4th District Congressional Debate—Kathy Barnette and Madeleine Dean." *Around Ambler*, October 5, 2020. Available at https://aroundambler .com/video-4th-district-congressional-debate-kathy-barnette-and-madeleine-dean/.

Transparency USA. n.d. "Montgomery County Republican Women's Leadership: Pennsylvania Political Action Committee." Accessed January 26, 2021. Available at https:// www.transparencyusa.org/pa/pac/montgomery-county-republican-womens-leader ship-pac-2009457/payments.

INTERVIEWS

Amuso, Peter. Montgomery County Chair, PA Veterans for Biden. October 6, 2020.

Baptiste, Andrea. Chair, Collegeville Democratic Party. November 29, 2020.

Bittner Mazza, Beth Ann. Republican Candidate, 150th State Representative District. December 18, 2020.

Dailey, Jim. Chair, Springfield Township Republican Party. November 17, 2020.

Drummond, Liz. Campaign Manager, Joe Webster for the 150th State Representative District. December 2, 2020.

Gillies, Robert. Campaign Chair, Barnette for Congress. November 30, 2020.

Hager, Doug. Area 4 Leader, Montgomery County Republican Party. December 16, 2020.

Harbison, Jeff. Springfield Township Commissioner and Committeeperson, Springfield Township Democratic Party. October 6, 2020.

Lockard, Carol. Chair, Springfield Township Democratic Party. November 24, 2020.

McDowell, Lexy. Campaign Chair, Dean for Congress. December 18, 2020.

Michelbacher, David. Member (Montgomery County), Pennsylvania State Republican Party. November 16, 2020.

Nelson, Napoleon. Democratic Candidate, 154th State Representative District (with Campaign Staffer Anne Martin-Montgomery). October 12, 2020.

Wilkerson, Ashley. Area 4 Leader, Montgomery County Democratic Party. December 1, 2020.

5

Campaigns in the Eighth Congressional District

What Does It Mean to Be "One of Us"?

BENJAMIN T. TOLL

Northeastern Pennsylvania (NEPA) is known for its long memory and for locals who ask newcomers about their family's national origin. It is an area that became prominent for its coal production and for its role in *The Office*. The region maintains political clout by having a U.S. senator from the area, as well as being the boyhood home of President Biden. At the same time, it constantly compares itself negatively to other places, recently being labeled the unhappiest region in the United States (Glaeser, Gottlieb, and Ziv 2014). Yet, it is also known for natural beauty and a well-developed civic culture, which local boroughs and communities have built over many years.

The history of the region remains important to residents, and it still informs the way many see themselves vis-à-vis the outside world, how people understand hard work, and encourages a sense of distrust for elites. Coal-mining was the main form of economic activity for much of the region in the nineteenth and early twentieth centuries, and that meant the presence of a myriad of immigrant groups (Shackel 2016). As one interviewee for this chapter remarked, "Everyone who comes here says they have never seen so many little churches in one town and that is because the Polish have their own church, and the Slovaks have their own church, and the Welsh have their own church. Even though they are all Catholic, it is an ethnic thing." Many of these communities retain their distinctive nature and national origins to this day (Bradlee 2018). Because the mining companies would keep ethnic communities isolated to their own enclaves for the sake of control, it has paradoxically created an environment in which many are wary of new arrivals and immigrants (Shackel 2016).

This historic distrust of nonlocals also translates into skepticism for elites and those who attempt to devalue lived experience. The battle for worker's rights and unionization remains integral to the history and current culture of NEPA (Golias 2020). Recent events, like the "Kids for Cash" scandal (Urbina 2009), have only exacerbated the distinction between those seen as the "common man" and the elites in the area. One interviewee declared, "Local residents do not trust experts who come in and tell us what to do. And, we have felt that way since before Trump came into power." People from the region are culturally conservative even though the area has historically voted for Democratic candidates. They are proud of having to work for things in life, and they value those with whom they have personal history.

Politics today is characterized by increasingly negative partisanship (Abramowitz and Webster 2018), leading to political affiliation becoming a mega-identity (Mason 2018). It is a maxim among political scientists that Americans have a paucity of knowledge about the political system (Delli Carpini and Keeter 1996), and that they know even less about state and local governments (Rosen 2018). In this context, it is logical to assume that local campaigns are solely interested in national-level issues.

This chapter argues that campaigns in NEPA represent a mixture of national and local interests. The 2020 campaign, locally and around the country, focused almost exclusively on two things: President Trump and the COVID-19 pandemic. Conversations routinely turned to the pandemic, how businesses were being hurt by "Democratic policies," and what proper leadership would look like. The pandemic also affected how Democrats, much more so than Republicans, campaigned nationally and locally. It created opportunities for Republican messaging to speak to the popularity of their movement, compared to a "lack of enthusiasm" among Democrats for their candidates. In this way, the campaigns in NEPA were nationalized.

The pandemic affected the way candidates spoke about the perennial issues of jobs, the economy, and how this region will compete in a changing business climate. While the issues of the economy and jobs are important throughout the country, they take on a specific context in NEPA due to the region's largely depressed economy. Trust in government officials remains important, as it does elsewhere, but it takes on a different meaning when trust is more about knowing a candidate's history and family than about what the candidate promises to do in office. More than any issue, candidates fought over who really was from the area and routinely attempted to portray the other one as not really a local.

In NEPA, being "one of us" is a determining factor between who will win elections and who will lose. The 2020 campaign focused on national issues like the pandemic, the economy, and views of President Trump. But in order to be heard, these candidates first needed to prove that they understood the local climate. Being seen as one who "gets" the region, or is "from here," allows a candidate to speak more clearly about the issues facing NEPA; but it also allows the candidate to be trusted more fully as someone who will look out for the "little guy." As a result, the campaigns in NEPA were talking about issues facing the nation, but the issues were predicated in their own local context.[1]

Demography, Geography, and Politics of the Region

The Eighth Congressional District was constructed for the 2018 cycle from parts of the old Tenth, Eleventh, and Seventeenth Districts. It encompasses part or all of five counties in NEPA. Three of these counties—Lackawanna County, which is the home of Scranton; Pike County; and Wayne County—sit entirely in the Eighth District. Roughly half of the precincts in Monroe County are in the district. Finally, the largest county in the district, Luzerne County, has 156 of the 186 precincts in the district.

The demographics of the Eighth District differ from the state in small but important ways, as seen in Table 5.1. It has a smaller percentage of those identifying as black, but a larger percentage who identify as Hispanic. The median income is lower than in the rest of the state, and a smaller percentage of the district has at least a bachelor's degree. Compared to the nation, the Eighth District has a higher percentage of white people and a smaller percentage of those identifying as black. It also has a lower percentage of individuals with a college degree or higher. As is common around Pennsylvania, individuals are more likely to be registered as Democrats than Republicans in the Eighth District.

On the other hand, elections favor Republican candidates—except in Lackawanna County, as the last time it voted for a Republican presidential candidate was 1984. At the local level, ten of the eleven Lackawanna County elected positions are held by Democrats. The largest county in the Eighth District in terms of population is Luzerne County, with around 320,000 residents in the 2020 census. Historically, Luzerne County has voted for Democratic candidates, but it has become more Republican over time. It is one of the three "pivot counties" in Pennsylvania that voted for Barack Obama in 2008 and 2012 but voted for Donald Trump in 2016. The county voted for Trump again in 2020, and the county commission became majority-controlled by the Republican Party for the first time in 2019.

Monroe County elects Republicans for local positions but has voted for Democrats at the state and federal levels. Around half of the county's precincts are in the Eighth District, and they come from the northern and more

TABLE 5.1 DEMOGRAPHIC AND REGISTRATION CHARACTERISTICS OF PENNSYLVANIA'S 119TH AND 120TH STATE HOUSE DISTRICTS, EIGHTH CONGRESSIONAL DISTRICT, PENNSYLVANIA, AND THE UNITED STATES IN 2019

	PA 119th State House District[a]	PA 120th State House District[b]	Eighth Congressional District[c]	Pennsylvania[d]	United States[e]
Population density: people/ square mile	331.1	1,025.3	262.1	286.1	92.3
Population white	83%	89%	78%	76%	60%
Population black	2%	4%	6%	11%	12%
Population Hispanic	11%	5%	13%	8%	18%
Foreign-born	5.5%	2.9%	6.7%	7.0%	13.5%
Median household income	$50,676	$55,888	$56,149	$63,463	$64,994
Bachelor's degree or higher	18.9%	27.6%	24.3%	32.3%	32.9%
Registered Democrat[f]	48.2%	48.6%	48.5%	46.5%	
Registered Republican[f]	38.4%	39.0%	36.9%	39.0%	
Registered none/other[f]	13.4%	12.3%	14.5%	14.5%	

Sources:
(a) Compiled from U.S. Census Bureau. n.d. "Census Reporter: State House District 119, PA." Accessed March 29, 2021. Available at https://censusreporter.org/profiles/62000US42119-state-house-district -119-pa/.
(b) Compiled from U.S. Census Bureau. n.d. "Census Reporter: State House District 120, PA." Accessed March 29, 2021. Available at https://censusreporter.org/profiles/62000US42120-state-house-district -120-pa/.
(c) Compiled from U.S. Census Bureau. n.d. "Census Reporter: Congressional District 8, PA." Accessed March 29, 2021. Available at https://censusreporter.org/profiles/50000US4208-congressional-district -8-pa/.
(d) Compiled from U.S. Census Bureau. n.d. "Census Reporter: Pennsylvania." Accessed March 29, 2021. Available at https://censusreporter.org/profiles/04000US42-pennsylvania/.
(e) Compiled from U.S. Census Bureau. n.d. "Census Reporter: United States." Accessed May 23, 2022. Available at https://censusreporter.org/profiles/01000US-united-states/.
(f) Compiled from Pennsylvania Department of State. n.d. "Voting and Election Statistics." Accessed March 29, 2021. Available at https://www.dos.pa.gov/VotingElections/OtherServicesEvents/VotingElection Statistics/Pages/VotingElectionStatistics.aspx.

rural parts of the county, which are more Republican than the rest of the county. The two smallest counties, Pike and Wayne, are largely supportive of Republican candidates for statewide and federal offices. These counties have a smaller voting population with around 60,000 combined voters, but Republican candidates can count on roughly 60% of those votes in most elections.

119th House Seat

The 119th State House District, which sits in Luzerne County, encompasses 38 of the 186 precincts and is located entirely inside the Eighth Congressional District. The northern part of the district is west of Wilkes-Barre, encompassing Larksville, Plymouth, and Nanticoke. Then, the district stays in rural areas of the county going south and including Foster Township, Rice Township, and Wright Township. Finally, the district includes the small boroughs around the north of Hazleton, but not the city itself. This is an expansive state legislative district, which is increasingly rural and Republican.

The median income in the 119th District is lower than the Eighth Congressional District or the state, and fewer people in the 119th District have a bachelor's degree compared to residents of the Eighth District or the state (Table 5.1). Home values and poverty rates also indicate that the 119th District is more economically depressed than the Eighth District and the state overall. The 119th District was chosen for a few specific reasons. The incumbent was a Democrat, Gerald Mullery, who won a close election in 2018. However, President Trump received 63.7% of the vote in 2016 and many local Republicans believed this would be the year to unseat the incumbent. Having a vulnerable Democrat in an increasingly Republican district presents an interesting case study because it compares similarly to the congressional district.

120th House Seat

The 120th State House District is also located entirely within Luzerne County, mostly in the northeast section of the county, and consists of 36 of the county's 186 precincts. The western terminus of the district is in Jackson Township, and it extends east along the north side of the county. The district encompasses Exeter, Kingston, Luzerne, West Pittston, Wyoming, and West Wyoming. Politically, the district has been represented by a Republican, Aaron Kaufer, since 2014.

The 120th District has higher educational attainment than the Eighth Congressional District and is comparable in median income. Individuals in the district are more likely to identify as white, and are more likely to have been born in the United States when compared to the Eighth District or the state (Table 5.1). The 120th District was chosen because it had a Republican incumbent who faced a well-funded challenger. The district was split fairly evenly in electoral outcomes at the presidential level in 2016. Thus, many local Democrats believed this could be a district where an incumbent Republican would lose heading into the 2020 cycle.

The Candidates

Donald Trump spoke the language of anger, which many people in the region found refreshing, and they liked that he was not a "typical politician" (Saul 2016; Bradlee 2018). Joe Biden has well-known ties to the Eighth Congressional District, as he was born and spent his early years in Scranton before he and his family moved to Delaware (Lakhani 2020). A consistent campaign theme from Biden was that Scranton greatly influenced his worldview (Pirini 2020).

Matt Cartwright is the Democratic candidate and incumbent for the U.S. House of Representatives. Cartwright is not originally from NEPA but married into a well-known legal family in the Scranton area; he moved to Scranton and practiced law there for the next twenty-five years. Cartwright was elected to Congress in 2012, representing the Seventeenth District. He won this seat by primarying Tim Holden due to the change in district composition following redistricting for 2012. Most of the Seventeenth District was moved into what is now the Eighth District following the state Supreme Court ruling on gerrymandering. According to DW-NOMINATE scores, Cartwright is a median Democrat and he has begun to serve in positions of leadership within the Democratic caucus.[2]

The 2020 GOP candidate for the Eighth District was Jim Bognet, who touts that he was born and raised in Hazleton, which sits just outside the district. Bognet had been active in politics for many years before his run for Congress in 2020. He had interned with Rick Santorum, worked for Lou Barletta (Bognet for Congress website), and went on to work for many statewide and presidential campaigns throughout his career (Democratic Congressional Campaign Committee 2020). Bognet served at the Export–Import Bank of the United States during the first part of President Trump's administration, and he resigned around the time of Trump's first impeachment proceedings to run for Congress.

Gerald Mullery, the incumbent Democrat in the 119th State House race, grew up in Nanticoke, which is in the district. He attended a local university and practiced law in the area before he was first elected in 2010. His messaging focuses on being a local product and emphasizes the importance of being rooted in the community. Over the last several cycles the 119th District has been tightly contested, with the 2018 cycle being the closest as

Mullery defeated the challenger with 53.1% of the vote. Mullery's challenger in 2020 was local business-owner and mayor of West Hazleton John Chura. Chura owns a used automotive dealership and got into politics only in 2017 when he was elected mayor. As will be highlighted below, Chura did not take advantage of technology throughout his campaign, even though he appeared to be a strong challenger on paper.

In the 120th State House race, Aaron Kaufer is the Republican incumbent. He is a native of the district who lost his first run for office in 2012 at the age of 24. Kaufer won an open-seat election in 2014 and has served ever since. Kaufer presents himself as a bipartisan individual who seeks policy over party. He refused to publicly state whom he was voting for in the 2016 presidential election (Buffer 2016), although he did attend a Trump rally in 2020. The challenger to Kaufer was another native of the area, Joanna Bryn Smith, who grew up in Jackson Township. After earning her law degree, she returned to the county and has served as a public defender for Luzerne County. The 2020 campaign represents her first attempt to win public office.

The Presidential Campaign

President Trump's messaging strategy of bringing back coal-industry jobs and "making American great again" played well in the region and contributed to his victory in the state in 2016 (Bradlee 2018; Rhys and Gardner 2020). In 2020, President Trump returned to these themes and argued that Democratic policies were harming the economic recovery following COVID lockdowns. Neither his willingness to discuss his wealth or the lack of growth in the coal industry affects the image of Trump as one who cares about the little man (Prose 2020). While Trump has no ties to the region, many felt that he understood them in a way that other politicians do not.

One campaign volunteer from Wayne County stated, "Trump understands people like us. He isn't fancy like other politicians, but he isn't a radical socialist like Biden." A candidate for a state office in the Eighth District stated that he did not trust the mainstream media because of how they negatively covered a "true patriot like Trump." Even more moderate Republicans, like a volunteer from Luzerne County, argued that President Trump "cares about the little guy, like people from Luzerne County, a lot more than the Democrats do."

The Trump campaign made several stops in the area throughout 2020. He participated in a town hall in Scranton in early March (Freking 2020). He visited the district two more times (*Upstate New York News*), and members of the campaign visited throughout the area, including during the final push before Election Day (Kalinowski 2020). The messaging strategy of the local Republican Party largely followed the talking points of the Trump campaign throughout the cycle. A local columnist described it as "the protection of rights, gun rights, the rights of the unborn child, homeland security and protecting the borders."

The Trump campaign and its surrogates sought to portray Biden as someone who left the area and never returned. A Wayne County Republican volunteer made it clear that Biden was not really from NEPA, since he had moved away at the age of ten. In many conversations with local conservatives, I was reminded that the Scranton Biden left in the 1950s was very different from the city today. In other words, being from the area does not mean a person is really "one of us." A Republican challenger within the Eighth District reminded me that Trump was supported by "a true local, Lou Barletta."

Mike Buffer, a local columnist, believes that Trump's approach in the 2020 cycle resonates with latent views that many locals hold. He states, "There is an us-versus-them approach, but I think people are looking at their neighbors differently. It is more of us against liberal coastal elites. Trump framed everything through that lens and I think that is why Trump won a lot of support from older people who used to be Democrats who are religious (prolife) Democrats. I think Trump's framing of everything [as] "us versus them"— the liberal coastal elites look down on you and they don't want to help you and they want to keep you down—helped him here."

There was a contrast in the expected outcome of the national and state elections within the Republican Party leading up to the election. A researcher working with the Luzerne County GOP spoke of the different views of what would happen on Election Day. He noted that the volunteers, described by many local journalists as "very Trumpy," were convinced Trump would win Pennsylvania in a landslide because they did not know anyone voting for Biden, while the paid staffers, on the other hand, believed that Trump would lose the election. The strategist I interviewed believed that Trump would lose Pennsylvania because of Biden's roots in the state, and was surprised at how close the state vote was. The two Republican candidates for local office believed that Trump would win, but they hedged their bets before the election by stating that it requires Trump voters to show up in record numbers.

Throughout the 2020 campaign, and throughout his career, Biden referred to his childhood as being formative for him. Locally, the Biden campaign played up this long-standing connection to the area. In NEPA, it was more important to portray him as a local product than it was to remind people of his record of service, including his time as vice president. A Democratic volunteer from Lackawanna County spoke of the strong relationship that Biden has with this area, and she stated, "Joe Biden is Lackawanna County. He grew up here. He understands what normal people want and need."

According to Kathy Bozinski, the chair of the Luzerne County Democratic Party, the Democratic messaging strategy was consistent between the Biden campaign, the state party, and the county party. The main themes that each focused on were jobs, the failures of Trump on COVID, protecting unions, and protecting the social safety net.

Biden's campaign was slowed due to the pandemic (Milligan 2020), but he did visit the district in October and on Election Day. The vice presidential candidates also visited the district in the last two months before the election. Some, however, felt that the Biden campaign did not spend enough time in the area. One local columnist states, "I think people want in their national candidates and their statewide candidates to see these people. They want to see that they care enough to come visit them in their home areas or counties. I repeatedly made that point with the Biden campaign. We hadn't seen any of them or surrogates and finally near the end of the campaign Biden did show at the high school in Dallas and Harris had the rally in Pittston."

Democrats in the area were quietly optimistic about the outcome of the 2020 election, as a local columnist described their mood as very different than it was during the Hillary campaign throughout 2016. The local volunteers and candidates all believed that Biden would win the state, but the real question was whether Biden would win the Eighth District. The two volunteers and the Democrat challenging for a state seat I spoke with believed he would win the district, whereas the Democratic incumbent thought he would lose narrowly.

The outcome, with Trump winning the Eighth District, is not surprising to many neutral observers of the election. A columnist for the local *Times Leader* said, "There were all sorts of rallies being held if not weekly, almost on a daily basis, on Trump's behalf. The mini parades that would start at Walmart and go through the valley with trucks and flags and horns. That was almost constant . . . Trump was still going to get all the people who voted for him in 2016. He could get all those votes and still lose the election as we saw because the Democrats were more excited and energized." Other elites were not surprised by the final vote tallies, but were surprised with how much ground Biden seemed to make up in the Eighth District, as he did 2.8 percentage points better than Clinton had in 2016.

In summary, both candidates sought to capitalize on issues that are important locally during the 2020 cycle, and COVID impacted the strategy and messaging employed by both candidates. President Trump wanted to focus on attracting more blue-collar jobs to the area with the promised resurgence of the coal industry. The Biden campaign was most affected locally by COVID, but his campaign sought to portray the Republican Party as reckless on the issue.

The Eighth Congressional District

The Cartwright campaign sought to focus more on local issues and constituency service throughout the campaign, in an effort to win election as a Democrat in a district that supported President Trump. Cartwright routinely sought to connect with locals in his use of campaign messaging and television advertisements. With his opponent portraying him as an out-of-touch elitist, it was important for Cartwright to show that he values this area and is truly a representative for NEPA.

Among local Democrats, Matt Cartwright is known for his constituency service and for being rooted in the community. One Democratic incumbent running for a local position remarked that he looks at Cartwright as an example of what legislators should do in their districts. A Republican strategist whom I interviewed that works outside of the Eighth district, stated that Cartwright is known for his strong local roots—and because of that, "Bognet had to appeal to his roots in the community even more, but they were more strained for Bognet than they were for Cartwright." Kathy Bozinski added, "You see the relationships he [Cartwright] has built within the community. . . . He is in Hazleton on a Saturday afternoon helping to pass out boxes of food during a pandemic to families in need at a drive-through." Research indicates that this is a valuable campaign strategy to employ, as it helps connect the incumbent with people in the district regardless of policies (Campbell et al. 2019).

Another way Cartwright sought to highlight his constituent service was through his use of social media to tout the money brought back to the area in the last two years. Figure 5.1 shows just one example of Cartwright using

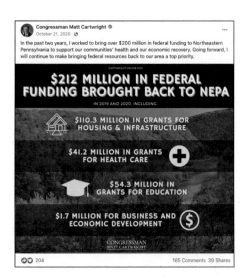

Figure 5.1 Cartwright and local investment. (Facebook, Congressman Matt Cartwright.)

social media to take credit for bringing economic investment back into the district. Cartwright's Twitter account posted 116 tweets from September 1st through November 2nd, and 15.5% of the tweets contained a discussion of the money he had brought back to the district or a discussion of the work he had done to secure a benefit for the Eighth District (Table 5.2).

Cartwright's most common social media posts addressed how to vote differently due to the pandemic, as 33.6% of his tweets contained information on this. While none of his television ads directly discussed this component, the information was a major source of direct-mail advertising from the Pennsylvania Democratic Party in the area. As a result, it was one of the most consistent messaging strategies of the Cartwright campaign.

Next, Cartwright routinely focused on the poor job the Trump administration had done in dealing with the COVID pandemic, and highlighting Cartwright's version of a better way forward. A general theme was that Cartwright felt the federal government was not responding effectively to the issues faced by the pandemic and was not helping health care workers enough in a time of crisis. Of his 116 tweets, 23.3% discussed fighting the pandemic or fixing the health care system (Table 5.2). Figure 5.2 is one example of Cartwright calling on the Trump administration to do more in relation to a national testing strategy for COVID. Among his television spots, in 28.7% of them COVID was the number one issue discussed. As a result, this was the most consistent issue he discussed throughout the campaign across different platforms.

TABLE 5.2 MOST TWEETED CONTENT

	Cartwright (D)	Bognet (R)
1st	Voting information (33.6%)	Matt Cartwright (53.4%)
2nd	Donate or volunteer (19.0%)	Donald Trump (38.3%)
3rd	Endorsement (16.4%)	"Radical left" (26.3%)
4th	Localized content (16.4%)	Joe Biden/Kamala Harris (24.1%)
5th	Constituent service/earmark (15.5%)	Nancy Pelosi (24.1%)
6th	COVID (13.8%)	Defund the Police/Back the Blue (17.3%)
7th	Middle-class/working families (13.8%)	Cities/riots/violence (15.8%)
8th	Unions (10.3%)	Donate/event (12.0%)
9th	Health care (9.5%)	Jobs (9.0%)
10th	Economic crisis/Jobs (6.9%)	China (5.3%)

Source: Data compiled by author. Analysis of all tweets from September 1, 2020, to November 2, 2020.
Note: Matt Cartwright's campaign account (@CartwrightPA) tweeted 116 times, and Jim Bognet's campaign account (@Bognet4congress) tweeted 133 times. Tweets could be counted multiple times, as each reference was recorded.

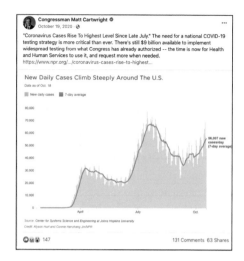

Figure 5.2 Cartwright and COVID. (Facebook, Congressman Matt Cartwright.)

On social media, another common theme was to connect the history of unionization in the area to the desire for increasing middle-class jobs in the United States. In 28 of 116 tweets, or 24.1% of the time, Cartwright mentioned either his support for unions or the importance of protecting the middle-class and working families in America (Table 5.2). This was most pronounced around the Labor Day holiday, but it was discussed regularly afterward.

Another consistent theme in Cartwright's television advertisements was his response to Jim Bognet's ads that related to law enforcement issues. Almost 25% of his own television spots responded directly to Bognet's claims that Cartwright wanted to defund the police. The one that received the most airtime, entitled "Bogus Commercials," included the chief of police from Hazleton countering Bognet's claims (Cartwright 2020a).

According to local journalists, the Cartwright campaign was almost surprised by this line of attack from the Bognet campaign. Buffer states, "I think the Cartwright campaign was on defense a lot in trying to say, 'I am not an extreme left-wing Democrat, I am a moderate mainstream Democrat and Joe Biden is a moderate mainstream Democrat. I deliver for the community and you know me. I have been the incumbent for a long time and you can trust me.'" Another local journalist added, "Well, I think Cartwright tried to stay focused on real issues. Economy, jobs, things like that." This finding [incumbent service, challenger attacking negatively] is consistent with research that argues incumbents are more likely to focus on what they have done rather than focusing on specific issues (Druckman, Kifer, and Parkin 2020).

Cartwright was constantly focusing on the way he brought money back home to the district and how he supported local NEPA-based businesses, as seen in Figure 5.1. His closing television ad, "Earned My Vote," combines his local roots with sharing the desire for his children to raise families in the area with his history of constituency service (Cartwright 2020b). It was important for Cartwright to continue focusing on his roots, and this focus was rewarded as one of the reasons he received endorsements from the local newspapers on October 12. Almost one of every six tweets sent by the campaign had a localized theme that would not translate to national-based issues. Thus, while Cartwright certainly discussed national issues, he spent considerable time trying to tie things back to the local community and how he had served the community in the past.

Jim Bognet's campaign focused almost immediately on nationalizing the 2020 Eighth District election. This approach was evident as early as the primary election. As Mike Buffer, a local reporter with the *Citizen's Voice*, said, "It was all about who was going to be the Trumpiest. It was all about who was Trump's most loyal soldier."

After winning the primary, Bognet continued following the talking points issued by the Trump campaign, whether this was on Twitter, in television ads, in direct mailers, or in press releases to local media. A Republican strategist, not connected with this race, indicated that Bognet "did not have anything original to add outside of being on team Trump." Volunteers within the Republican Party could not think of a way in which Bognet differed from Trump. Local Republican candidates spoke of the pressure to support Trump vocally in order to be in the "good graces of the party and the Bognet campaign."

Local journalists also pointed out that Bognet, when he was not attacking Cartwright, was attempting to connect himself almost fully to Trump. Buffer states, "My impression of the Bognet campaign is that they really went all in on nationalizing the campaign approach where they tried to link Cartwright to AOC, defund the police, crazy socialism, Bernie Sanders, etc. etc. Which, anyone who knows Matt Cartwright knows that is a stretch. They really tried to ride the Trump coattails . . . the Bognet campaign was trying to be the mini-Trump campaign . . . the Bognet campaign emails were the same talking points from the Trump campaign."

Another local columnist agrees: "Yeah, he [Bognet] wants to paint himself as a Trump ally. And, I think he is attaching his wagon to Trump's horses and trying to play that to victory." He adds, "The GOP and RNC is targeting Cartwright, thinking that it is a seat they can win, and Cartwright has a lot of advertising as well because he has a lot of money to spend." Indeed, both candidates had money to spend, as Bognet reports raising $1,519,527, but

Cartwright raised $3,885,136. Outside groups reported spending more than $1,500,000 on behalf of Cartwright, and almost $500,000 on behalf of Bognet (OpenSecrets.org 2021).

An analysis of Bognet's activity on Twitter, where he posted more regularly than Facebook, indicates the reporters were correct (Table 5.2). Bognet mentioned Matt Cartwright in more than half of his tweets, and Donald Trump in more than one-third of his tweets. Even more, Bognet routinely tried to connect Cartwright to Nancy Pelosi, calling him her lapdog, and one to the radical left as well. Figure 5.3 highlights just a few of Bognet's tweets from the last week of the campaign, showing the themes of Cartwright being out of touch with the community, Cartwright being rich, and Bognet supporting Trump's policies. When Bognet did focus on issues, they were almost always nationalized; only a small number of his tweets focused on issues perceived as important in the local area only, with five tweets posted about the importance of fracking and energy jobs.

Bognet also used this strategy in his television ads. During the summer unrest in Portland, Oregon, Bognet bought media time in Portland, telling families and businesses that they should move to NEPA (Krawczeniuk 2020). Several direct mailers in the area tied Trump and Bognet together as fighting for the same things against liberal politicians like Biden and Cartwright. This theme continued in the press releases of the Bognet campaign. Buffer stated, "I think Bognet had some issues when it came to his campaign emails and press releases. I've never seen someone running for Congress like that. . . . He had no message to get free media coverage and could not pick issues that we would write about. Instead, he kept repeating Trump talking points." Another local staff reporter stated, "Bognet seemed to be focused on venomous attacks on Cartwright as far as him being wealthy, him owning more than one home, him owning a boat and an airplane. He repeatedly used that in his commercials, and I don't think that played well for him at all."

Figure 5.3 Selected Bognet tweets. (Twitter, @Bognet4congress.)

It is not surprising that campaigns focus on issues they believe will help them win elections (Petrocik 1996). The Cartwright campaign did focus on the issues of COVID, working families, and protecting unions. However, it was more common that the Cartwright campaign wanted to remind people how to vote, to highlight an endorsement, or to remind constituents that "he is one of us and represents us." In many ways, then, Cartwright's campaign was localized in scope. Bognet's campaign was largely nationalized. Very rarely did he focus on issues that applied only to NEPA, and he was more focused on connecting Matt Cartwright to the "radical left" or to Nancy Pelosi. The issues that did matter to Bognet were issues that President Trump campaigned on, like fighting the movement to defund the police, the violence in cities, and the economic strength of the Trump years.

The race for being "one of us" appears to have helped Cartwright win reelection against Bognet. A staff writer and columnist for the *Times Leader* stated, "I think that native, a son or daughter, is important. I think that also played against Bognet even though he tried to paint himself as a Hazleton high school football star. I don't think anybody knew who he was until he came into this race . . . so I think there was a much stronger connection with Cartwright than there was with Bognet."

The outcome of the election was far from certain, as the last two cycles had been close. In 2016 Cartwright won his district with 53.8% of the vote. The 2018 cycle was a comfortable victory for Cartwright, but 2020 promised to be closer with the specter of a popular President Trump on the ballot as well (Table 5.3). Once again, turnout increased significantly between 2016 and 2020 throughout the district. But the increase was more pronounced on the Democratic side than it was on the Republican side. Cartwright received more votes in the Eighth District than Biden did, which speaks to his popularity within the district.

The 119th State House Campaign

For Republicans, the most important takeaway from the 119th State House race should be one of disappointment. President Trump performed very well in the district, winning it with 61% of the vote. It is a district where the incumbent representative won a narrow election in 2016 and 2018. And, on paper, the Republican challenger was a strong candidate. However, Gerald Mullery won reelection in another close contest partly because his challenger rarely campaigned. A Republican incumbent running in another race said, "If we had someone who actually campaigned, that is a seat we would have picked up. Mullery is a good person, but that district should be Republican." As one Republican strategist told me, "The Republican challenger's campaign should make Republicans angry because they should have won."

TABLE 5.3 COMPARISON OF 2020 PRESIDENTIAL ELECTION RESULTS WITH EIGHTH CONGRESSIONAL DISTRICT, 119TH STATE HOUSE AND 120TH STATE HOUSE RESULTS

Eighth Congressional District[a]	Trump (R)	Bognet (R)	Difference	Biden (D)	Cartwright* (D)	Difference
	184,804 *(52.2%)*	166,229 (48.2%)	Bognet −4.0	169,107 (47.8%)	*178,442* *(51.8%)*	Cartwright +4.0
	Trump (R)	Chura (R)	Difference	Biden (D)	Mullery* (D)	Difference
PA 119th State House District[b]	*17,569* *(61.0%)*	13,478 (47.4%)	Chura −13.6	11,217 (39.0%)	*14,943* *(52.6%)*	Mullery +13.6
	Trump (R)	Kaufer* (R)	Difference	Biden (D)	Bryn Smith (D)	Difference
PA 120th State House District[b]	*16,988* *(52.6%)*	*20,397* *(63.1%)*	Kaufer +10.5	15,339 (47.4%)	11,913 (36.9%)	Bryn Smith −10.5

Sources: Data accessed March 29, 2021. Compiled from the following:
(a) Department of Elections/Voter Registration Page, Lackawanna County. Available at https://www
.lackawannacounty.org/index.php/departmentsagencies/elections/voter-registration/certified-election
-results.
Election Results Archive, Luzerne County. Available at https://www.luzernecounty.org/404/Election
-Results-Archive.
Monroe County Election Results, Monroe County. Available at http://agencies.monroecountypa.gov
/elections/.
Elections Office, Pike County, Available at https://www.pikepa.org/elections.
General Election Results, Wayne County. Available at http://www.waynecountypa.gov/Archive.aspx?
AMID=36.
(b) Election Results Archive, Luzerne County. Available at https://www.luzernecounty.org/404/Election
-Results-Archive.
Note: Winning percentages are in bold italics. Star indicates the incumbent.

John Chura, the Republican challenger, ran almost no campaign in his bid to unseat Mullery. A local staff reporter said, "As far as campaigning, we didn't hear anything from Chura at all." Buffer adds, "I know very little about John Chura. He is from West Hazleton and his career in politics was sparse. We invited him to come in and talk to the editorial board regarding an endorsement and he declined. He seemed to have some sort of animosity toward the local press. . . . We don't really know what he stood for or what his campaign message was about."

Chura's social media activity was similarly sparse. He had no campaign Twitter or Instagram account, but instead relied on a Facebook account where he posted a total of six times from September 1st to November 2nd. Of those six posts, one was a response to an attack by Mullery about paying taxes, and another was about gun control. His website, which was taken down shortly after the election, focused on the importance of stopping gun control policies, ending property taxes, and repealing the "rain tax."

Chura's campaign should be seen as evidence of what could have been for the Luzerne County GOP. His campaign raised just over $10,000, but the state party provided over $470,000 in in-kind contributions (Pennsylvania Department of State n.d.). The House Republican Campaign Committee also spent $80,000 on a television ad attacking Mullery. Yet, there was very little to show for all of this. It is difficult to ascertain whether Chura ran a localized campaign or a nationalized campaign, simply because he did not really have a campaign.

Mullery, on the other hand, ran what could easily be characterized as a local campaign. He was active in several different venues and took positions that would not fit within the broader Democratic Party. He supports gun rights, and he reports supporting House Bill 76 to eliminate property taxes. Finally, he wants to work toward the elimination of the "rain tax." Thus, the three main issues that Chura campaigned on provided no difference in policy preference between himself and Mullery.

When speaking of Mullery's policy positions, Bozinski states, "You have to realize, that's a difficult district. He is walking that fence with pockets of solid Democratic supporters who tend to be more rural. . . . He has to walk that fine line where he wants to help the community, but he has to be pro-gun and pro-hunting and that district by gerrymander is designed that [way] and sprawls across Luzerne County. . . . I, as his chair . . . may not totally agree but I would understand why he needed to do that in that district."

His official Facebook page focused almost entirely on earmarks for the legislative district, updates about school closings due to COVID, and bi-weekly COVID tracking data. The campaign account, Citizens for Mullery, focused on local issues in almost one-third of all posts (32.3%) and highlighted his work for the district in 22.6% of posts. The political issues he mentioned most were support for education (9.7%), support for first responders (9.7%), and support for gun rights (6.5%). Mullery raised over $27,000 and spent more than $13,000 (Pennsylvania Department of State n.d.). He was the recipient of over $100,000 in outside spending (given by the state Democratic Party) that highlighted his support from law enforcement or attacked Chura.

Mullery's messaging strategy was to focus on areas of commonality with his district and combine this with strong constituency service. The *Times Leader* columnist says, "Mullery throughout the last two years did a lot of constituent visits. He went to a lot of the towns throughout his district and he spent time trying to identify what their concerns were, their issues were, and what they would like to see. He became much more visible during the two years in between and I think that probably helped him a lot." Buffer said, "He [Mullery] emphasizes constituent service, and his background in the community, and people know him and like him."

Mullery won by just over 5 percentage points (Table 5.3). One local columnist said, "I think that going into this race, Mullery would tell you himself that he didn't expect to win. I think he thought the district had become much more in line with the Republican Party and Trump especially. So, I don't think it was surprising that it was a close election. I think a lot of the votes that went to him [Chura] were Trump votes and those that were dissatisfied with the Democratic positions." Buffer concluded, "He [Mullery] kind of encourages ticket-splitting on that basis and that is how he survived the last three elections. I think he was fortunate to go up against a particularly weak candidate this last go around."

Mullery did retain his seat by just over 1,000 votes. But the increase in GOP votes should be concerning for Democrats as they look forward in this district. In Table 5.3, it is interesting to note that Chura underperformed the Trump vote by more than 4,000 votes, and Mullery outperformed Biden in the 119th by more than 3,500 votes. Thus, the race for the 119th District appears to be one where the GOP should have picked up a seat, but there was an unpopular or unknown Republican challenger and a well-liked Democratic incumbent. Mullery was successful through his localized campaign against a challenger who really did not run.

The 120th House Campaign

The 120th State House pitted a three-term incumbent, Aaron Kaufer, against a local public defender, Joanna Bryn Smith. Bryn Smith connected herself to progressive politics and Democratic Party positions throughout the campaign. Her social media presence on Facebook was identical to her presence on Twitter, and her posts were more likely to discuss the presidential campaign (17.6% of tweets), endorsements from unions and local residents (12.1%), and the importance of protecting voting rights (11%) than any other topics. She was a regular at the state and local party Zoom rallies held throughout the fall, as the party was trying to encourage her campaign as much as possible. Bryn Smith raised over $225,000 and spent nearly $200,000 in her campaign for the PA-120th seat, with nearly $200,000 in in-kind contributions from the Pennsylvania Democratic Party (Pennsylvania Department of State, n.d.).

One of the reasons for Bryn Smith being active on social media is that the Democratic Party did not allow in-person campaign activities. Bozinski states, "Her entire campaign had to shift to social media and digital, which is great except for long-time traditional voters who happen to live in that district. They don't do social media." In terms of messaging, Buffer states, "I think Bryn Smith tried to link him [Kaufer] to Trump. That was her strategy, thinking there were more anti-Trump voters in the district than there are. I think she had a tough campaign and that was really the only strategy she could employ. Biden did win Kingston and Forty Fort, which are two of the larger municipalities in the district, but there just aren't enough anti-Trump voters to win with an anti-Trump message." One must conclude, then, that Bryn Smith was more likely to nationalize the election, with a focus on party politics and partisan issues more than on issues that were local in nature.

Kaufer focused his campaign more on his experience, bipartisanship, and familiarity with the district. One local staff reporter says, "Kaufer has been a pretty diligent representative during the time he's been in Harrisburg. I think he has crossed party lines more than once. I think he has tried to vote constituent concerns more than party concerns." Buffer adds, "Ever since Kaufer has started running, he has presented himself as Mr. Nonpartisan. . . . That has become his trademark. That has become his message and he has stuck to it every election he has ever run in. . . . As more people in the district voted for Trump, that benefited Kaufer. Even though he never appeared to be a Trump-style Republican. . . . Because he has this independent Republican background, he gets endorsement from PSEA [Pennsylvania State Education Association] . . . It kind of builds your credibility of being nonpartisan or being willing to embrace all sides of the aisle."

Kaufer did not use social media in his campaign, instead relying on yard signs, local get-togethers, and his familiarity with local voters. He did not post on Twitter during the campaign, and he posted only twice to his campaign Facebook page: once to tout a local newspaper's endorsement and the other time to highlight a bipartisan set of endorsements from local mayors. Kaufer raised more than $120,000 and spent almost $112,000 in his reelection campaign (Pennsylvania Department of State n.d.). As a result, one concludes that Kaufer's style was localized and focused on constituency service and being a known entity to the local community.

Table 5.3 shows that Kaufer won the seat in the 2020 election handily. Bozinski concedes, "When you don't know a candidate even though she has great qualities, and you have Kaufer who is pretty good and most people think he is pretty good and feel like they know him, the easy thing to do is vote for the person you know even if you are Democrat." Kaufer outperformed Trump in the 120th District significantly, and Bryn Smith underperformed compared to Biden. Kaufer received 3,500 more votes than Trump, and Biden received 3,400 more votes than Bryn Smith (see Table 5.3).

Discussion

A few broad themes emerge in the elections in NEPA. First, incumbents were more likely than challengers to focus on localized issues and to break with the national party, while challengers were more likely to use the talking points of the national party. Matt Cartwright, Gerald Mullery (Democrat-119th), and Aaron Kaufer (Republican-120th) focused on reminding residents that they work hard for the area and that they have been successful in bringing money home to the district. Through social media posts, endorsements, and the issue positions they took, each of them also touted their willingness to work across partisan lines. Challengers Jim Bognet and Joanna Bryn Smith, who both put significant effort into campaigning, focused on issue positions similar to those of the national party. They both were more likely to address the out-party and grievances with them than they were to take positive political positions. While it is no surprise that this is the strategy, we see the power of incumbency highlighted in these outcomes as well.

Second, we see the importance of understanding the local climate and being "one of us" in the 2020 campaign. Voters prefer candidates with local roots to those who lack strong ties to the area (Campbell and Cowley 2014). Throughout the campaign cycle, candidates routinely tried to paint themselves as having local roots and truly understanding the common man in the area. This can be seen even at the presidential level; as Buffer states, "The Trump message was that Biden is a puppet being controlled by AOC and Bernie Sanders. But I think a lot of people who know Joe Biden . . . and know he is from Scranton, like Joe Biden and what he has been about in his 50-year career in politics . . . they just didn't buy that."

When Biden sought to distinguish himself from President Trump at a values-based level, he would remind people of being the "little guy" against people like Trump who only care about big corporations and other wealthy people (Woodall 2020). On the other hand, Trump claimed that Biden abandoned Scranton literally by moving away, and figuratively with his support of free-trade policies (Calefati 2020). In short, Scranton became a symbol of what both candidates wanted to portray about themselves to voters throughout the state of Pennsylvania and the nation (Erickson 2020; Meyer 2020).

In the state house races, being perceived as "one of us" also played an important role in how people talked about the election. All four of the major party candidates for the two seats are from the area, which means that residency was not sufficient to prove "you are one of us." The two incumbents, Mullery (Democrat-119th) and Kaufer (Republican-120th), emphasize constituency service and being familiar. The *Times Leader* columnist also said, "Those families [Mullery and Kaufer] have been in this area long. I never heard of the Chura family or Bryn Smith and her family before. So, I think that played some role in the voters' minds—that they are familiar with these names." Throughout the Eighth District, being someone who is known and seen as "one of us" consistently played an important role in how people perceive a campaign.

Third, the importance of COVID in the 2020 election in NEPA cannot be overstated. Republicans were more likely to view COVID-19 with a skeptical lens, but it played an important part in how they campaigned. To them, the main concern with COVID-19 was the effect it had on business and normal life. A Republican strategist said, "The winning message in Pennsylvania is focusing on Tom Wolf harming small businesses even though he didn't do much to stop COVID in nursing homes." Local volunteers were not as subtle. A volunteer from Luzerne County said, "Democrats want to ruin our livelihoods in the name of politics."

Democratic messaging focused more on the way in which President Trump failed as a leader during the COVID-19 pandemic. Local candidates for office spoke of the need to reopen businesses, but only when it was safe. One challenger pointed to a "failed national strategy, from a failed leader" as the reason the pandemic was so bad in the United States compared to other countries. A campaign volunteer in Lackawanna County pointed out that "Trump and the Republicans want you to think this pandemic is fake. They don't care about real people, but are only worried about the economy so he can win reelection."

In terms of campaigning, the Republican Party did not change much about their strategy, but the Democrats did. Republican candidates continued to hold rallies throughout the campaign, and they used Democratic reticence to do so against them. Buffer stated, "That is the big Trump approach: we are going to show our strength in numbers. And, we are going to have rallies in the middle of a pandemic and we don't care if it turns out to be a super spreader event because we want to show numbers. Then, we are going to mock the Biden campaign because there are only sixty cars at a Biden rally."

Even if the parties differed on how real the pandemic was, and how important it should be from a policy perspective, all interviewees highlighted that it played a role in how people viewed the election. The Republican volunteers and strategist believed that NEPA residents would see that Democrats wanted to control how we live. The Republican challenger said, "We can't survive if Democrats keep things closed. They are killing local businesses." Democratic volunteers believed the pandemic would help their candidates win office because "people see how reckless Republicans are with life." Bozinski made the argument that COVID-19 is one of the reasons Joanna Bryn Smith fared so poorly in her race, as it took away her opportunity as the challenger to truly introduce herself to the community, which made it tough to succeed against a popular incumbent.

Finally, the primary theme of discussion among those interviewed is how partisan the presidential election was in this area. A local staff writer told me, "There are a lot of lines that have been drawn between the Republicans, or Trumps, and the Democrats that are not to be crossed. Nobody expected anyone to convince a Trump supporter to vote for Biden. Trump has created this cultlike phenomenon of base support." Most of the local journalists routinely discussed the difficulty of finding someone who truly was undecided in their vote choice throughout the campaign. And this was a common refrain from international journalists who were traveling through the region because of its importance in the 2016 cycle.

None of the volunteers I spoke with could name any friends of theirs who were planning to vote for the nonpreferred candidate. While this is anecdotal, it does speak to the nationalized divisions within local communities. The Wayne County Republican volunteer spoke about Democrats as people who want to kill babies, do not support police officers, and are afraid to live their lives due to COVID. The Luzerne County GOP volunteer I spoke with was convinced that President Trump would win reelection. After the election they continued to believe the election had been stolen, and in early December they told me that January 6 would be the day Biden's campaign came crashing down and the truth would show.

Conclusion

There are two broad themes to take away from this analysis. First, the elections in the Pennsylvania Eighth District were both nationalized and local at the same time. As many interviewees showed, President Trump and the pandemic were on everyone's mind throughout the campaign. It was impossible to not talk about Trump and Biden, even when asking local candidates about their own campaign. At the same time, it was the challengers who were most likely to use nationalized framing, but they lost all three elections. Nationalization does not appear to help challengers defeat incumbents, at least from this analysis.

The second broad theme is that candidates in both parties focused on the same set of issues. The Republicans and Democrats offered competing notions of who would do better at growing the economy in this region and bringing back middle-class jobs. To Democrats this was protecting unions, and to Republicans it was helping to rebuild the coal industry. Republicans in the area were much more likely to focus on COVID restrictions harming local businesses, and Democrats used the public health frame. The local candidates won personal votes because they are known and are considered to be representative of the area, and people were happy to cross the aisle to vote for them. So, while the election was intensely national because that was all people could talk about, people still voted based on localized interests and knowledge of the candidates.

NOTES

1. This chapter draws on a collection of nineteen interviews with twelve individuals and looks at the nationalized and local context of three elections in the area. I spoke with candidates running for office, members of campaign staff, local party leaders, local party activists, and local journalists. Most (seven) of those interviewed were spoken to before and after the election, two interviewees spoke only before the election, and three spoke with me only after the election. Where allowed, I provide names for the quotes, but for many of the interviews I refer to the interviewees in general terms.

2. DW-NOMINATE stands for "Dynamic, Weighted Nominal Three-Step Estimation" and was created by Keith Poole and Howard Rosenthal. See their book *Ideology and Congress: A Political Economic History of Roll Call Voting*, 2nd ed (New York: Routledge, 2017).

REFERENCES

Abramowitz, Alan I., and Steven W. Webster. 2018. "Negative Partisanship: Why Americans Dislike Parties But Behave Like Rabid Partisans." *Advances in Political Psychology* 39, no. 1: 119–35.

Bognet for Congress. 2022. "Meet Jim." Accessed May 20, 2022. Available at https://www.bognetforcongress.com/meet-jim/.

Bradlee, Ben, Jr. 2018. *The Forgotten: How the People of One Pennsylvania County Elected Donald Trump and Changed America*. New York: Little, Brown.

Buffer, Michael P. 2016. "Race for 120th House Seat Highly Competitive." *Citizens' Voice*, November 1, 2016. Last modified June 18, 2020. Accessed May 10, 2021. Available at https://www.citizensvoice.com/news/race-for-120th-house-seat-highly-competitive/article_85ed64c8-c813-535e-a060-f46f049fd0e3.html.

Calefati, Jessica. 2020. "Fact-Checking Trump's Frequent Claim That Joe Biden 'Abandoned Scranton.'" *Philadelphia Inquirer*, August 31, 2020. Available at https://fusion.inquirer.com/politics/election/joe-biden-scranton-roots-trump-fact-check-20200829.html.

Campbell, Rosie, and Philip Cowley. 2014. "What Voters Want: Reactions to Candidate Characteristics in a Survey Experiment." *Political Studies* 62, no. 4: 745–65.

Campbell, Rosie, Philip Cowley, Nick Vivyan, and Markus Wanger. 2019. "Why Friends and Neighbors? Explaining the Electoral Appeal of Local Roots." *Journal of Politics* 81, no. 3: 937–51. Available at http://dx.doi.org/10.1086/703131.

Cartwright, Matt. 2020a. "Bogus Commercials." Accessed May 10, 2021. Available at https://host2.adimpact.com/admo/viewer/2970117.

———. 2020b. "Earned My Vote." Video. Accessed May 10, 2021. Available at https://youtube/bMgTqlTLYDo.

Delli Carpini, Michael X., and Scott Keeter. 1996. *What Americans Know About Politics and Why It Matters*. New Haven, CT: Yale University Press.

Democratic Congressional Campaign Committee. 2020. "Jim Bognet: Republican Candidate in Pennsylvania's 8th Congressional District." Last modified February 2020.

Accessed January 29, 2021. Available at https://dccc.org/wp-content/uploads/2020/05 /Bognet-Research-Memo-ONLINE.pdf.

Druckman, James N., Martin J. Kifer, and Michael Parkin. 2020. "Campaign Rhetoric and the Incumbency Advantage." *American Politics Research* 48, no. 1: 22–43. Available at https://doi.org/10.1177/1532673X18822314.

Erickson, Bo. 2020. "Joe Biden's Scranton Is Filled with Signs and Anxious Democrats." *CBSNews*, October 16, 2020. Accessed May 10, 2021. Available at https://www.cbsnews .com/news/joe-bidens-scranton-is-filled-with-signs-and-anxious-democrats/.

Freking, Kevin. 2020. "Trump Defends His Rhetoric in 1st TV Town Hall of 2020." *Associated Press*, March 5, 2020. Accessed May 10, 2021. Available at https://apnews.com /article/c03cd0c8f2a41ad0300092fff48ee4f4.

Glaeser, Edward L., Joshua D. Gottlieb, and Oren Ziv. 2014. "Unhappy Cities." *National Bureau of Economic Research*. Accessed January 29, 2021. Available at https://www.nber .org/papers/w20291.

Golias, Paul. 2019. "Labor's Legacy: 125 Years of Toil, Triumph for Organized Labor in NEPA." *Citizens' Voice*, March 2, 2019. Last modified April 17, 2020. Accessed January 29, 2021. Available at https://www.citizensvoice.com/lifestyles/labor-s-legacy125-years -of-toil-triumph-for-organized-labor-in-nepa-will-be-celebrated/article_7ad0a134 -dc47-5663-94b6-4db547fb6875.html.

Kalinowski, Bob. 2020. "President Trump, First Lady, VP Nominee Harris to visit NEPA in Final-Hour Campaign Blitz." *Citizens' Voice*, October 30, 2020. Last modified November 1, 2020. Accessed January 29, 2021. Available at https://www.citizensvoice.com /news/election/president-trump-first-lady-vp-nominee-harris-to-visit-nepa-in-final -hour-campaign-blitz/article_56d88550-5b8e-5ff6-936a-3c90c1340d89.html.

Krawczeniuk, Borys. 2020. "Bognet Buys Commercial Time in Oregon for Local Election." *The Times-Tribune*, August 18, 2020. Last modified February 6, 2021. Accessed May 10, 2021. Available at https://www.thetimes-tribune.com/news/election/bognet-buys -commercial-time-in-oregon-for-local-election/article_ce41b9a8-685e-50ce-a819 -91820e4326cb.html.

Lakhani, Nina. 2020. "Joe Biden Returns to Childhood Home in Scranton: 'From This House to the White House.'" *The Guardian*, November 3, 2020. Accessed May 10, 2021. Available at https://www.theguardian.com/us-news/2020/nov/03/joe-biden-scranton -pennsylvania-election-day-polls.

Mason, Lilliana. 2018. *Uncivil Agreement: How Politics Became Our Identity*. Chicago: University of Chicago Press.

Meyer, Katie. 2020. "Trump, Biden Battle for the Soul of Scranton." *WHYY News*, August 20, 2020. Accessed May 10, 2021. Available at https://whyy.org/articles/trump-biden -battle-for-the-soul-of-scranton/.

Milligan, Susan. 2020. "Where's Joe Biden?" *U.S. News and World Report*, August 7, 2020. Accessed May 10, 2021. Available at https://www.usnews.com/news/elections/arti cles/2020-08-07/wheres-joe-biden-not-on-the-campaign-trail.

OpenSecrets.org. 2021. "Pennsylvania District 08 2020 Race." Accessed March 29, 2021. Available at https://www.opensecrets.org/races/outside-spending?cycle=2020&id=P A08&spec=N.

Pennsylvania Department of State. n.d. "Campaign Finance Online Reporting." Accessed June 22, 2021. Available at https://www.campaignfinanceonline.pa.gov/pages/CFRe portSearch.aspx.

Petrocik, John R. 1996. "Issue Ownership in Presidential Elections, with a 1980 Case Study." *American Journal of Political Science* 40, no. 3: 825–50.

Pirini, Jay. 2020. "The Biggest Lesson Scranton Taught Joe Biden." *CNN News*, August 16, 2020. Accessed May 10, 2021. Available at https://www.cnn.com/2020/08/16/opinions/joe-biden-scranton-biggest-lesson-parini/index.html.

Prose, J. D. 2020. "Has Trump Delivered on 2016 Steel & Coal Campaign Promises for Pa.? What the Numbers Say." *Times*, October 15, 2020. Accessed May 10, 2021. Available at https://www.timesonline.com/story/news/2020/10/15/2020-election-pa-trump-campaign-steel-coal-not-happening/3636195001/.

Rhys, Dane, and Timothy Gardner. 2020. "In Pennsylvania Coal Country, Miners Forgive Trump for Failed Revival." *Reuters*, September 30, 2020. Accessed May 10, 2021. Available at https://www.reuters.com/article/us-usa-election-trump-coal-insight/in-pennsylvania-coal-country-miners-forgive-trump-for-failed-revival-idUSKBN26L1SB.

Rosen, Jill. 2018. "Americans Don't Know Much About State Government, Survey Finds." *JHU HUB*, December 14, 2018. Accessed May 10, 2021. Available at https://hub.jhu.edu/2018/12/14/americans-dont-understand-state-government/.

Saul, Josh. 2016. "Why Did Donald Trump Win? Just Visit Luzerne County, Pennsylvania." *Newsweek*, December 5, 2016. Accessed March 29, 2021. Available at https://www.newsweek.com/2016/12/16/donald-trump-pennsylvania-win-luzerne-county-527861.html.

Shackel, Paul, A. 2016. "The Meaning of Place in the Anthracite Region of Northeastern Pennsylvania." *International Journal of Heritage Studies* 22, no. 3: 200–13.

Upstate New York News. August 20, 2020. "In PHOTOS: President Trump Visits Small Town in Pennsylvania." Accessed December 22, 2021. Available at http://jeffersoncountyalerts.com/2020/08/20/in-photos-president-trump-visits-small-town-in-pennsylvania/.

Urbina, Ian. 2009. "Despite Red Flags About Judges, a Kickback Scheme Flourished." *New York Times*, March 27, 2009. Available at https://www.nytimes.com/2009/03/28/us/28judges.html.

Woodall, Candy. 2020. "'I Am Home': Biden's Pa. Roots Could Run from a Scranton Kitchen Table to the Presidency." *York Daily Record*, October 22, 2020. Available at https://www.ydr.com/story/news/politics/elections/2020/10/22/joe-biden-pa-scranton-pennsylvania-white-house/6004490002/.

INTERVIEWS

Bozinski, Kathy. Chair of the Luzerne County Democratic Party. September 10, 2020.
———. January 14, 2021.

Buffer, Mike. Reporter for Wilkes-Barre *The Citizens' Voice*. September 24, 2020.
———. January 15, 2021.

Democratic challenger for state-level office. October 1, 2020.
———. January 15, 2021.

Democratic incumbent for state-level office. December 15, 2020.

Democratic volunteer for Lackawanna County. October 13, 2020.
———. December 17, 2021.

Democratic volunteer for Monroe County. October 8, 2020.
———. January 13, 2021.

Republican challenger running for state-level office. September 3, 2020.

Republican incumbent for state-level office. September 17, 2020.

Republican strategist from Harrisburg. December 17, 2020.

Republican volunteer for Luzerne County. September 10, 2020.

———. December 17, 2021.

Republican volunteer for Wayne County. October 6, 2020.

———. December 10, 2021.

Staff reporter for Wilkes-Barre *Times Leader*. January 13, 2020.

6

Campaigns in the Tenth Congressional District

Competitiveness, Professionalism, and
Asymmetric Nationalization

SARAH NIEBLER AND SOPHIE ACKERT

With the Pennsylvania Supreme Court's redrawing of the congressional districts in the Commonwealth, the district represented by Republican Scott Perry became more competitive. Prior to the 2018 redistricting, Perry represented the Fourth Congressional District, which was more Republican than the new Tenth Congressional District. The district is thought to be one of the more competitive districts in Pennsylvania, and Republican Scott Perry, who was the incumbent running for reelection in 2020, carried it by less than 3 percentage points in 2018.

In this chapter, we examine the degree of nationalization in the Tenth Congressional District (PA-10), between the Republican incumbent Scott Perry and the Democratic challenger, state auditor general Eugene DePasquale. We also look at nationalization in the down-ballot races in the Pennsylvania State House Districts 105 and 199 (HD-105 and HD-199). First, we provide geographic, political, cultural, and economic context of the U.S. congressional and Pennsylvania State House districts. Then we discuss nationalization based on the different types of data we observed and collected, including debates and rallies, advertising, social media and websites, direct mail, and interviews with local media experts and representatives from the campaigns we followed.

We ultimately found a fair amount of localization in our races, but there is evidence of significant nationalization as well. The PA-10 race was somewhat nationalized due to its federal nature, and the candidates were more nationalized when talking about their opponents than when talking about themselves. In down-ballot races, nationalization occurred much more in HD-105 than in HD-199, in part, we argue, because HD-105 was more competitive. Even within HD-105, however, evidence of nationalization was higher when we looked at funding sources and endorsements as compared to discussion of the issues. Across all three of the races we examined, the Republican incumbents largely talked about local issues when promoting their own campaigns and accomplishments; they were much more nationalized when discussing their opponents, attempting to connect their Democratic challengers to unpopular national Democratic figures.

TABLE 6.1 DEMOGRAPHIC AND REGISTRATION CHARACTERISTICS OF PENNSYLVANIA'S 105TH AND 199TH STATE HOUSE DISTRICTS, TENTH CONGRESSIONAL DISTRICT, AND PENNSYLVANIA IN 2019

	PA 105th State House District[a]	PA 199th State House District[b]	PA Tenth Congressional District[c]	Pennsylvania[d]
Population density: people/square mile	1,058.5	278.8	689.3	286.1
Population white	74%	87%	73%	76%
Population black	12%	4%	11%	11%
Population Hispanic	5%	4%	9%	8%
Foreign-born	9.1%	4.6%	7.5%	7.0%
Median household income	$74,626	$64,204	$67,155	$63,463
Bachelor's degree or higher	38.4%	30.5%	32.2%	32.3%
Registered Democrat[e]	40.2%	34.6%	39.9%	46.5%
Registered Republican[e]	44.6%	48.5%	44.0%	39.0%
Registered none/other[e]	15.2%	16.9%	16.2%	14.5%

Sources:

(a) Compiled from U.S. Census Bureau. n.d. "Census Reporter: State House District 105, PA." Accessed March 29, 2021. Available at https://censusreporter.org/profiles/62000US42105-state-house-district -105-pa/.

(b) Compiled from U.S. Census Bureau. n.d. "Census Reporter: State House District 199, PA." Accessed March 29, 2021. Available at https://censusreporter.org/profiles/62000US42199-state-house-district -199-pa/.

(c) Compiled from U.S. Census Bureau. n.d. "Census Reporter: Congressional District 10, PA." Accessed March 29, 2021. Available at https://censusreporter.org/profiles/50000US4210-congressional-district -10-pa/.

(d) Compiled from U.S. Census Bureau. n.d. "Census Reporter: Pennsylvania." Accessed March 29, 2021. Available at https://censusreporter.org/profiles/04000US42-pennsylvania/.

(e) Compiled from Pennsylvania Department of State. n.d. "Voting and Election Statistics." Accessed March 29, 2021. Available at https://www.dos.pa.gov/VotingElections/OtherServicesEvents/Voting ElectionStatistics/Pages/VotingElectionStatistics.aspx.

PA-10

Pennsylvania's Tenth Congressional District comprises Dauphin County (including Harrisburg), the eastern half of Cumberland County (including Carlisle), and the northern part of York County (including the City of York). The entire central region of the state is thought to be conservative, but the inclusion of Democratic-leaning cities of Harrisburg and York into the same congressional district as Republican-leaning rural townships makes PA-10 more competitive than any south central Pennsylvania congressional district has been in nearly twenty years. Had PA-10 existed in 2016, Republican Donald Trump would have carried it by 9 points (52% to 43%) over Democrat Hillary Clinton (Daily Kos 2018). In 2016, Republican Scott Perry won the same percentage of the vote as Trump (52%), but Democratic challenger George Scott earned more votes than Clinton. The final vote margin between the two candidates was less than 3 percentage points, making PA-10 the second-closest congressional race in Pennsylvania that year (Pennsylvania Department of State 2018).

The demographic composition of PA-10, HD-105, and HD-199, as well as voter registration statistics of the three districts, can be found in Table 6.1. Major employers in the district include federal and state governments as well as the medical industry (specifically, the Milton S. Hershey Medical Center in Dauphin County, the WellSpan York Hospital in York County, and Penn State Health Holy Spirit Medical Center and Highmark Health Services in Cumberland County). Cumberland County also houses a number of warehouses, making Giant Food Stores LLC and Amazon.com LLC among the top employers in the area (Cumberland Area Economic Development Corporation 2015).

HD-105 and HD-199

HD-105 is in Dauphin County and encompasses the townships of Lower Paxton, South Hanover, and West Hanover, which are all east of the city of Harrisburg. HD-199 is in Cumberland County and is made up of the boroughs of Carlisle and Newville and the townships of Dickinson, Lower Frankford, Lower Mifflin, Middlesex, North Middleton, Silver Spring (part), Upper Frankford, Upper Mifflin, and West Pennsboro.

We selected HD-105 for inclusion in this study because prior to the election, it was predicted to be one of the most competitive districts in the Commonwealth. In 2018, the seat was open and Republican Andrew Lewis defeated Democrat Eric Epstein by 1.6 percentage points (50.8% to 49.2%) (Dauphin County Pennsylvania 2018). The 2020 general election featured Lewis as the Republican incumbent against Democratic challenger Brittney Rodas. Both

Lewis and Rodas were uncontested in their parties' primary elections. Andrew Lewis is a veteran of the U.S. Army, having served nearly ten years. After completing his military service, he joined his family's construction business and earned his bachelor of arts degree from Thomas Edison State College. He also has a graduate certificate in public policy, a master's degree in legislative affairs, and a master of business administration (Pennsylvania House Republican Caucus 2021a). Prior to her candidacy, Brittney Rodas worked at the Pennsylvania House of Representatives as a policy and research analyst. She was also the South-Central Region Director for the Pennsylvania Young Democrats. She earned her bachelor of science and master of public administration degrees from Penn State University (Brittney Rodas for PA State Representative 2020).

We selected HD-199 largely because it is the district where Dickinson College is located, but in recent years the district has been relatively uncompetitive. In 2018, Republican Barb Gleim defeated Democrat Sherwood McGinnis by just under 20 percentage points (58.8% to 39.4%) (Cumberland County PA 2018). In 2020, Gleim ran as the incumbent against Democratic challenger Janelle Kayla Crossley; both of them ran uncontested races for their parties' primaries. Prior to her first election in 2018, Gleim held a variety of positions at local businesses in addition to owning a family cattle farm with her husband. She has a bachelor's degree from the University of Maryland and a master of business administration from Delaware Valley University (Pennsylvania House Republican Caucus 2021b). Crossley worked in health care facility management for twenty-five years and attended Cumberland Perry Technical School (Vote USA 2020). She is the first openly transgender woman to run for elected office in the Commonwealth (Janelle for PA-199 2020).

Nationalization in the 2020 Elections

The Presidential Race

Before discussing the congressional and state house races, we briefly consider the presidential race, specifically focusing on the September 26, 2020, rally that President Donald Trump held at the Harrisburg International Airport (HIA), which is located in PA-10. The rally occurred on the same day Trump announced Amy Coney Barrett as his choice to fill the open seat on the U.S. Supreme Court, and less than a week before he and Hope Hicks tested positive for COVID-19. Trump's speech at HIA did not refer much to down-ballot races, instead focusing on his nomination of Coney Barrett, lockdowns related to the coronavirus, law enforcement, and the economy (Barr 2020). Not surprisingly, throughout his speech Trump made many direct references to Biden, but in doing so he attempted to tie Biden to the more progressive wing of the Democratic Party, saying, for example, that Biden's potential judicial nominees would be "hand-picked by socialists like Representative Alexandria Ocasio-Cortez. AOC. AOC plus three. And Ilhan Omar" (Barr 2020, 1:53). Trump also made a broad reference to Biden having to negotiate with Democrats in Congress in order to pass legislation, saying, "Did you see their plans? The manifesto? That's the Bernie Sanders and AOC manifesto" (Barr 2020, 21:52).

When Trump did reference down-ballot races, he did so simply by thanking congressional Republicans and candidates for attending the rally, saying, "Also with us are a group of warriors from Washington that are fantastic and love you" (Barr 2020, 42:20). Then he referenced representatives Dan Meuser (PA-9), Scott Perry (PA-10), Lloyd Smucker (PA-11), Fred Keller (PA-12), John Joyce (PA-13), and Mike Kelly (PA-16) and candidate Jim Bognet, who challenged Democrat Matt Cartwright in PA-8. Trump's most specific praise was reserved for former congressman Lou Barletta, who has strong ties to the mid-state, having represented most of Cumberland and Dauphin Counties from 2011 through 2018. With his comments, however, Trump was focused not on Barletta's issue positions, but on Trump's own assertion that Barletta predicted Trump would win Pennsylvania in 2016, long before others thought it possible.

Trump's speech was focused almost exclusively on national-level politics and issues. He had little time to stump for down-ballot Republicans, mentioning them in only superficial ways and not articulating why Republican voters should support them. Other than the approximately three minutes he spent listing the names of down-ballot Republicans (Barr 2020, 42:20–45:07) and the two minutes at the very end of the speech (Barr 2020, 1:09:52) in which he talked about Pennsylvania's geography and history—saying "This is the state where our founding fathers declared American independence. It's where the army weathered its brutal winter at Valley Forge. Where General George Washington led his men on a daring mission across the Delaware. And where our union was saved by the heroes of Gettysburg"—Trump's speech at HIA could have been given in nearly any state in the country.

Pennsylvania Tenth Congressional District

Moving to the Tenth Congressional District (PA-10) race, we find neither a fully nationalized campaign nor a fully localized one. Both Scott Perry and Eugene DePasquale highlighted their backgrounds and local issues when discussing themselves, while trying to paint their opponents in a negative light using national issues and personalities. In television advertising, direct mail, and social media, the candidates frequently attacked one another, which meant there were higher levels of nationalization in those venues. During their two debates, however, nationalization was somewhat reduced, because the candidates tended to focus more on their own accomplishments.

As regards television advertising in PA-10, we see evidence of nationalization simply by looking at the sponsors of ads in the district. While a slim majority of the spending came from candidates and the political parties, nearly 48% came from outside groups. Table 6.2 shows the breakdown of spending by sponsor and whom the sponsor supported with the advertisement. While some of these groups supported only Perry or only DePasquale (see Table 2.5), Federal Election Commission and OpenSecrets data suggest that the vast majority of the groups that paid for ads in the PA-10 race also paid for ads in support of other candidates. In this way, the spending of outside interest groups and national political parties nationalized the race.

TABLE 6.2 TELEVISION ADVERTISING IN THE TENTH CONGRESSIONAL DISTRICT

Sponsor	Type of Group	Amount Spent	Favored Candidate
DePasquale for PA CD-10	Candidate	$2,417,305	DePasquale
Perry for PA CD-10	Candidate	$1,229,759	Perry
DCCC	Political party	$1,586,485	DePasquale
NRCC	Political party	$1,194,504	Perry
DCCC/DePasquale	Coordinated (candidate and party)	$95,760	DePasquale
NRCC/Perry	Coordinated (candidate and party)	$99,050	Perry
American Action Network	Outside group	$229,000	Perry
Club for Growth Action	Outside group	$872,480	Perry
Congressional Leadership Fund	Outside group	$1,429,560	Perry
Future Progress PAC	Outside group	$373,301	DePasquale
Gun Owners of America	Outside group	$636	Perry
House Freedom Action	Outside group	$508,356	Perry
House Majority Forward	Outside group	$307,022	DePasquale
House Majority PAC	Outside group	$2,240,105	DePasquale
Patriotic Veterans Inc	Outside group	$2,685	Perry
Special Operations for America	Outside group	$119,281	Perry
The Conservative Caucus	Outside group	$10,520	Perry
The Principles Project	Outside group	$8,963	DePasquale

Source: AdImpact.

Examining the content of ads, we see large differences in the level of nationalization based on the tone of the advertisements, especially on the Republican side. When ads paid for by Perry and the National Republican Congressional Committee (NRCC) are positive in nature, they talk about Perry's military experience, his mother's role in his upbringing as evidence for his commitment to protecting Social Security, and his opposition to a congressional pay raise in 2019 (Marcos 2019). In some of Perry's and the NRCC's ads attacking DePasquale, the ads are focused on local issues like COVID cases in Pennsylvania nursing homes and high tolls on the Pennsylvania turnpikes. However, a number of these ads also attempt to tie DePasquale to national figures like Nancy Pelosi and Alexandria Ocasio-Cortez. In one ad, the NRCC says, "Proud liberal . . . DePasquale [will] go to Washington and push up your taxes again by four trillion to fund Nancy Pelosi's socialist wish list."

In probably the most well-known Perry ad of the 2020 campaign season, called "Plain Crazy," Perry says, "Socialized medicine takes away your private insurance and leads to long waits to see a doctor. The Green New Deal kills Pennsylvania's energy industry while giving China a huge competitive advantage. And defunding our police? That's just plain crazy. Yet AOC and Eugene DePasquale support all these plans." As Perry talks about the Green New Deal, a picture of Alexandria Ocasio-Cortez, flanked by Bernie Sanders, is on the screen. When Perry says, "AOC and Eugene DePasquale support all these plans," close-ups of the two politicians appear on the screen with a red-colored, raised, clenched fist and the words "radical socialist agenda" between them (Cole 2020).

Interestingly, despite the nationalized nature of the groups paying for them, ads paid for by outside groups opposing DePasquale did so in a localized manner, largely criticizing DePasquale for taking campaign contributions from a Philadelphia union leader.

In ads paid for by the DePasquale campaign or the Democratic Congressional Campaign Committee (DCCC), messaging was largely positive and localized as it focused on DePasquale's upbringing, family, and experience as auditor general. Even when referring to Perry, the ads were not particularly nationalized, instead attacking Perry for voting to give tax breaks to corporations and cutting unemployment insurance during the pandemic, arguing overall that Scott Perry "doesn't care about 'us.'" Ads paid for by outside groups in support of DePasquale were more negative in tone, but were not any more nationalized. Again, the ads focused on votes Perry took that favored "millionaires and wealthy corporations" instead of supporting everyday Pennsylvanians. Overall, ads that were positive toward Perry, regardless of sponsor, tended to be focused on local issues. Advertisements that were negative toward DePasquale were nationalized when paid for by

Perry or the NRCC and were more local when funded by outside groups. Ads that were supportive of DePasquale and those that were negative toward Perry were all relatively localized.

Patterns of nationalization in direct mail largely mirrored those found in the television advertising, in that tone and sponsor affected levels of nationalization. The vast majority of the direct-mail pieces we examined were paid for by the state political parties. The Republican Party of Pennsylvania and Patriots for Perry—Scott Perry's campaign committee—also sent out some mail on his behalf, but none of the direct mail supporting DePasquale came solely from his own campaign committee. Other sources of direct mail in the PA-10 were Americans for Prosperity Action and the National Rifle Association in support of Perry, and the American Federation of State, County & Municipal Employees Public Employees Organized to Promote Legislative Equality (AFSCME PEOPLE), the Pennsylvania State Education Association (PSEA), and Planned Parenthood in support of DePasquale. DePasquale also had support from a variety of national postcard-writing efforts that focused on expanding the Democratic majority in the U.S. House of Representatives. Only one of the six postcards we collected had any sponsor information; this came from Postcards To Voters (https://postcardstovoters .org/), whose aim is to send "handwritten reminders from volunteers to targeted voters giving Democrats a winning edge in close, key races coast to coast."

In some of the direct mail paid for by the Perry campaign and the State GOP supporting his own candidacy, Perry appeals to more local politics, discussing the economy and the response to COVID-19. When talking about the work he is doing to help the economy get back on track, he says he continues to "support our small businesses, and move manufacturing out of China and back to York, Cumberland, and Dauphin Counties." In his references to COVID-19, Perry implicitly appeals to local politics when he talks about nursing homes and protecting seniors.[1] However, the overarching theme in Perry's direct mail is that the country is headed toward socialism, and that reelecting him is one way to stand up to the "radial Left" agenda, which connotes a more nationalized politics. Mailers that highlight Perry's opposition to a "government-run socialist-style healthcare system proposed by the radical Left" and state that he "continues to fight against Nancy Pelosi's radical agenda in Washington" are particularly nationalized. Additionally, despite having been a member of the U.S. House of Representatives since 2013 and the incumbent in this race, Perry sets himself apart from "Washington" with statements like "Unlike Washington, Scott puts his money where his mouth is." Despite the nationalized nature of most of his direct mail, in only one fundraising letter does Perry explicitly associate himself with any other national figures. In this letter, he includes a picture of himself shaking the hand of President Trump and says it is imperative that voters "re-elect President Trump to a second term and send Nancy Pelosi and the Alexandria Ocasio-Cortez radicals back to the minority." Interestingly, when Perry's mail opposing DePasquale does not explicitly feature Pelosi, it tends to focus on more local issues, referencing votes that DePasquale took to raise taxes as a member of the Pennsylvania House of Representatives in 2009 and a vote on a transportation bill in 2007 that Perry says led to increased tolls on the Pennsylvania Turnpike (which runs through PA-10).

Equating Democratic politics to socialism and the "radical Left" can be seen even more clearly in the Republican Party's direct mail opposing the candidacy of DePasquale. Nancy Pelosi is featured in nearly every piece of negative mail produced by the Pennsylvania Republican Party. In one mailer, Bernie Sanders, Alexandria Ocasio-Cortez, and Adam Schiff stand in the background while a figure removes a Halloween-style face mask to reveal Nancy Pelosi underneath. The text on the mailer says, "Eugene DePasquale has been hiding who is behind his campaign. . . . Now we know . . . Nancy Pelosi," and it specifically ties DePasquale to a "radical agenda" featuring "$125 trillion in new taxes, the Green New Deal, Medicare for All, and Defund[ing] the Police."

Direct mail paid for by the Pennsylvania Democratic Party in support of DePasquale's candidacy emphasizes localized topics, but with some connections to national issues. The party focuses extensively on DePasquale's connections to south central Pennsylvania and the characteristics of the people who live in the district, saying he is running for Congress because "South Central PA is full of honest, hardworking people [who] deserve a representative in Washington, DC who works just as hard as [they] do." He focuses on his working-class roots, his brother's muscular dystrophy and its associated health care challenges, and his father's drug addiction. Along those lines, DePasquale's mailers discuss his experience as auditor general and how he "reduced the backlog of rape kits" and "expos[ed] more than $1 billion in wasteful government spending." DePasquale's mailers also address the COVID-19 pandemic, but make no reference to national figures, instead saying he would "listen to experts. . . . Fight for Pennsylvania to get the tests we need. . . . Work to rebuild the economy safely . . . and reform our health care system." Postcards written by individual voter volunteers on behalf of DePasquale did not mention expanding the Democrats' majority in the U.S. House, but they did indicate that a vote for DePasquale would be a vote "to protect social security, the environment, and health care."

DePasquale's mail opposing Perry had a slightly more nationalized tenor to it, but not much. Instead, DePasquale sought to depict Perry as someone who did not help the average south central Pennsylvania resident and was out of touch with his constituents. One mailer said that "Pennsylvanians are struggling, and Scott Perry isn't doing anything to help." It took particular aim at Perry's claims of being fiscally responsible, saying that he voted "FOR massive tax giveaways for millionaires, but now he's voting AGAINST extending unemployment insurance." Another criticized the sources from which Perry got his campaign funding, concluding that taking money from PACs and the pharmaceutical and insurance industries made Perry someone who voted for "corporations and special interests, not for us." Still another, this one directed toward voters of color, highlighted statements Perry had made that systemic racism does not exist. An additional one of DePasquale's mailers provided a PolitiFact fact check "exposing Scott Perry's lies" related to his statements misrepresenting DePasquale's [lack of] support for "socialized medicine, the Green New Deal, and defunding the police." In some ways, this mailer was the most nationalized, as it refuted claims we referenced earlier in Perry's mail when he attempted to connect DePasquale to policies supported by Pelosi, Ocasio-Cortez, and other House Democrats.

Direct mail paid for by outside groups in support of Perry contained a mix of localization and nationalization. Mail from Americans for Prosperity is neither particularly localized nor nationalized, but instead is more vague, arguing that Perry will "fight for economic recovery" and "ensure you can keep your health care" while electing DePasquale will lead to "higher taxes, less opportunity" and will facilitate "government-run health care." Mail from the National Rifle Association (NRA) specifically nationalizes the issue of gun ownership, saying that "billionaire Michael Bloomberg and the anti-gun elite are trying to buy this Pennsylvania election . . . and eliminate your right to self-defense by implementing Nancy Pelosi's radical gun control." The NRA mailer also contains a postscript reminding voters to vote for Donald Trump for president and (Republican) Heather Heidelbaugh for Pennsylvania attorney general.

AFSCME mailers in support of DePasquale's candidacy focused on the perceived failings of Scott Perry, showing differences between the candidates on issues of drug costs, health care coverage of preexisting conditions, and the COVID-19 response. Planned Parenthood sent direct mail focused on health care, and it placed pictures of both Joe Biden and DePasquale on the mailer, saying the two candidates were "the best leaders for our health care." Finally, the Pennsylvania State Education Association sent a postcard with a photo of a Pennsylvania teacher, identified as the recipient's neighbor, encouraging the recipient to vote for DePasquale as a "pro-education candidate who supports safe, healthy schools and increased education funding." Thus, mail paid for by Perry and the Republican Party was highly nationalized, especially when it attacked DePasquale. Mailers from DePasquale and the

Democratic Party, on the other hand, were more localized, while mail from outside groups was mixed.

In terms of social media,[2] across all platforms, Perry attempted to nationalize DePasquale by criticizing party elites in the Democratic Party. As he did in direct mail and in televised campaign ads, on social media Perry frequently claimed that DePasquale would be supportive of the national Democratic Party agenda, which he argued was embodied by figures like Speaker Nancy Pelosi and Representative Alexandria Ocasio-Cortez. While Perry most often criticized Pelosi, and other national Democrats, he also occasionally nationalized his own campaign by announcing his allegiance to and support for President Trump's statements, actions, and policy positions—something he rarely did in other campaign materials. On November 1st, Perry posted photographs on his campaign Facebook site of himself at a crowded Trump rally with hundreds of "Make America Great Again" signs behind him, alongside photos of sparse crowds at a socially-distanced Democratic rally, with the caption "Anyone else sensing an enthusiasm gap?" (@ScottPerryForCongress, 11/1/20). Despite the fact that the rally Perry attended was with President Trump, Perry did not tag Trump or use Trump's name in the post. Perry also regularly retweeted posts by other members of the U.S. House Republican caucus, like Representative Steve Scalise, criticizing Pelosi and other Democratic House members.

Overall, there were few occurrences of localized issues on Perry's social media feeds, except for when he criticized Democratic governor Tom Wolf for Wolf's handling of COVID-19 or talked about how COVID has affected Pennsylvania. Perry's social media posts were much more about "our nation" than about Pennsylvania specifically. The only content that is consistently focused on local issues on his social media are his weekly Facebook videos, where he talks about what issues are most prominent in the district. Even though these also have a national tone to them, talking about Washington and what was going on in the House, Perry did often tie this content back to what was happening in PA-10.

DePasquale's social media and web presence shows signs of both nationalization and localization. The biography on his campaign website notes that DePasquale is "dedicated to reforming Washington and focusing on the issues that are most important to people in Pennsylvania's Tenth Congressional District" and that he is "going to fight for people here at home" (Eugene DePasquale for Congress 2020). In nearly all his social media, even in posts about national issues like COVID, Social Security, and health care, DePasquale attempted to find a local angle on the issue, talking about how the issue affects local people or businesses in PA-10. A tweet from the DePasquale campaign on October 15th reads, "#PA10 residents like Mike rely on protections for pre-existing conditions to get the health care coverage they need. @RepScottPerry voted 12 times to take those protections away and supports a lawsuit that could eliminate them in the middle of the COVID crisis. We deserve better." This tweet appeared alongside a video of Mike telling his personal story. DePasquale did nationalize his own campaign via social media, however, by touting endorsements from national figures and organizations; the most prominent was the endorsement DePasquale received from Pete Buttigieg, which he posted multiple times across different platforms, while also sharing posts related to a fundraising event he hosted alongside Buttigieg.

While DePasquale largely focused on local angles of issues when promoting his own agenda, he did nationalize Perry when attacking and criticizing his opponent. DePasquale's social media paints Perry as a Washington elite and insinuates that Perry is someone whose views do not align with the average south central Pennsylvania voter. For example, in a Twitter post on October 10th, including a clip from their October debate, DePasquale says that "in Washington, [Perry] sold us out." Two days later, the DePasquale campaign posted an advertisement talking about how Perry takes money from big industries, saying he cares about his job and not "us." Additionally, in another Twitter post that included an advertisement clip for himself, DePasquale states that "#PA10 families face an uphill climb while Washington politicians are busy tending to the corporations and political insiders that bankroll their campaigns. In Congress, you can count on me to have your back because I'll never forget where I came from" (@DePasqualePA). DePasquale also posts pictures of himself door-knocking, attending local sporting events, and talking to district voters at the polls. These local events are often accompanied by a caption about the importance of making all voters' voices heard. These posts, along with his criticism of Perry in advertisement clips and other social media content, show that DePasquale is trying to nationalize Perry to be a Washington elite who forgets about the district and the voters' needs, and is localizing himself to seem like someone who knows the place and the people and will stick up for them. Overall, with respect to social media, DePasquale had more localized content than did Perry, but his accounts still included many posts about national issues, organizations, and political figures.

While COVID-19 limited the number of in-person rallies held by the candidates, the PA-10 race featured two debates between DePasquale and Perry, each hosted by and broadcast on local television channels. The first debate took place on Thursday, October 8th, and the second three weeks later, on Thursday, October 29th. The debates featured many of the same talking points from each candidate. Most content was localized in the sense that the candidates focused on their own backgrounds and experiences, and on the ways in which even more nationalized issues, like #BlackLivesMatter, trade relationships with China, Social Security, and election law, related to residents of south central Pennsylvania.

In the rare moments when DePasquale did make more nationalized references, he did so by tying Perry to a Washington, D.C. that is broken, saying things like "Congressman Perry and all of Washington are simply out of touch" (ABC27, part 1, 2:14), and "It is clear that we have a capital city, Washington, DC, that is not looking out for everyone" (WGAL8, part 3, 10:02). An additional part of DePasquale's campaign narrative was to attempt to paint Perry as out of touch with the average constituent in PA-10. He did so by referencing Perry's membership in what he called the "far-right Freedom Caucus," saying, "He's the most conservative member in the entire congressional delegation. He actually believes in more partisanship" (ABC27, part 1, 12:35).

When Perry focused on national issues, which he did more than DePasquale, he did so by trying to tie DePasquale to more liberal members and ideas present within the Democratic Party, saying things like "Well, my opponent can say that all day long [that he does not support defunding the police], but we are well aware of people, even in this state, that said they were going to do one thing when they ran and then did another thing when they went to Washington, DC. And I will just tell you this . . . the policy that's coming out of Washington, DC, run by the squad—AOC, Rashida Talib— are exactly the ones who defund the police. So when he goes to Washington, DC, he's going to fall in line" (ABC27, part 2, 10:12). Perry also specifically tried to tie DePasquale to the Democratic majority and House Speaker Nancy Pelosi, saying, "But this is the problem when you have a far-left Speaker like Nancy Pelosi and you've got a lapdog in my opponent who's going to go down there and support her" (ABC27, part 2, 12:00), and "Speaker Pelosi, Nancy Pelosi did a fundraiser for my opponent down in Philadelphia because he knows that her policies and the things she believes in are not going to sell very well in this district" (WGAL8, part 1, 18:08)

Finally, in speaking with a local journalist who covers Pennsylvania state government, politics, and policy, his first comment with respect to nationalization in PA-10 was "It is no exaggeration to say that . . . the nationalization is off the charts there. The DCCC and NRCC are active and on the ground at all times" (Journalist Interview, 2:10).

Overall, we draw three conclusions about nationalization in PA-10 based on the evidence we gathered. First, we argue that, to an extent, spending from national political parties and outside groups nationalized this race, even if the issue content of ads and direct mail was more localized, especially because many of the outside groups advertising in PA-10 also supported candidates in other parts of the country. Second, both candidates touted their own accomplishments and policy positions in a highly localized manner, while talking about their opponents in a more nationalized way. Our third takeaway, however, is that the race featured asymmetric nationalization; DePasquale was the more nationalized candidate because Perry and the Republican Party made him such. While some of DePasquale's attacks on Perry were critical of Perry's response to more localized issues, nearly all the attacks mounted by Perry attempted to tie DePasquale to a "radial left" agenda directed by Nancy Pelosi, Bernie Sanders, and Alexandria Ocasio-Cortez. Interestingly, we observed no attempts on the part of Perry or the Republican Party to associate DePasquale with Democratic presidential nominee Joe Biden.

State House District 105

In many ways, the campaign in HD-105 mirrored the race in PA-10. Both races featured Republican incumbents who had won their previous elections by small margins, both races were expected to be highly competitive, and both races were targeted by political parties and groups as contests that might influence the overall partisan control of the legislative bodies. Perhaps not surprisingly, then, many of the conclusions we draw about nationalization in PA-10 also hold true in HD-105. Throughout the contest, $1.4 million was spent on television advertisements, 74% of which was paid for by the candidates or by the candidates in coordination with their political party. Table 6.3 shows spending and favored candidate by sponsor.

The content of the ads aired by the candidates and their coordinated party committees was localized when the candidates were talking about themselves, but it was more nationalized when the candidates were attacking their opponents. In HD-105, in ads paid for by the Andrew Lewis campaign promoting his own candidacy, Lewis talked about "protecting taxpayers and standing with law enforcement." When attacking Brittney Rodas, Lewis

TABLE 6.3 TELEVISION ADVERTISING IN HOUSE DISTRICT 105

Sponsor	Type of Group	Amount Spent	Favored Candidate
Lewis for PA HD-105	Candidate	$355,209	Lewis
PA HDCC/Rodas	Coordinated (candidate and party)	$691,680	Rodas
Commonwealth Leaders Fund	Outside group	$62,351	Lewis
Pennsylvania Fund for Change	Outside group	$298,675	Rodas

Source: AdImpact.

claims that her "radical special interest" supporters are lying about him and that Rodas will support their agenda. In another ad, Rodas is labeled as a "career insider." We argue that the language of "political insider," "career insider," and "liberal" and explicit statements like "Rodas *and her allies* will defund police, oppose property tax reform, support more spending, and higher taxes and job killing policies" (italics added for emphasis) nationalize the message, even when the issues (like property tax reform) are more local in nature.

In terms of direct mail sent in HD-105, the vast majority we collected was in support of Lewis but was paid for by the Republican Party of Pennsylvania or by interest groups. The only literature that came from Lewis himself was a constituent newsletter. Mailers from the Republican Party in support of Lewis were highly localized, touting Lewis's background in the U.S. Army and National Guard and as a small-business owner. While the issues discussed are somewhat national in nature, they are not explicitly so. Instead, the accomplishments listed are more general, such as Lewis "responsibly addressing COVID-19, putting taxpayers first, working to safely restart our economy, fighting for better healthcare and education, protecting our country, and creating jobs." Most of the fliers coming from the Republican Party were not solely supportive of Lewis, but instead had one side highlighting Lewis's accomplishments and the other side attacking Rodas. In interesting ways, the issues used to attack Rodas were more nationalized than the issues promoting Lewis. The fliers tended not to mention Washington, D.C., or any federal political figures, but instead attempted to use Rodas's time as a Pennsylvania congressional staffer to paint her as a "political party and government insider." The most explicitly nationalized references came when Lewis and the GOP referred to Rodas's campaign funds, which they said came from "liberal California mega donors" and "dark money special interests" that support "higher taxes on families, government takeover of healthcare, and defunding our police."

Direct mail paid for by interest groups supporting Lewis was also mostly localized. The NRA focused exclusively on gun rights, touting Lewis's "proven record of fighting to protect our Second Amendment rights"; but like the NRA mailer supporting Perry, the one for Lewis also encouraged voters to cast ballots for Trump and Heidelbaugh (for attorney general of Pennsylvania). A door-knocker from Make Liberty Win talked about very localized issues, including "end[ing] the rainwater tax" and defending Dauphin County against "looting and violence." The Commonwealth Leaders Fund also followed this pattern, using local issues to highlight their support for Lewis, but then connecting Rodas to other political figures, whether in Harrisburg or in Washington. On one of its fliers, this group put a black-and-white photo of Rodas shaking hands with Nancy Pelosi, while saying that Rodas "supported forced closure of businesses," was "backed by politicians who worked to keep our economy closed," and "support[ed] more taxes and higher spending." The only direct mail we were able to collect in support of Rodas's campaign was from the group End Citizens United, which focused its efforts solely on attacking Lewis for attempting to "create a commission that would change the rules and undermine the democratic process."

Clear differences existed between the two campaigns' uses of social media, as Rodas had far more posts and different platforms across which she posted regularly. Most of Lewis's social media content consisted of general posts about patriotism, his experience in and respect for the military, and the United States in general. While patriotism might be viewed as a national issue, it is also a personal one for Lewis, given his military background and experience. When sharing content, Lewis occasionally engaged with national issues, often characterizing Black Lives Matters protestors as "rioters," posting about voting in person versus by mail, and affirming his support for the nomination of Amy Coney Barrett to the U.S. Supreme Court. He also nationalizes his campaign in much the same way Perry does, by criticizing the campaigns of national Democrats. For example, on Facebook Lewis shared a *Fox News* video titled "Biden Campaign Faces Backlash for TV Ad Depicting Michigan Tech CEO as Struggling Bar Owner," and he says that "*Actual* struggling bar and restaurant owners know exactly who's responsible for the harsh lockdowns driving them out of business—and spoiler alert, it's not Donald Trump" (@AndrewLewisPA, 10/20/20).

In other instances, Lewis localized national issues to be more specific to Pennsylvania and his district. For example, one Facebook post reads, "Here in the 105th, we value our American freedoms, a government that is limited and efficient, low taxes, world class schools, and communities that are safe and strong. Our way of life is on the ballot next Tuesday. Five more days" (@AndrewLewisPA, 10/29/20). Occasionally, Lewis took an explicitly national post from an outside organization and localized it to his own district. On Facebook on October 22nd, he shared an advertisement from People For the American Way talking about police brutality, but he states that the ad "sinks to a new low [Lewis has] never seen in our local politics. . . . The police in 'our community' are from the Lower Paxton Township Police Department and PA State Police—they're some of the best." Overall, Lewis's goal appeared to be similar to Perry's: to discuss local issues when promoting his own candidacy, while attacking his Democratic opponent by trying to connect her to Biden or criticizing Democrats as a party. In fact, Lewis shared multiple posts from Scott Perry, including the advertisement comparing DePasquale to Alexandria Ocasio-Cortez and Bernie Sanders.

When Brittany Rodas's social media feeds are examined, her campaign appears nationalized, as she both aligned herself with national Democratic figures and expressed her criticism for national Republican figures. She attempted to associate Lewis with national Republican figures, including, but not limited to, Donald Trump. In a tweet sent on August 28th, Rodas writes, "If you don't want to re-elect Trump then don't support State Legislators who embrace him" (Rodas Twitter, 8/28/20), explicitly connecting voting for Lewis to voting for the Republican agenda up and down the ballot. Additionally, in a tweet about Lewis's finances, she states, "This cycle my opponent has raised $385,000. Of that, $150,000 has come from Betsy DeVos-backed private charter interests" (Rodas Twitter, 10/25/20). The mention of Betsy Devos is a clear indication that Rodas is vilifying Lewis for taking money from sources tied to the national Republican Party.

Unlike most of the other candidates we followed during the 2020 campaign cycle, Rodas not only talked about national issues when attacking her opponent but also evoked national issues and partisans when promoting her own candidacy. Rodas was endorsed by many national figures and organizations, such as Joe Biden, Barack Obama, Planned Parenthood, and EMILY's List, and she regularly shared those endorsements on all her social media platforms. Beyond the sharing of endorsements, she often retweeted or quoted tweeted posts from the Trump campaign and other national Republican figures, expressing her disagreement and criticism while commenting favorably on retweets of posts from the Biden campaign. If there was any question that she was running a nationalized campaign, Rodas confirmed it just a few days before Election Day by sharing a photo of herself on Instagram after voting. In the post, she was wearing a face mask that reads "VOTE" and holding up a sign for the Biden campaign (@rodasforpa, 10/23/20). Although there were certainly some social media posts that localized the Rodas campaign—specifically, images and posts of her door-knocking in the district throughout the campaign season—the majority of her social media content is about national issues and figures: posts about herself and her campaign and about her opponent and his campaign.

While no debates between Lewis and Rodas took place, we were able to speak with a campaign staffer from the Rodas campaign. We first asked what issues the campaign focused on, hoping to gain an understanding of whether the Rodas campaign saw itself as appealing to voters based on local issues or on more national ones. The Rodas campaign indicated their three primary issues were COVID-19 response, health care, and education, which they believed to be "standard for a state legislative campaign," especially one in Pennsylvania due to the Commonwealth's "lack of prescription drug price caps . . . [and the fact that] Dauphin county has some of the most unequal schools in Pennsylvania" (Rodas Campaign Interview, 2:29). With respect to the COVID response, the Rodas campaign chose to focus on this issue specifically because Lewis appeared in the Capitol four days before he began experiencing "mild flu-like symptoms" and six days before testing positive for COVID-19 (Gabriel 2020). From the very beginning of our interview, the Rodas campaign highlighted the ways in which even more national issues applied to the local district they were seeking to represent.

While the issue focus of the campaign was highly localized, the Rodas campaign did try to coordinate GOTV efforts with both the DePasquale and Biden campaigns in the district. However, they were somewhat frustrated with what they felt was the state Democratic Party's lack of interest in down-ballot races. The Rodas campaign referenced specific instances of phone calls being made by the Pennsylvania Democrats where they reportedly asked, "Can Joe Biden and Kamala Harris count on your support?" followed by "What's your vote plan?" (Rodas Campaign Interview 7:02) without ever mentioning even the names of down-ballot Democrats running for the U.S. House or the Pennsylvania Assembly.

The local journalist we spoke with saw evidence of nationalization largely coming from outside groups attempting to help Pennsylvania Democrats take control of the Assembly as a whole. Our source noted that "Planned Parenthood is in [spending money in PA] . . . EMILY's list is now in, and Everytown is now spending money" (Journalist Interview, 15:34). He continued, saying that Rodas was mentioned specifically in at least two of the three groups' press releases about their involvement and spending of money on Pennsylvania Assembly races. In terms of issues highlighted by the Rodas and Lewis campaigns, our source noted that due to the pandemic, issues were probably a lot more nationalized than they otherwise would have been. Overall, then, nationalization in PA-105 worked similarly to that in PA-10 in that the candidates themselves tried to emphasize local issues and their personal experiences. The Republican incumbent, Lewis, like Scott Perry, attempted to tie his Democratic challenger, Rodas, to national political figures and "political insiders," again resulting in asymmetric nationalization of the two candidates.

State House District 199

Turning now to HD-199, the first thing we note is that there was significantly less campaign activity in this contest than in the other two races we followed. Neither campaign aired any television advertisements, direct mail was minimal, and there were no debates. We were able to speak with a representative from the Crossley campaign, however, which helped us understand Crossley's approach to the campaign.

As mentioned, direct mail in the PA-199th was negligible. Crossley sent just one postcard, while Gleim sent a constituent newsletter and one piece of campaign direct mail. In Crossley's postcard, she simply listed a host of issues she would work on if elected. These were relatively vague, so they are neither national nor local, except for a reference about working toward fair redistricting in Pennsylvania. Otherwise, her issues were "improved nursing home care and staffing; equality, fair representation, respect; strengthen environmental protections; school funding & school safety; support universal health care; and end homelessness."

Gleim's campaign mailer touted her "honest and trusted leadership" while focusing on local issues of "keeping our families safe, representing your interests and values in Harrisburg, and supporting small businesses." She specifically played up her accomplishments during the COVID-19 pandemic, focusing on helping her "constituents in receiving federal and state aid, while fighting for transparency, accountability, and responsibility" and her authoring of legislation that would have provided "liability protections for farmers, businesses and healthcare providers impacted by the pandemic." Gleim's constituent newsletter was almost entirely about the implications of the COVID-19 pandemic for her district and her efforts to support her constituents, small-businesses owners, and children and families affected by the pandemic. The newsletter is critical of Democratic governor Tom Wolf, but it makes no reference to the federal government or to any national political figures outside of referring to federal funding such as the Coronavirus Aid, Relief, and Economic Security (CARES) Act.

As with other forms of campaign activity, Gleim and Crossley had less social media activity than the other candidates we followed. Gleim posted only on Facebook throughout the election season, using both her public personal account and her official PA State Representative webpage, while Crossley had social media accounts on more platforms and built an email listserv that she used to distribute a weekly "Walk With Janelle" newsletter.

Gleim used her campaign Facebook page mainly for sharing her endorsements. On her official state legislative Facebook page, she posted about specific legislation being considered by the General Assembly, mostly about farming and agricultural issues, which are of particular interest to her. Gleim also posted about the impact of COVID-19 and efforts in the legislature to provide economic relief to small businesses, but she did so in a way that was explicitly local, saying things like "Déjà vu: House Democrats flip their votes—this time to kill legislation to save our restaurant industry, which is so crucial to the Carlisle area economy!" (@RepGleim, 10/21/20). Gleim frequently criticized Democratic governor Tom Wolf's handling of COVID-19 in Pennsylvania. She rarely referenced Trump or Biden, either explicitly or implicitly, but occasionally she posted about a national political figure, like Ben Carson or Karen Pence, visiting the Commonwealth. In one of the only posts to explicitly reference Trump, she shared a photo of a "Trump train" that someone had created on their farm (post since deleted).

Despite Crossley's social media presence on multiple platforms, her posts were relatively limited, likely due to the minimalist nature of her campaign overall. When her social media content was most localized, Crossley posted advertisements for and recordings of her weekly "Listening Hours," where she heard directly from constituents about their concerns. Another example of explicitly local content from the Crossley campaign was a tweet that came a week before the election, outlining her support for the "Rural Bill of Rights for Pennsylvania," in which she said, "Rural people are too often ignored in Harrisburg" (@JanelleForPA199, 10/31/20). Overall, however, most of her social media posts were broad, talking about national issues like COVID-19, health care, and voting security and the election; these posts rarely mentioned Pennsylvania or HD-199 specifically. She also shared and retweeted a significant amount of her content from Democratic presidential nominee Joe Biden and the Democratic National Committee.

In our interview with a representative of the Crossley campaign, we found that the campaign focused almost exclusively on issues that were personal to the candidate herself. The Crossley campaign talked about the importance of advocating for nursing home residents, especially with respect to ensuring an appropriate number of staff as well as making sure the staff were treating nursing home residents with respect and care. "School funding and school safety is a big issue . . . homelessness is a big issue . . . infrastructure is another big thing . . . and environmental issues" (Crossley Campaign Interview, 21:27). Regarding environmental issues, the campaign mentioned the Green New Deal (Crossley Campaign Interview, 21:41), but also talked about environmental concerns related to "all the warehouses that are going up and all the trucks that are sitting around idling" (Crossley Campaign Interview, 21:32). The campaign emphasized, however, that the issues the candidate cares about are not what is most important—that the campaign needs "to know the concerns of the people" (Crossley Campaign Interview, 23:10) and that the "people's platform needs to come first" (Crossley Campaign Interview, 23:27). When asked specifically whether the campaign was trying to focus on local issues, the campaign member replied, "Yeah, absolutely" (Crossley Campaign Interview, 24:11).

In addition to running a very local campaign with respect to issues, the Crossley campaign, like the Rodas campaign, felt as though they were doing much of the work of campaigning (GOTV, door-knocking, etc.) without much support from the national or even county-level political parties. The Crossley campaign specifically noted difficulties they had getting their door-hangers distributed by up-ballot campaigns, but they did note that Crossley had endorsed Eugene DePasquale and vice versa (Crossley Campaign Interview, 15:41). The Carlisle, Pennsylvania Democrats did some door-knocking in the borough of Carlisle, which is the most Democratic part of PA-199, dropping off door-hangers with the names of the Democratic candidates in all seven races that would appear on the ballot on November 3rd—including Joe Biden and Kamala Harris, Eugene DePasquale, and Janelle Crossley.

Finally, in talking with us about this race, the local journalist echoed our findings that Gleim and Lewis attempted to make the race more local, especially with respect to their own candidacies. However, he again noted that while normally in Pennsylvania Assembly races, "it's schools, it's jobs, it's taxes . . . [this year] at both levels [congressional and assembly] the pandemic just swallowed everything (Interview 3, Journalist, 20:20).

2020 Election Results

All three Republican incumbents we followed—Perry, Lewis, and Gleim—won their respective races, and outpaced President Trump's vote percentage in their respective districts, while Democratic challengers underperformed against Joe Biden. Table 6.4 presents these results; in PA-10, Perry received 53.2% of the vote, while Trump received 50.6%. Biden lost the district by 3 points, earning 47.6% of the vote, but DePasquale earned just 46.6% of the votes cast in the district.

TABLE 6.4 COMPARISON OF 2020 PRESIDENTIAL ELECTION RESULTS WITH TENTH CONGRESSIONAL DISTRICT AND PENNSYLVANIA 105TH AND 199TH STATE HOUSE DISTRICT RESULTS

Tenth Congressional District	Trump (R)	Perry (R)	Difference	Biden (D)	DePasquale (D)	Difference
	50.6%	*53.2%*	Perry +2.6	47.6%	46.6%	DePasquale −1.0
PA 105th State House District	Trump (R)	Lewis (R)	Difference	Biden (D)	Rodas (D)	Difference
	48.3%	*51.7%*	Lewis +3.4	*49.9%*	48.1%	Rodas −1.8
PA 199th State House District	Trump (R)	Gleim (R)	Difference	Biden (D)	Crossley (D)	Difference
	57.5%	*63.5%*	Gleim +6.0	40.7%	36.4%	Crossley −4.4

Sources: Authors' calculations from data accessed on March 30, 2021: Cumberland County: https://www.ccpa.net/3135/Election-Results; Dauphin County: https://www.dauphinc.org/election; York County: https://yorkcountypa.gov/voting-elections/elections-results.html.
Note: Winning percentages are in bold italics.

The closest race of the three was in HD-105, where Lewis defeated Rodas by just 3.5 percentage points (51.7% to 48.1%). In HD-105, however, Biden garnered a higher percentage of votes than did Trump (49.9% to 48.3%). Lewis overperformed against Trump's vote percentage by 3.4 percentage points, while Rodas earned 1.8 percentage points less of the vote than did Biden in the district. Finally, in HD-199, Gleim was reelected by nearly 30 points (63.5% to Crossley's 36.4%). Not only was the vote differential between these two candidates the largest we observed; the degree to which they differed from the presidential candidates was also larger than in the other districts. Gleim earned 6.0 percentage points more of the vote than did Trump, while Crossly underperformed against Biden's vote total by 4.4 percentage points.

Discussion

Considering all our evidence—television advertisements, social media, direct mail, debates and rallies; interviews with campaign officials; and the election results themselves—we find that the PA-10 race between incumbent Republican Scott Perry and Democratic challenger Eugene DePasquale had aspects of both localization and nationalization, but was significantly more nationalized when the tone was negative and the candidates were attacking their opponents than when they were talking about themselves in a positive light. The Perry campaign was more negative overall, and it also likely faced more incentives to attempt to nationalize DePasquale than the DePasquale campaign did to nationalize Perry. Perry was, and is, an incumbent in the minority political party in the U.S. House, and in nearly all his campaign materials he touted his ability to stand up to the agenda of the Speaker of the House and other House Democrats while arguing that his opponent in the campaign would simply be a "lap dog" or a rubber stamp for the majority party agenda. Given the proclivity of a sizable percentage of American voters to support divided government (Frankovic 2020), being a minority party incumbent seems to lend itself to a strategy of attempting to nationalize one's opponent.

One question we need to consider, however, is whether it matters what party the president belongs to. For instance, would Perry have had the same incentives to nationalize his opponent if President Trump had been a Democrat rather than a Republican? We think yes, and in fact the incentives to nationalize might be even stronger if an incumbent is working to stand up to a majority party that controls even more aspects of government. Perry made only ancillary references to President Trump during his campaign, and he likely could have run a campaign very similar to the one he did, regardless of who the president was or what party the president was part of. Perry's strategy relied on touting his own accomplishments and policy positions through a local lens and attacking his opponent through a more national lens. We found it interesting, however, that in Perry's campaign materials he never mentioned Joe Biden, the Democratic presidential nominee, by name or by image. Overall, Perry's nationalization of DePasquale was not about Biden at all; instead, it was about House Democrats and the "radical-left" agenda. When a non-House figure, like Bernie Sanders, was pictured, it was because he more embodies the "radical-left." Featuring Biden instead could have created cognitive dissonance with respect to ideology.

Another factor affecting the nationalization of a race is the overall tone of the race. In contests, or aspects of contests, that are more negative, there tends to be more nationalization. We saw evidence of this particularly in PA-10. Perry was much more negative and also nationalized in his attacks of DePasquale in his direct mail pieces and television advertisements and on his social media accounts than he was in debate performances. Although Perry still attempted to tie DePasquale to national Democratic figures in the two televised debates, he did so in a less explicit, less negative fashion during the debates than in other contexts.

Looking at the Pennsylvania House races, we see that another factor leading to nationalization of a race is competitiveness, especially when possible control of the legislative chamber is at stake. Democrats across the country targeted the Pennsylvania General Assembly as a legislature that could potentially be flipped from Republican to Democratic control during 2020, which meant that Democratic challengers raised more money than Republican incumbents did. Of the thirteen state legislative candidates who raised over $1,000,000, ten of them were Democratic challengers (FollowTheMoney .org 2021). The national influence in HD-105 could also be seen in Rodas's endorsements and the materials she highlighted on her social media feeds. The nationalization in this contest, however, was not reciprocated by the Lewis campaign. Lewis ran largely a localized campaign, especially when promoting his own candidacy. His social media presence was limited, and in his direct mail and television ads he rarely mentioned his partisanship, instead focusing on his personal background and his support for owners of small businesses.

HD-199 featured very little explicit campaigning, as party registrations and recent historical election results suggested the race was safely in the hands of the Republican Party. Democratic challenger Janelle Crossley simply did not have the resources that Brittney Rodas did; no television ads aired on her behalf, and we believe she sent just one piece of direct mail to her voters. Crossley communicated with her supporters largely through her weekly newsletter, "Walk With Janelle," which she promoted on her social media accounts. Republican incumbent Barb Gleim also did not campaign aggressively; she did not air any ads, and the only mail we have evidence of her campaign sending is a constituent newsletter, which is not explicitly campaign material.

Even though the Republican Party controlled the Pennsylvania General Assembly, the strategy pursued by the Lewis campaign was similar to that undertaken by Perry. Both incumbents attempted to tie their Democratic opponents to their copartisans in the federal government rather than focusing on the specific policy positions of the candidates they were running against. This is not wholly unlike Trump's strategy, which often seemed to talk more about the more liberal members of the Democratic Party (AOC, "the squad", etc.) and not talk specifically about Biden. From an ideological perspective, though, perhaps this makes sense: Biden and DePasquale, in particular, both ran as moderates, and it was more appealing for Republican candidates to try to tie their Democratic challengers to more ideologically extreme members of the Democratic Party.

Finally, we see some evidence of a relationship between professionalization and nationalization of campaigns, but the relationship is complicated by the competitiveness of the contest. In races that are competitive, and especially when the outcome of one race might affect party control of the legislative body overall, the campaign is also more likely to be more professional because more money comes into the race. With just the races we observed, we are unable to disentangle the relationship between competitiveness, professionalism, and nationalization, but we suspect the relationship is nonlinear. We would argue that campaigns that are underresourced have no choice but to be localized; they cannot afford coordinated efforts that would permit nationalization, nor are they taken seriously by national actors. However, campaigns that are highly professionalized might also find reasons to be more localized, because they want to control their own narrative rather than being identified only by what partisans at the elite level are saying about their political party.

Conclusion

We cannot conclude this chapter without at least briefly discussing the events that took place at the U.S. Capitol on January 6, 2021. That morning, members of Congress and the vice president gathered at the Capitol to perform their normally ceremonial task of counting the Electoral College votes. At approximately 2:15 p.m., however, a "pro-Trump mob breache[d] the Capitol, breaking windows and climbing inside the building, then opening doors for others to follow" (Tan et al. 2021). After the insurrection was quelled, and Congress resumed its business, Representative Perry was the U.S. House member who formally objected to the certification of Pennsylvania's election results. In addition to contesting the election results in the Commonwealth, he also signed his name to the contestation of the results in Arizona. As part of his objection to Pennsylvania's results, he spoke on the floor of the U.S. House, decrying the deadline by which voters had to return their absentee/mail-in ballots, the way in which the secretary of state provided guidance with respect to precanvasing absentee/mail-in ballots, and the quality of the data in the Pennsylvania Statewide Uniform Registry of Electors system (U.S. Congressional Record 2021).

Two and a half weeks after the Capitol insurrection and just three days after the inauguration of President Biden and Vice President Harris, the role that Representative Perry played in former president Donald Trump's attempt to hold onto his office and invalidate results of the November 3, 2020, election became even more pronounced. According to a *New York Times* story, which Perry himself later confirmed, he introduced the former president to a "relatively obscure Justice Department official, Jeffrey Clark . . . [who] was sympathetic to Mr. Trump's view that the election had been stolen" (Benner and Edmondson 2021). It is this introduction and the subsequent conversation(s) between former president Trump, Representative Perry, and Mr. Clark that "set off a crisis in the Justice Department" (Benner and Edmondson 2021) that seemed as though it might end in the firing of acting attorney general Jeffrey Rosen. Rosen was unsympathetic to the Trump, Perry, and Clark plan that would have informed Georgia election officials that there was a Justice Department "investigation into voter fraud that could invalidate the state's Electoral College results" (Benner and Edmondson 2021).

While the evidence we presented throughout this chapter indicates that Perry campaigned on largely local issues, especially when discussing his own issue positions, his background, and his accomplishments, we cannot, after January 6th, characterize him as focused on only local issues. Even when centering his objection to the Electoral College results on the integrity of results in the Commonwealth, he was part of a larger, national plot that attempted to cast doubt on the election results of the 2020 presidential election, despite the fact that U.S. government officials deemed the November 3rd election "the most secure in American history" (Cybersecurity and Infrastructure Security Agency 2021).

APPENDIX

APPENDIX TABLE A SOCIAL MEDIA ACCOUNTS USED BY CAMPAIGNS

	Tenth Congressional District	
	Scott Perry	*Eugene DePasquale*
Facebook (government)	@repscottperry	
Facebook (campaign)	@ScottPerryforCongress	@DePasqualePA
Twitter	@RepScottPerry	@DePasqualePA
Instagram	@repscottperry	@eugene_depasquale
YouTube	Rep. Scott Perry	Eugene DePasquale for PA

	Pennsylvania House District 105	
	Andrew Lewis	*Brittney Rodas*
Facebook (government)	@RepAndrewLewis	
Facebook (campaign)	@AndrewLewisPA	@RodasforPA105
Twitter	@AndrewLewisPA	@RodasforPA
Instagram		@rodasforpa
YouTube		Brittney Sylvia-Rodas

	Pennsylvania House District 199	
	Barb Gleim	*Janelle Crossley*
Facebook (government)	@RepGleim	
Facebook (campaign)	@Barbara Gleim	@JanelleforPA199
Twitter		@JanelleForPA199
Instagram		@janelleforpa199

NOTES

1. In March 2020, during the very early stages of the COVID-19 pandemic, Assistant Secretary for Health Dr. Rachel Levine moved her then ninety-five-year-old mother out of an assisted living facility (McKelvey 2020). While Perry never directly references Secretary Levine or her mother, he does "call for a federal investigation into nursing home deaths here in Pennsylvania" and indicates that he "fought for crucial COVID-19 laws that saved lives while ensuring Seniors were protected from hurtful policies."

2. For a list of all social media platforms used by the candidates and their campaigns, see Appendix Table A.

REFERENCES

ABC27. 2020. "10th Congressional District Debate" *ABC27 News*. Accessed February 15, 2021. Available at https://www.abc27.com/10th-congressional-district-debate-2020/.

Barr, Barbara. 2020. "President Donald Trump Holds Rally at Harrisburg International Airport." *WGAL News*. Accessed February 15, 2021. Available at https://www.wgal.com /article/donald-trump-holds-rally-at-harrisburg-international-airport-tonight/34170872#.

Benner, Katie, and Catie Edmondson. 2021. "Pennsylvania Lawmaker Played Key Role in Trump's Plot to Oust Acting Attorney General." *New York Times*, January 23, 2021. Available at https://www.nytimes.com/2021/01/23/us/politics/scott-perry-trump-justice -department-election.html.

Brittney Rodas for PA State Representative. 2020. "About Brittney." Accessed February 1, 2021. Available at https://rodasforpa.com/about-brittney.

Cole, John. 2020. "PA10: Perry Links DePasquale to AOC in Opening TV Ad." *Politics PA*. Accessed February 15, 2021. Available at https://www.politicspa.com/pa10-perry-links -depasquale-to-aoc-in-opening-tv-ad/95708/.

Cumberland Area Economic Development Corporation. 2015. "Largest Employers in Cumberland County Pennsylvania." Accessed February 1, 2021. Available at https:// cumberlandbusiness.com/datamap-demographics/largest-employers/.

Cumberland County PA. 2018. "Election Results, 2018-11-06, Official Summary Report." Accessed February 1, 2021. Available at https://records.ccpa.net/weblink_public/9 /edoc/1142720/Official%20Summary%20Report.pdf.

Cybersecurity and Infrastructure Security Agency. 2021. "Joint Statement from Elections Infrastructure Government Coordinating Council & the Election Infrastructure Sector Coordinating Executive Committees." *CISA*. Accessed February 15, 2021. Available at https://www.cisa.gov/news/2020/11/12/joint-statement-elections-infrastructure-gov ernment-coordinating-council-election.

Daily Kos. 2018. "Elections 2008, 2012 & 2016 Presidential Election Results for Congressional Districts Used in 2018 Elections." Accessed February 1, 2021. Available at https:// docs.google.com/spreadsheets/d/1zLNAuRqPauss00HDz4XbTH2HqsCzMe0pR8 QmD1K8jk8/edit#gid=0.

Dauphin County Pennsylvania. 2018. "General Election Results, November 6, 2018." Accessed February 1, 2021. Available at https://www.dauphinc.org/electionarchive/Pre cinct?key=23.

Eugene DePasquale for Congress. 2020. "Meet Eugene DePasquale." Accessed February 15, 2020. Available at https://eugeneforcongress.com/about.

FollowTheMoney.org. 2021. "At A Glance: Pennsylvania 2019 & 2020 Elections." Accessed February 15, 2021. Available at https://www.followthemoney.org/at-a-glance?y=2020 &s=PA.

Frankovic, Kathy. 2020. "Voters Favor Divided Government, Even Though They Didn't Vote That Way." *YouGovAmerica*. Accessed February 15, 2021. Available at https:// today.yougov.com/topics/politics/articles-reports/2020/11/16/divided-united-gov ernment-voters-poll.

Gabriel, Trip. 2020. "A G.O.P. Lawmaker Had the Virus. Nobody Told Democrats Exposed to Him." *New York Times*, May 28, 2020. Available at https://www.nytimes.com/2020 /05/28/us/politics/andrew-lewis-brian-sims-pa-house-coronavirus.html.

Janelle for PA 199. 2020. Accessed February 1, 2021. Available at https://janelleforpa199 .com/.

Marcos, Cristina. 2019. "Lawmakers Push to Block Pay Raises for Members of Congress." *The Hill*, June 7, 2019. Accessed February 15, 2021. Available at https://thehill.com /homenews/house/447490-lawmakers-push-to-block-pay-raises-for-members-of-con gress.

McKelvey, Wallace. 2020. "Health Secretary Rachel Levine's Removal of Mom from Care Home Amid Pandemic Draws Scrutiny." *PennLive*, May 14, 2020. Accessed March 31, 2021. Available at https://www.pennlive.com/news/2020/05/health-secretary-rachel -levines-removal-of-mom-from-care-home-amid-epidemic-draws-scrutiny.html.

Pennsylvania Department of State. 2018. "2018 General Election Official Results." Accessed February 1, 2021. https://www.electionreturns.pa.gov/General/OfficeResults? OfficeID=11&ElectionID=63&ElectionType=G&IsActive=0.

Pennsylvania House Republican Caucus. 2021a. "PA State Rep. Andrew Lewis, About Andrew." Accessed February 1, 2021. Available at http://www.replewis.com/about.

———. 2021b. "PA State Rep. Barb Gleim, About Barb." Accessed February 1, 2021. Available at http://www.repgleim.com/about.

Tan, Shelly, Youjin Shin, and Danielle Rindler. 2021. "Visual Timeline: How One of America's Ugliest Days Unraveled Inside and Outside the Capitol." *Washington Post*, January 9, 2021. Available at https://www.washingtonpost.com/nation/interactive/2021 /capitol-insurrection-visual-timeline/.

U.S. Congressional Record. 2021. "Proceedings and Debates of the 117th Congress, First Session." January 6, 2021. Accessed February 15, 2021. Available at https://www.congress .gov/117/crec/2021/01/06/CREC-2021-01-06.pdf.

Vote USA. 2020. "November 3, 2020, Pennsylvania General Election, Candidates for State Representative District 199, Pennsylvania." Accessed February 1, 2021. Available at https://vote-usa.org/CompareCandidates.aspx?State=PA&Election=PA20201 103GA&Office=PASTATEHOUSE199.

WGAL8 News. 2020. "WGAL Hosts Debate between Scott Perry and Eugene DePasquale." *WGAL8 News*, October 20, 2020. Accessed February 15, 2021. Available at https://www .wgal.com/article/wgal-hosts-debate-between-scott-perry-and-eugene-depasquale-us -house-10th-district/34412866#.

7

Campaigns in the Sixteenth Congressional District

How Partisan Incentives Shape Nationalization
in Northwestern Pennsylvania

Andrew Bloeser and Tarah Williams

If you were to travel through northwest Pennsylvania during election season, America's national political divisions would quickly become visible. Erie, the region's largest and most populous city, continues to be a Democratic stronghold. Yet in the small towns and rural areas that make up most of the region, pro-Trump signs, flags, and billboards have become fixtures of the landscape. Support for the Republican Party—and for President Trump in particular—has become steadfast. Northwest Pennsylvania is visibly shaped by the divisions of national-level politics.

Even so, the challenges facing northwest Pennsylvania are unmistakably wedded to a popular, place-based narrative of what this region has been and aspires to be again. Northwest Pennsylvania has long been a region defined by manufacturing, and the decline of manufacturing jobs has hit many local communities hard. Many small municipalities are facing financial hardship and struggling to identify local solutions. This economic trend may be part of a national narrative (Wasserman 2020; Gonyea 2020; Gonyea 2019; Zarroli 2016), but the consequences are profoundly local.

For candidates seeking office in this region, this confluence of nationalized, partisan politics and pressing local issues creates competing priorities. On one hand, local challenges require local solutions, and this creates an incentive for politicians to explain how they can help create a path forward. There is a reason, after all, that the adage "all politics is local" has long stood as conventional wisdom. On the other hand, there are also clear incentives for calling attention to the national, partisan conflicts. When many people think about politics, they think about conflicts between the two major parties at the national level (Hopkins 2018). Elections for state office and even for congressional office also tend to be low-information elections. In these situations, citizens rely on their perceptions of each national party, rather than on information about policy (Schaffner and Streb 2002). For these reasons, down-ballot candidates may have an incentive to connect their electoral fortunes to national leaders. Taken to an extreme, this incentive to nationalize campaign messages may crowd out efforts to communicate with voters about specific plans to address local issues.

The question is this: Do candidates embrace the nationalization of politics, even at the expense of messaging about specific, local policies? Or is it still the case that, despite the salience of national politics, all politics remains local? In this chapter, by observing the congressional race in Pennsylvania's Sixteenth Congressional District and the races for the Pennsylvania State House in the 6th and 9th Districts, we examine which strategies campaigns adopt. We investigate whether candidates adopt a nationalized approach to their campaigns or whether they instead try to emphasize local issues. We also attempt to discern why campaigns make the strategic choices they do. Campaigns, of necessity, have a practical interest in understanding what voters *really* want from political representatives. Because of this interest, they may have something to teach us about *how* American politics has become nationalized and what possibilities remain for a place-based approach to politics that emphasizes regional and local concerns.

Northwest Pennsylvania at a Glance: Its Problems and Its Political Trends

Northwest Pennsylvania is a region that is experiencing some significant challenges. The city of Erie, the largest city in the region, has experienced a 30% drop in population since 1960 and its population continues to decline (Mahon 2019; Rink 2019). Of the ten counties commonly considered to be part of the region, nine have experienced declines in population since 2015. This loss of population follows the decline of manufacturing jobs in metals production and locomotive production, which has occurred over a period of several decades (Wertz 2019; Northwest Pennsylvania Regional Planning and Development Commission 2016).

Related to this trend, household incomes in northwest Pennsylvania, on average, lag behind the rest of the state. As Table 7.1 highlights, the median household income in each of the electoral districts examined in this study is lower than the state median. Meanwhile, the region's unemployment tends

TABLE 7.1 DEMOGRAPHIC AND REGISTRATION CHARACTERISTICS OF PENNSYLVANIA'S 6TH AND 9TH STATE HOUSE DISTRICTS, SIXTEENTH CONGRESSIONAL DISTRICT, AND PENNSYLVANIA IN 2019

	PA 6th State House District[a]	PA 9th State House District[b]	Sixteenth Congressional District[c]	Pennsylvania[d]
Population density: people/square mile	113.1	331.1	204.8	286.1
Population white	93%	90%	89%	76%
Population black	2%	5%	4%	11%
Population Hispanic	2%	2%	3%	8%
Foreign-born	1.5%	1.6%	2.2%	7.0%
Median household income	$56,527	$47,324	$54,627	$63,463
Bachelor's degree or higher	27.6%	22.5%	28.3%	32.3%
Registered Democrat[e]	35.1%	44.9%	40.2%	46.5%
Registered Republican[e]	52.0%	43.5%	46.3%	39.0%
Registered none/other[e]	12.9%	11.6%	13.5%	14.5%

Sources:
(a) Compiled from U.S. Census Bureau. n.d. "Census Reporter: State House District 6, PA." Accessed March 4, 2021. Available at https://censusreporter.org/profiles/62000US42006-state-house-district-6-pa/.
(b) Compiled from U.S. Census Bureau. n.d. "Census Reporter: State House District 9, PA." Accessed March 4, 2021. Available at https://censusreporter.org/profiles/62000US42009-state-house -district-9-pa/.
(c) Compiled from U.S. Census Bureau. n.d. "Census Reporter: Congressional District 16, PA." Accessed March 4, 2021. Available at https://censusreporter.org/profiles/50000US4216-congressional-district -16-pa/.
(d) Compiled from U.S. Census Bureau. n.d. "Census Reporter: Pennsylvania." Accessed December 30, 2020. Available at https://censusreporter.org/profiles/04000US42-pennsylvania/.
(e) Compiled from Pennsylvania Department of State. n.d. "Voting and Election Statistics." Accessed March 4, 2021. Available at https://www.dos.pa.gov/VotingElections/OtherServicesEvents /VotingElectionStatistics/Pages/VotingElectionStatistics.aspx.

to be slightly higher than the state and national averages (Northwest Pennsylvania Regional Planning and Development Commission 2016). Although the region is also known for its connection to the thriving natural gas industry, the decline in manufacturing continues to sizably define the region's economic forecast. Accompanying these economic challenges are concerns about educational opportunities and access to affordable health care, which have long been priorities for workers experiencing job displacement and stagnant wages (Northwest Pennsylvania Regional Planning and Development Commission 2016).

The effects of the COVID-19 pandemic have also been felt across the region. Virtually all of the counties in northwest Pennsylvania experienced increases in COVID-19 cases through the summer and fall of 2020 (Dennis, Dupree, and Iati 2020; *Pittsburgh Post-Gazette* 2020). Like the people in so many places around the state and the entire country, northwest Pennsylvanians found themselves faced with both public health concerns and economic concerns related to the pandemic.

These challenges, experienced across the region, have become a recurrent focus of both Democratic and Republican campaigns in the Sixteenth Congressional District and the 6th and 9th Districts of the Pennsylvania State House.

The Sixteenth Congressional District

Since 2018, Pennsylvania's Sixteenth Congressional District has been a point of interest for both regional and national politics. In January 2018, the Pennsylvania Supreme Court ruled on a lawsuit, brought by the League of Women Voters of Pennsylvania, which alleged that the state's congressional districts had been unconstitutionally gerrymandered to favor Republican candidates. The court struck down the state's existing electoral map for its eighteen congressional districts, saying it "clearly, plainly and palpably" violated the state constitution (Wines and Gabriel 2018).

Prior to the 2018 congressional election cycle, the state redrew its district lines, and in the process created a belief among Democrats that incumbent Republican Mike Kelly could be defeated. Before being redistricted into the Sixteenth Congressional District (PA-16), Kelly, a business owner from Butler County, was first elected to represent Pennsylvania's Third Congressional District (PA-3). Historically, it had been a very safe Republican seat. The areas south of Erie in PA-3 leaned moderately to heavily Republican. Phil English, the first Republican to win PA-3 after the 2002 redistricting, averaged a 29-point margin of victory across his three consecutive electoral victories. Although Democrat Kathy Dahlkemper narrowly defeated English by 2.4 points in 2008, she served only one term. In 2010, Kelly defeated Dahlkemper by 10 points and won his next three elections in PA-3 by comfortable margins. After Kelly won reelection in 2014 by 20 points, the Democrats did not field a challenger in 2016 (Ballotpedia 2020a).

The 2018 redistricting, however, created an opportunity for Democrats when the city of Erie was concentrated in the newly redrawn Sixteenth District. This attracted a serious Democratic challenger, Ron DiNicola, who had narrowly lost a bid for Congress in 1996. In 2018, DiNicola received strong support, as predicted, in the city of Erie, while Kelly, as expected, maintained strong support from the more conservative, southern parts of the district. Although Kelly ultimately defeated DiNicola, the race was close. Kelly won by just 4 points, his narrowest electoral victory (Ballotpedia 2020b). When Kristy Gnibus, a political newcomer, mounted a challenge to Mike Kelly in 2020, she did so on the premise that a Democrat could win PA-16 by building greater support outside of Erie.

The 6th District, Pennsylvania State House

Encompassing parts of Crawford and Erie Counties, the 6th District of the Pennsylvania State House is populated by primarily small-town and rural communities whose economies have heavily depended on manufacturing. The district is also a Republican stronghold. The Republican Party has maintained control of the district since 1991, and the current Republican office-holder, Brad Roae, was first elected in 2006. Representative Roae ran unopposed by Democrats in his first two reelection bids but has encountered some electoral competition in recent years. Most notably, Democrat Pete Zimmer won 40% of the vote in 2016 despite being a first-time candidate who spent only two months campaigning. Zimmer, who ran a progressive populist campaign, received his greatest support in and around the city of Meadville, the largest and only Democratic-leaning city, in Crawford County. It is also noteworthy that Zimmer appeared to make substantial progress against powerful electoral headwinds. Although he lost the election by 20 points (Ballotpedia 2020c), Crawford County, which constitutes most of the district, voted to elect Trump president by a margin of 40 points (Politico 2016). For Democrats, this result suggested two lessons. First, Zimmer's double-digit loss signaled that the 6th District was not yet competitive, particularly in more rural areas outside of Meadville. Second, Zimmer performed better than previous Democrats and outperformed the Democrats' presidential nominee by 12 points despite a short campaign with limited outreach in rural areas. This second lesson motivated the Democrats' most recent candidate, Matthew Ferrence, to challenge Roae in 2020 with a campaign that began organizing earlier and with the importance of rural areas in mind.

The 9th District, Pennsylvania State House

Located entirely within Lawrence County, the 9th District of the Pennsylvania State House shares much in common with the 6th District. It consists of small towns and rural areas with economies that have long been connected to manufacturing. However, unlike the 6th District, the 9th District has historically elected Democrats to office, including the current incumbent, Chris Sainato of New Castle. Despite having many of the economic and demographic characteristics of districts that have flipped to Republican control (see Table 7.1), the 9th District has elected Sainato eleven times since 1995 (Ballotpedia 2020d). Even so, some evidence suggests that the district is potentially competitive for Republicans. In 2012, Republican Gary Cangey came within 2 points of defeating Sainato in a presidential election year in which Republican Mitt Romney won Lawrence County by 9 points (Politico 2012). Donald Trump won the county by a substantially larger margin—28 points—in 2016 (Politico 2016), during a cycle in which Sainato had run unopposed. This abundance of support for Trump suggested the viability of a Republican challenger in 2020.

Carol Lynne Ryan, a Trump delegate and outspoken supporter of the president, emerged as that challenger. A political newcomer, Ryan appeared to stake her candidacy on the trend toward nationalization in politics in a district that has increasingly supported Republicans at the national level. By all appearances, the 2020 election cycle provided an opportune moment for such a candidate. In 2020, President Trump once again carried Lawrence County by a wide margin, this time winning by 29 points. But Ryan was not the only candidate to run. Darryl Audia, a conservative candidate who ran as an independent, also entered the race. This provided the Democratic incumbent with two challengers who would each compete for, and ultimately divide, the conservative vote.

Examining the Possibility of Nationalized Campaigns

What Counts as Nationalization?

The central question of this chapter is whether campaigns in northwest Pennsylvania embrace the nationalization of politics as they engage with potential voters. For the purposes of our analysis, *nationalization* refers to campaign communication that does not mention local-level policy matters but instead emphasizes content that campaigns could run anywhere in the nation. This includes stating issue positions in broad terms without mentioning specific local problems.

Just as importantly, nationalized campaigning can also involve emphasis placed on the issue positions and political figures associated with the nation's two major political parties. As some foundational scholarship has noted, nationalization often occurs "when the political conflict and issues dominant at the national level are reflected in subnational competition and voter behavior" (Hopkins 2018, 22). As reported in Chapter 2, a majority of voters indicate that it is important to them that their preferred candidates in subnational elections align with the positions of their preferred presidential candidate. In this sort of political environment, embracing the national brand of one's own political party might be perceived as carrying electoral advantages. Similarly, candidates might also perceive incentives to highlight unpopular issue positions and political figures associated with their opponent's chosen party. This approach might have advantages, given the trend toward negative partisanship in the American electorate. *Negative partisanship* describes the tendency of citizens to form political opinions based on opposition to political parties they dislike (Abramowitz and Webster 2016). In either case, campaign materials that prime citizens to think about the national parties would constitute an important manifestation of nationalized politics. With respect to campaigns in northwest Pennsylvania, this approach to nationalized communication might be particularly useful for Republican candidates, given the partisan composition of the region's electoral districts.

In any case, regardless of what form nationalized communication may take and regardless of who is using this approach to communication, the central concern is this: To the extent that nationalization is occurring, it means that campaigns are forfeiting opportunities to address local-level matters in their communication with potential voters and, by extension, that voters are losing opportunities to hear about local-level issues as they select their representatives.

What Counts as Localization?

Although there are many reasons to suspect that nationalization could permeate races in northwest Pennsylvania, it also remains possible for campaigns to avoid invoking the nationalization of politics altogether. Avoiding nationalization, in fact, might even have special appeal for campaigns running in areas where their opponent's national party might be more popular. In northwest Pennsylvania, Democratic campaigns fall into this category. However, all campaigns may see the value in *localizing* their communication with potential voters to show their connection to the region and its people.

For example, campaigns can invoke the local or regional identities of potential voters. In the context of northwest Pennsylvania, these identities include a connection to industrial work, farming, and rural life. By invoking these identities, candidates are not merely noting that people have common life experiences but also signaling the values and personal character forged by those experiences. Campaigns can also localize their communication by highlighting how specific policies or policy proposals will affect a locality or region. Such policy-oriented communication could emphasize what candidates believe would be beneficial or detrimental to their locality or region; the distinguishing feature is that the content of campaign communication focuses on place-based considerations.

In our view, localized communication that features specific local policies is especially important because only this type of communication provides citizens with information about political choices that could immediately affect their region and their own lives. To the extent that subnational campaigns prioritize national-level considerations over local ones, they crowd out opportunities to convey information that citizens may not find elsewhere.

Did Campaigns in the Northwest Embrace the Nationalization of Politics?

To understand whether and to what extent campaigns engaged in nationalized communication, we primarily examined three sources of evidence: print and television advertisements[1] produced by the campaigns, remarks from candidates at public campaign events, and interviews with campaign staff about communications strategy. The first two forms of evidence give us a picture of what campaigns actually did. The third form of evidence—interviews with candidates and campaign staff—provides insight into why candidates chose to either embrace or avoid nationalization when communicating with specific audiences.

In the analysis that follows, we pay special attention to communication that focuses on "political conflict and issues dominant at the national level" (Hopkins 2018, 22), which, in practice, tends to reference conflict between the national parties. Across all of the races we examine, we find that Republican candidates—both incumbents and challengers—demonstrate a stronger tendency to nationalize their campaign communications.

Nationalization in the Sixteenth Congressional District Race

We turn first to the race for the Sixteenth Congressional District seat between Representative Mike Kelly (R) and Kristy Gnibus (D). Given that this race is for a seat in a national legislative body, one might reasonably anticipate that both candidates had abundant opportunities to engage in nationalized communication. After all, the issues addressed by the U.S. Congress are often national in scope.

In this approach to identifying nationalized communication, clear differences emerge along party lines. As anticipated, the stronger tendency to reference national-level partisanship emerged from Representative Kelly and his campaign. Several nationalized mailers produced by the Kelly campaign included photographs of Kelly with President Trump and mentioned Trump's endorsement of him. They also placed strong emphasis on issues heavily popularized by the incumbent president, including that Representative Kelly will "hold the Chinese Communists accountable for COVID-19 and the unfair trade practices that attack our workers." This comes as no surprise. Many parts of the Sixteenth Congressional District have supported Republican candidates for president in the last several election cycles and demonstrated particularly strong support for Trump. Drawing attention to Kelly's partisan credentials and his connection to the party's most prominent national figure is a rhetorical move that reflects an understanding of the district. Outside groups also drew upon national-level political narratives in their support for Kelly. Most notably, the National Rifle Association produced mailers and door hangers that emphasized his A+ rating and Gnibus's F rating on gun rights issues.

Campaign communication from the Kelly campaign was not entirely nationalized, however. Kelly made a point of demonstrating his connection to the local region in one of his campaign's most prominent television advertisements. The ad, which appeared in the weeks leading up to Election Day, featured an employee at Kelly's car dealership who has struggled with opioid addiction. The ad is narrated entirely by Kelly's employee, who recounts Kelly's willingness to give him a chance by employing him during a difficult time in his life. Although the ad does not discuss any policy proposals to address this problem, it does signal Kelly's attention to a regional problem, and his compassion for people who are struggling with addiction. It also signals the Kelly campaign's nuanced sense of nationalized politics. According to Melanie Brewer, Kelly's campaign manager, the candidate recognized that his deliberate association with President Trump carried both benefits and costs. President Trump remained a popular figure in the congressman's district, particularly with the Republican base. However, the campaign was also aware that many voters found the president's personal style to be offensive. For this reason, the campaign sought to differentiate Kelly from Trump by emphasizing Kelly's commitment to personally providing help to a resident of the district. Similarly, the campaign ran a second advertisement that features him making the case for why medicines like insulin should be affordable for everyone to whom they are prescribed. In this ad, Kelly speaks directly to the camera—and by proxy, to voters themselves—and strikes a tone of compassion for those who need help but cannot afford it.

These ads are notable given that they are likely to be among the most far-reaching modes of campaign communication and thus more likely to reach voters beyond the Republican base. The ads are also crafted in a manner that would not alienate the base. They differentiate Kelly from President Trump only in terms of personal qualities, rather than on the basis of key policy issues or core values associated with his national party. Combined with Kelly's direct mailers and mailers provided by outside groups, the ads enabled Kelly to craft an image of a compassionate version of a committed Trumpian Republican.

Kristy Gnibus's campaign, meanwhile, attempted to avoid nationalization in its campaign communication by muting Gnibus's connection to the national Democratic Party. In contrast to the Kelly campaign's approach, direct mail produced by Gnibus's campaign did not include photographs of the candidates alongside major figures of the national party, and the word *Democrat* appeared only once and in small lettering. Instead, mailers and handouts produced by the Gnibus campaign tended to focus on the candidate's personal story (such as working as a teacher in a local public school) and her commitment to lowering health care costs and creating jobs. Gnibus's mailers clearly attempted to localize her appeal to voters.

Likewise, a thirty-second spot run by Gnibus does not mention her party affiliation, and it emphasizes her personal history of overcoming adversity as a cancer survivor who has balanced working two jobs to make ends meet. Gnibus's emphasis on her hardworking character is consistent with a regional identity that emphasizes hard work and perseverance, and this likely is not an accident. Taken together with her campaign's direct-mail messaging, Gnibus consistently avoided the "political conflict and issues dominant at the national level" and instead prioritized telling her personal story in a localized manner that reflected her connection to the region.

This is consistent with her approach to interacting with potential voters at public campaign events. When fielding questions from those who attended these events, Gnibus pushed back against comparisons that linked her to a particular national figure of the Democratic Party—Representative Alexandria Ocasio-Cortez. At one event, attended primarily by progressive voters, Gnibus explicitly contrasted herself with Ocasio-Cortez, stating, "Some people say 'I'm a young woman. I'm like AOC.' I get that all the time. [But] I grew up on a farm. I am nothing like AOC." It also warrants noting that her campaign was prepared for voters to frame their political concerns in a nationalized way. A staffer on the Gnibus campaign explained that, when interacting with voters, Gnibus made an effort to explain how she differed from the party brand. She regularly drew contrasts between herself and major Democratic figures like Representative Ocasio-Cortez and House Speaker Nancy Pelosi and she emphasized her personal experiences as a mom and a schoolteacher. The staffer also expressed frustration about the ways the COVID-19 pandemic made it more difficult to communicate the differences between Gnibus and national Democratic figures. That differentiation would have been easier, the staffer argued, in a campaign environment where the candidate could engage more with voters at in-person events and reach beyond events that were predominantly attended by likely supporters.

Yet, despite attempts to distance herself from the national Democratic Party, Gnibus also encountered limits on her ability to do so. Gnibus was a first-time candidate who lacked both name recognition and the financial resources that incumbents, like her opponent, generally possess. While Gnibus spent $579,453 during the 2020 cycle, Representative Kelly was able to spend more than twice that amount, ultimately using $1,319,340 for campaign activities (OpenSecrets.org 2020). Outside money also disproportionately favored the incumbent. Representative Kelly received $341,807 in outside spending ($338,336 of it from the National Rifle Association) while outside spending for Gnibus totaled $3,785 (OpenSecrets.org 2020). This meant that Gnibus needed to rely on coordinated campaign communication with other Democratic candidates, and most notably the Biden campaign for president, to spread her name and message more broadly.

This, however, linked Gnibus to the national party and its most prominent figures in an unmistakable way. Most notably, a mailer that arrived shortly before Election Day came bundled with a mailer promoting Joe Biden. This is arguably the most prominent piece of direct mail from the Gnibus campaign, and although the material about Gnibus did not emphasize her partisan identity or include a picture with her beside Biden, the bundling with a Joe Biden mailer drew an unmistakable connection between the congressional candidate and the flag-bearer of her national party. Mailers sent by an outside group, the National Education Association, also drew a clear connection between Gnibus and Biden. These mailers did not mention any specifics about the candidates' local-level priorities. Rather, they connected the candidates to the national-level priorities of the Democratic Party. These instances of nationalized communication, however, stand in contrast with the dominant strategy of the Gnibus campaign itself.

If we pull back to examine larger patterns in the race for the Sixteenth Congressional District seat, two notable tendencies emerge. First, using the concept of nationalization adopted in this book, nationalized campaign communication emerged from both Republican and Democratic campaigns for the Sixteenth Congressional District seat and from groups that supported each candidate. Instances of communication that could have appeared anywhere in the nation emerged on both sides. Second, when it comes to the kind of nationalization that taps into "political conflict and issues dominant at the national level" (Hopkins 2018, 22), a stronger tendency emerged from the Republican campaign. Representative Kelly was aware that both he and President Trump had strong support in the southern parts of his district. He campaigned accordingly. Similarly, while running against a Republican candidate who strongly aligned with a Republican president in an area with many Republican voters, the Democratic candidate appears to have strategically avoided nationalization when possible.

Nationalization in the 6th and 9th District State House Races

Campaign communication from the candidates for state house also demonstrated some tendencies toward nationalization, particularly in instances when candidates brought partisan differences into focus. As with the Sixteenth Congressional District race, some of the strongest tendencies toward nationalization once again emerged from Republican candidates.

In the race for the 6th District house seat, incumbent Brad Roae exhibited relatively little campaign activity, but when he did, his messaging often blended an emphasis on his regional identity and his alignment with the values of the national Republican Party. Notably, during the only debate with his Democratic challenger, Roae used his opening statement to highlight his positions on several nationalized issues. He indicated that opposing tax increases, protecting gun rights, opposing abortion, and opposing illegal immigration were top priorities. But he also argued that these priorities simply reflected the preferences of his voters. Although he connected his opposition to taxes to state-level decisions, his discussion of other issues made no reference to state policy and instead echoed the positions of the national Republican Party. Similarly, Roae's discussion of state-level issues via his Facebook account also reflected his alignment with the national Republican Party. The most prominent example of this came in the context of one of the most salient issues of 2020: COVID-19. Nationally, Republicans adopted the position that COVID restrictions advocated by Democrats were too stringent and hindered national and local economies. On Facebook, Roae's position on this issue reflects where he stood on this nationalized political controversy.

Despite the candidate's frequent emphasis on national-level differences between the Republican and Democratic Parties, the Roae campaign did produce one piece of campaign communication that had a distinctively localized theme. A Roae mailer sent out just before Election Day emphasized his personal ties to the area, including that he has lived in northwest Pennsylvania for forty-two years, was an Eagle Scout in a local troop, and is a graduate of an area high school. This emphasis shows a local connection without addressing any local issues. Yet this approach also stands in contrast to the candidate's practice in public settings—as in his debate with his Democratic opponent—of emphasizing how his issue positions align with the Republican Party's national brand.

By contrast, Matthew Ferrence's campaign made a concerted effort to avoid nationalized messaging and to distance itself from the national Democratic Party. One of the most striking examples is a placard distributed at public events and door-to-door during "lit drops." The placard featured cartoons drawn by the candidate, including a caricature of the candidate himself and a drawing of the state that highlights northwest Pennsylvania. Next to the map, the cartoon contains the words "We can re-write the story of northwest Pennsylvania." The word *Democrat* appeared only once on the Ferrence placard, in small letters, and was dominated in size by the caricature of the candidate and the prominent map of northwest Pennsylvania. This instance of campaign communication clearly and deliberately had a localized, regional focus. In an interview about his run for the 6th District seat, Ferrence explained this strategy: "It's important to people that the candidate is *from here*, a person like them. . . . When you talk to more committed voters, the people who want to know who their candidates are, for them all politics is local." Importantly, the Ferrence campaign ultimately spent less than half the amount spent by the Roae campaign—$16,691.83 to $39,053—according to filings with the state (Pennsylvania Department of State, n.d.). For the Ferrence campaign, this meant thinking carefully about what to prioritize when spending limited funds. In this context, the Ferrence campaign's decision to invest its resources in messaging with a consistent regional focus suggests its strong belief in the efficacy of this approach.

Even so, when Ferrence's campaign materials turn to the candidate's policy priorities, they mention public education and affordable health care without mentioning any specific local challenges with respect to those issues. In effect, the campaign messages invoked a symbolic sense of regional identity but did not highlight any local-level policies the candidate endorsed. While specific references to regional identity were prominent, with respect to policy positions the content of the campaign materials could have appeared anywhere in the nation, even if it consistently avoided invoking conflicts between the political parties at the national level.

Ferrence was perhaps even more aggressive in his effort to differentiate himself from the national Democratic Party during his public debate with Roae. Ferrence's opening statement laid his orientation to partisan politics bare: "I am talking to you tonight not as the Democrat representative of the district, but to be the representative for all of the district." In a later interview, Ferrence argued that the lack of party support also made it clear that he would need to differentiate himself. He expressed frustration that the state and national Democratic Party would "blame Appalachian and rural voters for not voting for them but they will not show up to win votes in those places." His strategy relied on countering the Democrats' national party brand and national-level party narratives. "A race like this needs to be local, it needs to disrupt partisan identification." Offering an example, he spoke of how one supporter had put up a Ferrence yard sign right next to the Trump sign that had long adorned this supporter's front lawn. For Ferrence, this admittedly atypical action by a northwest Pennsylvanian was a signal of what is possible if Democrats focus on local-level concerns rather than nationalized party messaging.

The race for the 9th District house seat also saw pronounced partisan differences in nationalized campaigning. In this race, the Democratic incumbent, Chris Sainato, faced challenges from a Republican, Lynne Ryan, and from a conservative independent, Darryl Audia. Direct mail from the Ryan campaign was heavily nationalized and included Ryan's positions on nationalized issues, such as protecting the southern border of the United States, that had no obvious connection to district-level concerns. Ryan also embraced nationalized political language popularized by President Trump, such as "America First" and "drain the Harrisburg swamp." One of Ryan's mailers prominently featured her multiple visits to the Mexican border. We were able to collect almost no evidence of localization in any of the campaign materials from the Ryan campaign, apart from a few subnational messages like "PA strong" that appeared less prominently than slogans echoing nationalized rhetoric. Ryan clearly believed in the effectiveness of this approach. She filed one campaign finance report suggesting that she loaned her campaign $12,000 (Pennsylvania Department of State n.d.), some portion of which was likely spent on campaign communication. Ryan also used a candidate debate with Representative Sainato and challenger Audia to signal her partisan position on the government response to COVID and its economic implications: "I think we need to fire the lockdown liberals that have shut our state down."[2]

Darryl Audia, for his part, also reiterated messaging about the government's COVID response that echoed the national position associated with the Republican Party and with conservatives more broadly. Audia criticized the government's response to the pandemic on both religious and economic grounds. Responding to a question about this issue from the debate's moderator, he stated, "I go to church and it just upsets me that people are not permitted to be next to each other. Now, I am going to be candid with you. I had the coronavirus, and, yes, it was not easy, but . . . I got through it and I can tell you that you shouldn't stop the world economically and let us slip so far down that people will never recover. . . . It is dictatorial to change the lives of people who worked so hard." Despite running as an independent, Audia also signaled his conservative political beliefs on his campaign website. Among his issue priorities he included protecting the rights of the unborn and keeping taxes low—nationalized issue positions long associated with American conservatism and the Republican Party.

The Sainato campaign demonstrated a more balanced approach to campaign communication. Several direct mailers from the Sainato campaign could have run anywhere in the nation and were not discernibly partisan in tone. These included mailers that stressed his commitments to affordable health care and protecting veterans' benefits, but they did not emphasize any specific problems being experienced at the local level. Affordable health care and protecting veterans' benefits are popular positions nationwide, and although recipients of these mailers could infer that health care and veterans' issues are relevant to their locality, the content of the mailer did not explicitly direct attention to this. Yet, the Sainato campaign *also* produced several mailers that prominently emphasized how the candidate had worked to bring jobs back to Lawrence County and helped constituents with issues related to health care. These were clear examples of localization, even as they touched on issues that are not unique to Lawrence County. Given that the Sainato campaign spent $125,679.94—roughly 10 times as much as his nearest competitor—it also seems possible that communication from the Sainato campaign, and its greater emphasis on specific local issues, had a broader reach in the district relative to the communication of his opponents. This emphasis on how policy affected the locality made the Sainato mailers distinctive in this race and, indeed, distinctive among all of the campaign materials examined in this study.

Turning an eye to broader patterns in the State House races, we saw two familiar patterns. First, as in the race for the region's congressional seat, Republican candidates more frequently engaged in nationalized campaign communication that had a distinctly partisan flair. This was true of both Republican incumbents and challengers. This makes sense, given the abundance of Republicans in the electorate of the 6th and 9th State House Districts.

Second, although some localized messaging was available to voters, the campaign communication that focused on northwest Pennsylvania as a region tended to focus on symbolic matters rather than specific policy issues. This is particularly true of communication via direct mail and other printed materials, which often reach the largest number of potential voters (relative to messages at campaign events and statements made at candidate debates). With the exception of Sainato's locally tailored direct mail, most direct mailers and other printed materials tended to emphasize personal connections to a locality and campaign themes that called for citizens to participate in "re-writing" the story of their region, rather than highlighting specific local issues. In this broad sense, then, regional campaigns in northwest Pennsylvania often minimized localized communication about policies when communicating with the broadest swath of voters in their districts.

When Is Localized, Policy-Focused Communication Most Likely to Occur?

From the perspective of those who want to see more attention given to local-level political issues, the evidence discussed so far provides some cause for concern. Nationalized communication is prevalent in northwest Pennsylvania, particularly for Republican candidates, who can reference a national party brand that is popular within the region. Meanwhile, when both Republican and Democratic campaigns engage in more localized forms of communication, it often tends to be in the form of symbolic references to local identities rather than specific policies. One might therefore be compelled to wonder, *Do campaigns in northwest Pennsylvania ever focus on specific local policies?*

As it turns out, nearly all of the campaigns devoted sustained attention to specific local-level matters in one specific context. When candidates addressed live audiences—and especially in the context of debates moderated by *local media*—candidates put local-level concerns in the spotlight. In these debates, moderators asked questions that allowed and encouraged candidates to talk specifically about local issues. Often it was these questions that pushed candidates to move beyond broad identity-based connections to instead discuss the details of their policy positions. In all of the debates, candidates of both parties discussed specific policies that they would prioritize and they even explained their plans for implementation. In the congressional race, candidates discussed how to bring jobs to the area. In the 6th District race, candidates discussed challenges facing local schools and universities. In the 9th District race, candidates discussed how to support local businesses and how to help the town of New Castle transition out of financial distress. These questions pushed candidates away from nationalized messages in these forums and moved candidates from symbolic localized messaging to substantive localized messaging.

Of course, as the earlier discussions in this chapter highlighted, some candidates in these debates did, independently, respond to questions by invoking the issue positions and rhetoric of their national-level party. Nonetheless, questions from journalists about local issues created a context that prioritized policy ideas for the region. The fact that local journalists could create an opportunity for candidates to direct their communication in this way suggests that local media can play an important role in helping to preserve a sense of local accountability. Unfortunately, this news comes as local media is struggling for funding (Hendrickson 2019). Moreover, this is not the kind of campaign communication that most citizens are likely to encounter, unless they are especially motivated to seek out information about subnational politics. Television ads and direct mail are much more likely to reach the average voter, which helps to tip the scale even further toward nationalized messages.

This is not to say that local media was flawless with respect to emphasizing local issues during the campaign. Interviews with campaign staff for both Kelly and Gnibus revealed that both campaigns were interested in getting more news coverage for their positions on local policies. Kelly's campaign manager reported that Kelly had a difficult time getting the local media to cover the local grants that he delivered to his district. From her perspective, because local news outlets were not covering Kelly's efforts to bring funds back to the district, campaigning on this type of local issue became more challenging. A Gnibus campaign staffer mentioned something similar, arguing that the campaign found itself talking about national themes because the media devotes more attention to them than local issues. Gnibus herself brought this up at a local forum with college students in October 2020, arguing that wind energy could be an economic boon for the area but that getting media coverage of the issue remains difficult. These reports from the campaigns underscore that they regard local media as a conduit for information that could augment the content of television ads and direct mailers. Both campaigns noted that they still talked about matters of local policy when engaging with voters during campaign events, but the lack of media coverage hindered their ability to spread their messages about local policy further.

In sum, campaigns appeared interested in seeing more regular coverage that focused on local-level considerations. They also expressed frustration with what they perceived as a drift toward nationalization in the way local media covered their campaigns. These sentiments from the congressional campaigns suggest that, although local media did create opportunities to focus on local policy issues during candidate debates, the media could do even more to focus on local-level implications, and if they did, campaigns would make use of these opportunities.

The Results of the 2020 Elections: Did Candidates' Strategies Make Sense?

As noted earlier, when it comes to nationalizing and localizing campaign communication, Republican and Democratic candidates in northwest Pennsylvania took distinctly different approaches. Republican candidates more frequently engaged in nationalized campaign communication, while Democrats were more inclined toward localized themes. Given the partisan composition of the electoral districts examined in this study, this difference in approach makes considerable sense.

As noted in Table 7.1, Republicans maintain a 46.3% to 40.2% advantage with respect to registered voters in the Sixteenth Congressional District. Although this district is not as disproportionately Republican as Representative Kelly's previous district, it is nonetheless a district in which the largest plurality of registered voters is likely to be comfortable with messaging that is in-line with the brand of the national Republican Party. As noted in Table 7.2, the Sixteenth Congressional District also heavily favored President Trump, who won 58.3% of the district's vote. If voters apply a nationalized lens to evaluate candidates (Hopkins 2018) and candidates are adapting to this pattern among voters, one would expect Kelly to win by a similar margin over Kristy Gnibus, his Democratic challenger. Indeed, this is precisely what we see. Kelly's vote share is nearly identical to Trump's. This electoral result also sheds light on the wisdom of the Gnibus campaign's strategy, which involved focusing more on the candidate's personal attributes, particularly when those attributes suggested differences with icons of her national party. As a Democrat, Gnibus ran in a district where a nationalized, partisan message could have done more harm than good.

This same pattern emerges in the 6th District race for the state house. As Table 7.1 shows, 52% of registered voters in the district are Republicans. Representative Brad Roae, a Republican incumbent in a heavily Republican area, had name recognition and a solid base of Republican support. His approach to emphasizing his positions on issues strongly associated with his national party is an approach well tailored to the majority of voters in his district. By

TABLE 7.2 COMPARISON OF 2020 PRESIDENTIAL ELECTION RESULTS WITH SIXTEENTH CONGRESSIONAL DISTRICT AND 6TH AND 9TH STATE HOUSE DISTRICT RESULTS

Sixteenth Congressional District	Trump* (R)	Kelly* (R)	Difference		Biden (D)	Gnibus (D)	Difference
	58.7%	59.3%	Kelly +0.6		39.9%	40.7%	Gnibus +0.8
PA 6th State House District	Trump (R)	Roae* (R)	Difference		Biden (D)	Ferrence (D)	Difference
	62.0%	65.4%	Roae +3.4		36.6%	34.7%	Ferrence −1.9
PA 9th State House District	Trump (R)	Ryan (R)	Difference		Biden (D)	Sainato* (D)	Difference
	61.1%	39.9%	Ryan −21.2		37.7%	50.35%	Sainato +12.65

Sources: Butler County Bureau of Elections, Crawford County Voter Services, Erie County Board of Elections, Lawrence County, Mercer County Board of Elections, and the Pennsylvania Department of State.
Note: Winning percentages are in bold italics. Incumbents are indicated with an asterisk.

contrast, Democrat Matthew Ferrence had to contend with an electorate that was inclined to vote for his opponent as soon as they saw the "R" next to his name. By Ferrence's own account, he knew that, as a Democratic candidate, to make inroads with voters he would need to "disrupt partisan identification." That disruption proved difficult, however. Voters in the 6th District widely supported Trump in 2016 and did so again in 2020. If Republican voters, in particular, applied a nationalized lens to evaluate their state house candidates, one would expect Representative Roae's vote share to be very similar to Trump's, and it is. Trump received 62% of the vote in Roae's district. Roae won reelection with 65.2% of the vote.

Meanwhile, in the 9th District house race, both the power and the limitation of nationalized politics came into view. Republican Carol Lynne Ryan ran an intensely partisan and nationalized campaign, often echoing the issue positions and rhetoric of President Trump. Although not nearly as bold in his tone, Darryl Audia, a conservative independent, also highlighted positions on nationalized issues, including the government response to COVID. For both of these candidates, this approach made sense in a district where the electorate is trending Republican. Although there are roughly equal numbers of registered Republicans and Democrats in the district, Republican presidential candidates have been winning by comfortable margins in the last several election cycles. In this context, Ryan won 39.9% of the vote despite placing almost no focus on local issues in most of her campaign communication. Audia, for his part, managed to grab 10% of the vote with relatively little campaign activity. Taken together, then, these two conservative candidates achieved nearly 50% of the vote in a context in which voters could rely on little more than partisan and ideological cues. It is difficult to imagine this occurring if not for the nationalization of politics.

Nonetheless, as noted in Table 7.2, Democratic incumbent Chris Sainato managed to win 50.4% of the vote, displaying his continued ability to win majority support in a heavily Republican area of the state. Impressively, Sainato accomplished this in a district where Trump achieved a vote share of 61.1%. The name recognition and reputation that comes with incumbency is likely one reason for Sainato's victory. Yet Sainato's approach to campaigning is also notable. Sainato largely avoided messaging that invoked the brand of his national party and instead focused on efforts related to local policy and constituency service. He avoided nationalization even as his most significant challenger ran a relentlessly nationalized campaign on the coattails of a president who was very popular in the district. The nationalization of politics was certainly present in the 9th District house race, but by standing in contrast to it, Sainato demonstrated that a localized approach to campaigning can work, even under challenging electoral conditions.

Discussion: The Power of Nationalization and the Possibility of Localized Campaigning

In northwest Pennsylvania, subnational campaigns clearly nationalize their messages, particularly when communicating through direct mail and providing remarks during political debates. In all the races we examined, Republican candidates were especially likely to engage in nationalized communication, but in all races there are instances in which both parties' candidates emphasized issues that could resonate broadly across the country. When campaigns did localize their communication with voters, it often took the form of emphasizing a candidate's connection to the local area, rather than making specific policy proposals or touting political accomplishments that benefited the region.

This corresponds to findings about how citizens think of themselves in relation to politics. Because place-based identities tend to be built around geographical landmarks and not politics (Hopkins 2018), drawing on local identities and connecting them to politics presents candidates with a difficult challenge. Related to this, many citizens are low-information voters who often are not familiar with the policy issues facing their locality (Binder et al. 2016). Perhaps for these reasons, campaigns in northwest Pennsylvania tended to communicate their issue positions in broad terms. This may have created a context in which campaigns gravitated toward well-known nationalized themes rather than focusing on specific local-level considerations.

Just as importantly, our findings suggest that the use of nationalized campaign communication is conditioned by partisanship. Republicans were more likely to embrace partisan nationalization, while Democrats were more likely to strategically differentiate themselves from these messages. Although we cannot be certain about why this party line difference occurred, two possibilities warrant consideration. One possibility is that the Republicans' propensity for nationalization could reflect broader differences in the two major parties. Republicans in general often lean into a particular version of expressed ideology, whereas Democrats are more likely to score campaign points discussing specific policies rather than ideological values (Grossman and Hopkins 2016). This possibility is also suggested by events that occurred in the aftermath of the 2020 elections. One instance of partisan nationalization occurred when Representative Kelly advanced a lawsuit intended to challenge the mail-in ballots of Pennsylvanians, including his own voters. Another instance involved Representative Brad Roae, who joined the signatories of an amicus brief from Republican state legislators looking to change the vote count in Pennsylvania. This work, egged on by President Trump, demonstrates continued partisan signaling on a national issue, even in the aftermath of the 2020 election.

Another possibility is that candidates in the Republican Party had the benefit of electoral districts that favored Republicans. The two state house districts we examined went heavily for Trump in 2016 and 2020 and leaned Republican even before that. The recently redrawn Sixteenth Congressional District has become more competitive, but much of the district outside of Erie still remains a bastion of Republican support. This suggests that, in a bluer district, it might be Republicans who are incentivized to push back on nationalized messaging and differentiate themselves from nationalized figures while Democrats embrace their party's national brand. Coupled with the findings in Chapter 3, we believe this volume provides some evidence for this interpretation. Democrats, like Republicans, may be inclined to nationalize their messaging when they believe their party's national brand is strong in their locality or region. This suggests the enduring power of nationalization during these times.

Even so, campaigning that focused on local-level policies was not entirely absent from the campaigns we studied. In fact, we find evidence that virtually all of the campaigns in northwest Pennsylvania wanted to connect their campaigns to local identities and that all were prepared to discuss the specifics of local issues. We also found evidence that some campaigns wanted to engage in more of this communication. In all of the interviews that we conducted with campaign staff and candidates, interviewees made strong arguments that they wanted to localize their communication with voters in a way that connected policy ideas to the lives of citizens. However, this approach to campaign communication emerged most prominently during meet-and-greet events with potential voters and during debates moderated by local media. Notably, both of these venues allow candidates to give long-form statements that allow for more nuance than a thirty-second television spot or the bullet points on a piece of direct mail. Just as notably, these venues also allow citizens and journalists to pose questions that solicit responses containing some specifics about policy positions that affect the region. Journalists, it should be noted, were more disciplined than ordinary citizens about asking such questions, which suggests the important role local journalism can play in bringing localized information to citizens.

To be fair, journalists were not perfect custodians of localized politics. Campaign officials from both major parties stressed that local news outlets sometimes overlooked their candidates' efforts to discuss local matters. Yet even when campaigns could control their own message through advertising and direct mail, specifics about positions on local issues were often scant and messaging often drifted toward broad platitudes that could resonate in any locality in the nation. This may partly owe to the fact that subnational elections are generally "low-information" elections and to the fact that citizens primarily fixate on national-level political debates when they think about politics at all. In this environment, connecting with citizens may require a certain degree of nationalized communication.

Nonetheless, the effectiveness of nationalized communication is not without limits. As the Sainato campaign illustrates, candidates who consistently message about the specifics of local issues can win, even when the candidate differs from the partisan leanings of their district, and even when their opponent runs a primarily nationalized campaign. Although this is just one example, it nonetheless demonstrates that localized campaigning can work, even in an era when it seems that "all politics is national."

NOTES

1. Our analysis of television advertisements is limited to the congressional race. Neither of the state house races that we investigated used television ads to reach voters.

2. Ryan's direct mail also asserted this sentiment, in similar language.

REFERENCES

Abramowitz, Alan I., and Steven W. Webster. 2016. "The Rise of Negative Partisanship and The Nationalization of US Elections in the 21st Century." *Electoral Studies* 41:12–22.

Ballotpedia. 2020a. "Pennsylvania's 3rd Congressional District." Accessed January 10, 2021. Available at https://ballotpedia.org/Pennsylvania%27s_3rd_Congressional_District.

———. 2020b. "Pennsylvania's 3rd Congressional District." Accessed January 10, 2021. Available at https://ballotpedia.org/Pennsylvania%27s_16th_Congressional_District.

———. 2020c. "Pennsylvania's 3rd Congressional District." Accessed January 10, 2021. Available at https://ballotpedia.org/Pennsylvania_House_of_Representatives_District_6.

———. 2020d. "Pennsylvania's 3rd Congressional District." Accessed January 10, 2021. Available at https://ballotpedia.org/Chris_Sainato.

Binder, Michael, Matthew Childers, Andrew Hopkins, and Colleen Hampsey. 2016. "In Voters' Minds, Are All Politics Really Local? Comparing Voters' Knowledge of National and Local Politics." In *Conference Proceedings of the State Politics and Policy*, 1–35. Presented at the State Politics and Policy Conference, Dallas, Texas, May 19–21.

Dennis, Brady, Jacqueline Dupree, and Marisa Iati. 2020. "With Coronavirus Cases Spiking Nationwide, All Signs Point to a Harrowing Autumn." *Washington Post*, November 10, 2020. Available at https://www.washingtonpost.com/health/with-coronavirus-cases-spiking-nationwide-all-signs-point-to-a-harrowing-autumn/2020/11/10/d61fa050-238b-11eb-a688-5298ad5d580a_story.html.

Gonyea, Don. 2019. "In One Pennsylvania County, Economic Woes Impact Political Leanings." *NPR News*, March 8, 2019. Available at https://www.npr.org/2019/03/08/701671607/in-one-pennsylvania-county-economic-woes-impact-political-leanings.

———. 2020. "Swing Voters in Northwestern PA Weigh in on Fall Election." *NPR News*, September 14, 2020. Available at https://www.npr.org/2020/09/14/912612270/swing-voters-in-northwestern-pennsylvania-weigh-in-on-fall-election.

Grossmann, Matt, and David A. Hopkins. 2016. *Asymmetric Politics: Ideological Republicans and Group Interest Democrats*. Oxford: Oxford University Press.

Hendrickson, Clara. 2019. "Local Journalism in Crises: Why America Must Revive Its Local Newsrooms." *Brookings Institution*. Accessed January 16, 2021. Available at https://www.brookings.edu/wp-content/uploads/2019/11/Local-Journalism-in-Crisis.pdf.

Hopkins, Daniel J. 2018. *The Increasingly United States: How and Why American Political Behavior Nationalized.* Chicago: University of Chicago Press.

Mahon, Ed. 2019. "Erie Lost People for Decades. Now, Leaders There Hope a New Tax Break Will Transform the City." *WITF News*, October 15, 2019. Available at https://www.witf.org/2019/10/15/erie-lost-people-for-decades-now-leaders-there-hope-a-new-tax-break-will-transform-the-city/.

Northwest Pennsylvania Regional Planning and Development Commission. 2016. "Northwest Pennsylvania Comprehensive Economic Development Strategy." Accessed December 8, 2020. Available at https://northwestpa.org/wp-content/uploads/2016/12/CEDS-Final-2016-12.27.16.pdf.

OpenSecrets.org. 2020. "Pennsylvania District 16 2020 Race." Accessed April 4, 2021. Available at https://www.opensecrets.org/races/summary?cycle=2020&id=PA16.

Pennsylvania Department of State. n.d. "Campaign Finance Online Reporting." Accessed April 4, 2021. Available at https://www.campaignfinanceonline.pa.gov/pages/CFReportSearch.aspx.

Pittsburgh Post-Gazette. 2020. "Western Pa. Reports 303 New Cases with Allegheny County's 200 Leading the Way," July 12, 2020. Available at https://www.post-gazette.com/news/health/2020/07/12/COVID-19-coronavirus-Allegheny-County-Western-Pennsylvania-cases-deaths-data-pandemic-38/stories/202007120123.

Politico. 2012. "2012 Pennsylvania Presidential Election Results." Accessed January 12, 2021. Available at https://www.politico.com/2012-election/results/president/pennsylvania/.

———. 2016. "2016 Pennsylvania Presidential Election Results." Accessed January 12, 2021. Available at https://www.politico.com/2016-election/results/map/president/pennsylvania/.

Rink, Matthew. 2019. "The City of Erie's Population Slide Continues." *Erie Times-News*, September 26, 2019. Available at https://www.goerie.com/news/20190926/city-of-eries-population-slide-continues.

Schaffner, Brian F., and Matthew J. Streb. 2002. "The Partisan Heuristic in Low-Information Elections." *Public Opinion Quarterly* 66, no. 4: 559–581.

Wasserman, David. 2020. "The 10 Bellwether Counties That Show How Trump Is in Serious Trouble." *New York Times*, October 6, 2020. Available at https://www.nytimes.com/2020/10/06/opinion/biden-trump-bellwether-counties-.html.

Wertz, Jim. 2019. "State of Erie Industry 2019." *Erie Reader*, March 27, 2019. Available at https://www.eriereader.com/article/state-of-erie-industry-2019.

Wines, Michael, and Trip Gabriel. 2018. "Pennsylvania Congressional District Map Is Ruled Unconstitutional." *New York Times*, January 22, 2018. Available at https://www.nytimes.com/2018/01/22/us/pennsylvania-maps-congress.html.

Zarroli, Jim. 2016. "Bringing Back Manufacturing Jobs Would Be Harder Than It Sounds." *NPR News*, August 18, 2016. Available at https://www.npr.org/2016/08/18/490192497/bringing-back-manufacturing-jobs-would-be-harder-than-it-sounds.

INTERVIEWS

Brewer, Melanie. Campaign Manager for Representative Mike Kelly. October 9, 2020.

Campaign Staffer for Kristy Gnibus, candidate for the Sixteenth Congressional District. October 14, 2020.

Ferrence, Matthew. Candidate for Pennsylvania State House, District 6. October 16, 2020.

8

Campaigns in the Seventeenth Congressional District

Handling Pressure from National Eyes while Maintaining Local Ties

KRISTEN COOPIE AND OLIVIA O'DONNELL

During a January 2020 campaign stop in Iowa, Democratic presidential candidate Joseph Biden thanked the Pennsylvania congressional representative who made his introduction. "He reminds me so much—excuse me for saying this—of my son Beau," Biden says. 'They both ended up majors, they both ended up deployed, and they both ended up serving their country from their heart as well as their head" (Ball 2020). Biden was speaking of Conor Lamb, the second-term congressman from western Pennsylvania. Two years earlier, Biden endorsed Lamb's first foray into politics; this time, it was Lamb who stumped for Biden, whom he publicly endorsed for the Democratic nomination earlier that month (Levy 2020).

If previous election cycles have any predictive value, Pennsylvania was poised to serve as a bellwether state in 2020, with Lamb's Seventeenth Congressional District a key race to watch. Turnout in the large, urban population centers of Philadelphia and Pittsburgh was usually enough to carry Democrats statewide, but an increase in Republican support across the state doomed Clinton in 2016 (Davis and Detrow 2017). The importance of Pennsylvania in 2020, especially the competitive district PA-17, was renewed, and the presidential candidates did not disappoint in showering western Pennsylvania—and its congressional contenders—with their attention.

In this chapter, we explore the degree of nationalization in PA-17, analyzing the impact of the contest between President Trump and former vice president Joe Biden on one of the most active, vitriolic, and consequential congressional races in the country. We find strong evidence of nationalization in both congressional campaigns. We also investigate two very different races for the Pennsylvania General Assembly in Districts 28 and 30, where a low-key incumbent Republican fought to keep her seat in a localized race, and the resignation of a prominent Republican led to a feisty, seminationalized, open-seat contest.

To Know 17, You Must Understand 18

To understand the political environment of Pennsylvania's Seventeenth Congressional District during the 2020 election cycle, it is important to revisit the electoral events of 2018. As legal battles over an alleged partisan gerrymander played out in court, voters were tasked with selecting a new representative in a special election. Incumbent congressman Tim Murphy, who had represented the then Eighteenth District for fifteen years, resigned his seat soon after revelations by the *Pittsburgh Post-Gazette* that not only was Murphy having an affair but the prolife Republican had encouraged his mistress to terminate her pregnancy (Ward 2017b). Murphy, who earlier declared his intention to retire after the 2018 election, resigned shortly thereafter. His premature departure set up a special election, but Republicans, including National Republican Congressional Committee chair Steve Stivers, were confident the party would hold the district (Blade and Sherman 2017).

In Pennsylvania special elections, nominees are appointed by state party committees. State Representative Rick Saccone was actively running for the U.S. Senate but was chosen by Republican conferees from Allegheny, Westmoreland, Washington, and Greene Counties on the second ballot as the congressional candidate (Engelkemier 2017). An Air Force veteran and an expert on North Korea, Saccone was the most conservative of the candidates considered.

Local Democratic Committee members made a more moderate selection in Conor Lamb, a Marine Corps veteran and prosecutor, and former assistant U.S. attorney in Pittsburgh. In the second round of balloting, he beat out Westmoreland County Commissioner Gina Cerilli (Ward 2017a). Although this was Lamb's first candidacy for any office, his family has deep connections in Pennsylvania politics. His uncle, Michael, served as Pittsburgh city controller, and his grandfather Thomas was a Democratic leader in the state senate and, later, a close legislative aide of governor Robert P. Casey (Ward 2017a). Lamb also connected with Joe Biden through campaign staff member Mike Donilon, who served as a senior counselor to the vice president from 2009 to 2013, which helped secure Biden's appearances for, and endorsement of, Lamb (Weigel and Dawsey 2020).

Despite the practical importance of filling Murphy's vacant seat, the election was potentially "inconsequential" (Fischer-Baum and Uhrmacher 2018) in the short term due to the Pennsylvania Supreme Court's redistricting decision. The electoral winner would, months later, be required to run in another primary in their new district. Saccone's new home district, PA-18, now encompassed the city of Pittsburgh and much of Allegheny County, safe Democratic strongholds in an increasingly red part of the state. Following redistricting, Lamb's home was in PA-17, represented by incumbent congressman Keith Rothfus; in 2016 this new district had voted for Trump by only 3 points over Clinton (Fischer-Baum and Uhrmacher 2018).

On March 13, 2018, Lamb narrowly defeated Saccone by 755 votes, 49.9% to 49.5%. Republicans began to distance themselves from their candidate and the loss even before Election Day. Alex Isenstadt of *Politico*, one week before the election, wrote this:

> As election day grows closer, the national GOP is increasingly pinning the blame on Saccone. In interviews with nearly two dozen administration officials, senior House Republicans and top party strategists, Saccone was nearly universally panned as a deeply underwhelming candidate who leaned excessively on the national party to execute a massive, multimillion-dollar rescue effort. It was complete with visits from the president, vice president and several Cabinet members. (Isenstadt 2018)

The GOP had a chance to unseat Lamb seven months later in the 2018 midterms, which, because of the new map, featured the only two-incumbent race in the country. Rothfus represented PA-12 since 2013, but his Sewickley home was now a part of the redrawn Seventeenth Congressional District. Described as "relatively quiet," the race was dominated by Lamb. He "outraised his opponent by a 2-to-1 margin between July and September, for example. And, outside Republican groups pulled back spending in the district in the months leading up to the election," despite Trump endorsing the incumbent in October (Herring and Perkins 2018). Lamb significantly increased his vote margin, beating Rothfus 56.3% to 43.7%. Having faced significant losses twice in the same year, candidate selection and messaging became a top priority for the GOP in 2020, especially in such a highly contested district. Both parties also realized the need to become more cognizant of the new demographic realities of their constituencies. Lamb's 2018 victories were viewed not only as a test of a failed GOP strategy in the area with working-class voters but also as a reconnection of Democrats with the economic issues that motivate many working families (Bowman 2018).

The Federal and State Candidates of the New PA-17

Lamb ran in a considerably different district in 2020 than in 2018. The "new" PA-17 encompasses much of northern Allegheny County and all of Beaver County, with a small portion of southwestern Butler County (U.S. Census Bureau 2017). The socioeconomic characteristics of the district trend higher than in other districts across the state (see Table 8.1). Health care and social

TABLE 8.1 DEMOGRAPHIC AND REGISTRATION CHARACTERISTICS OF PENNSYLVANIA'S 28TH AND 30TH STATE HOUSE DISTRICTS, SEVENTEENTH CONGRESSIONAL DISTRICT, AND PENNSYLVANIA IN 2019

	PA 28th State House District[a]	PA 30th State House District[b]	Seventeenth Congressional District[c]	Pennsylvania[d]
Population density: people/square mile	1,049.3	1,205.6	882.9	286.1
Population white	86%	94%	87%	76%
Population black	2%	1%	6%	11%
Population Hispanic	2%	1%	2%	8%
Foreign-born	8.8%	4.3%	5.2%	7.0%
Median household income	$110,430	$91,459	$70,857	$63,463
Bachelor's degree or higher	65.7%	50.7%	42.5%	32.3%
Registered Democrat[e]	38.0%	44.1%	48.5%	46.5%
Registered Republican[e]	44.9%	42.0%	37.1%	39.0%
Registered none/other[e]	17.1%	13.9%	14.4%	14.5%

Sources:
(a) Compiled from U.S. Census Bureau. n.d. "Census Reporter: State House District 28, PA." Accessed July 9, 2021. Available at https://censusreporter.org/profiles/62000US42028-state-house -district-28-pa/.
(b) Compiled from U.S. Census Bureau. n.d. "Census Reporter: State House District 30, PA." Accessed March 22, 2021. Available at https://censusreporter.org/profiles/62000US42030-state-house -district-30-pa/.
(c) Compiled from U.S. Census Bureau. n.d. "Census Reporter: Congressional District 17, PA." Accessed March 30, 2021. Available at https://censusreporter.org/profiles/50000US4217-congressional-district -17-pa/.
(d) Compiled from U.S. Census Bureau. n.d. "Census Reporter: Pennsylvania." Accessed December 30, 2020. Available at https://censusreporter.org/profiles/04000US42-pennsylvania/.
(e) Compiled from Pennsylvania Department of State. "Voting and Election Statistics." Accessed November 1, 2020. Available at https://www.dos.pa.gov/VotingElections/OtherServicesEvents/Voting ElectionStatistics/Pages/VotingElectionStatistics.aspx.

services are by far the largest employment sectors, reflecting the strong presence of health care services and hospitals in the area; retail, accommodation services, manufacturing, and management round out the top five industries.

The new district boundaries create a more competitive environment for the parties. Prior to redistricting, Republicans enjoyed a 20-point advantage; this was significantly decreased down to a meager +2.5 Republican rating (Singer 2018). An analysis of 2016 votes within the new district boundaries finds that President Trump would have won the new PA-17 by only 2 points (Gonzales 2018). Democrats, however, hold a 49%-to-37% registration advantage, with 14% of voters remaining unaffiliated (D. Moore 2020a). In 2020, immediately before the election, the *Cook Political Report* (2020) rated the district as Likely Democratic, favoring Lamb to win reelection.

The vitriolic and combative nature of the federal campaigns was represented at the local level as well. Nestled within District 17 are 11 of the 203 state house districts. In the 2020 electoral cycle, seven featured incumbent Democrats, three had incumbent Republicans, and one seat, in District 28, was open due to the sudden resignation of Speaker Mike Turzai. As government relations professional Alexandra Kozak notes, "The district is changing just like so many in PA. This particular district has been Republican for over 50 years but Democratic registration is climbing. Wolf actually won the district in 2018, as did Senator Bob Casey."

Although Turzai, a Republican who was first elected in 2001 and worked his way up to the Speaker position, had declared that he would not be running for reelection, he surprised many by announcing his early resignation in June 2020 (Scolforo 2020). Some claim that this quick departure was the result of accusations that Turzai and other Republican House leadership "intentionally withheld information about a GOP representative's coronavirus diagnosis" (Czachor 2020), although Turzai claimed his intention was to "move into the private sector" at some future point (Scolforo 2020). This created an even more competitive atmosphere in the district, as Turzai's favored candidate to replace him, West Point grad and Army veteran Rob Mercuri, waged an active campaign with his Democratic opponent, former screenwriter and nonprofit founder Emily Skopov. Skopov announced her candidacy in 2019 expecting to again challenge Turzai, having taken many lessons from a failed campaign to unseat him in 2018.

Pennsylvania District 30 features the only state Republican incumbent in this chapter, Lori Mizgorski, who ran a much more muted and under-the-radar campaign than fellow candidates Sean Parnell and Rob Mercuri. Her opponent, first-time Democratic candidate Lissa Geiger Shulman, utilized her classroom experience as a teacher in Pittsburgh Public Schools to craft education policies while serving as chief of staff to state representative Dan Miller (Lissa Giger Shulman for State Representative 2020). After three years as his legislative director, Geiger Shulman sought to take her passion for education into public office.

Nationalization in the Congressional Contest

Ready to quell Lamb's 2020 reelection effort was retired Army infantry captain and *Fox News* contributor Sean Parnell. Before he formally announced his candidacy, his name was tossed into the ring by President Trump himself during an official White House visit to Pittsburgh in October 2019 (Potter 2019). Prolife, promilitary and veteran, and pro-Second Amendment, Parnell is as enthusiastic about President Trump and his policies as he is critical of his opponent and the Democratic Party. The presence of nationalization in this race began early on, with candidates and incumbent politicians launching specific criticisms of both the opponent (Lamb) and the Democratic Party in general.

In a campaign ad released in June 2020, Parnell states that "Conor became Pelosi's little lamb the moment he got to Washington. . . . Lamb supports Joe Biden who wants to put AOC in charge of Pennsylvania's energy jobs. That's like putting Bill Clinton in charge of your intern program" (Wallace 2020). This connection between Lamb and House Speaker Nancy Pelosi has been made many times by Republicans, with the president even incorrectly tweeting in May that "Connor Lamm" voted to support "Crazy Nancy Pelosi" for Speaker (Kiely 2020). Lamb is no stranger to Trump's criticisms, as the president actively campaigned against "Lamb the Sham" at a Saccone rally in Moon Township, Pennsylvania, during the 2018 special election (C-SPAN 2020). Even from his initial election, Conor Lamb was on the radar of the president, who, through his speeches, tweets, and comments, placed Lamb, his party, his district, and his challengers onto the national stage.

With the strong national attention being paid to the candidates, the framing of candidates in a negative manner using national issues, and the frequent visits by both presidential candidates to the area, we find strong evidence of nationalization of the congressional contest in PA-17. The 2020 race was viewed as representative of the national political climate, with the district being called an "incubator for American politics" (D. Moore 2020b). Speaking about both Lamb and Parnell, Republican consultant Mike DeVanney told *Roll Call* that "you have people who are viewed potentially as the future of the party: Conor Lamb, who ran as a centrist. And then you have Sean Parnell, who has run as being part of the party that has been energized by President Trump" (Bowman 2020b). Tying the congressional candidates to the presidential contenders is strong evidence of nationalization, as the parties, the media, and the candidates themselves frequently tied their electoral fortunes together.

On social media, Parnell's frequent tweets in support of Trump and his policies have closely aligned him with the president; conversely, his campaign statements and advertisements aim to align Lamb closely with Nancy Pelosi and more progressive Democrats. However, GovTrack (2021) finds that Lamb's voting record positions him as one of the more moderate members of Congress. The Parnell ad released in June, mentioned above, featured Parnell carrying a stuffed lamb around a factory, past portraits of "crazy socialist" Senator Bernie Sanders and House Speaker Nancy Pelosi. While these criticisms were specific to Lamb, the nature of the complaints and statements about the Democrats or the Democratic Party at large could have been used to frame any Democratic candidate. Yet Parnell was cognizant of the importance of his success not only for his own political fortunes but also for those of the president, a figure to whom Parnell closely ties his electoral fortunes. "Look, the entire fate of Pennsylvania rests on PA-17's shoulders, the district that I am running for," Parnell said in an interview with *Brietbart News Saturday*. "If I win PA-17, the president wins PA-17, he wins the state of Pennsylvania. The end" (Boyle 2020).

The economy, jobs, and health care (including the handling of the COVID-19 pandemic) retained their distinction as some of the major issues that voters care about across the ballot. But in western Pennsylvania, a subset of issues prominent in local minds carried as much importance, if not more, in the 2020 election, and interestingly, some were tied directly to the national conversation. The frequent personal attacks and the focus on partisan political issues—as well as issues in the national debate—led to this being a strongly nationalized race.

For many across western Pennsylvania, the economy means fracking jobs and economic security. The industry has brought over 30,000 jobs to the state and has increased median home prices in the area (Said and Yurkevich 2020). With fracking having such a significant impact on the local economy, the position of each candidate and party on fracking had the potential to be a main driver of vote choice. President Trump was highly vocal on the issue and spoke frequently on the subject to drive support for his own campaign. He reiterated that he has long supported American oil and gas industries and that he retracted many policies detrimental to their businesses. During an August 2019 visit to the building site of a Shell-sponsored manufacturing complex located in Beaver County—the centerpiece of which is an ethane-cracker plant—Donald Trump played up his support of fossil fuels and the oil and gas industries to his attendees. However, these blue-collar workers who carried Trump to a 16-point victory in the county in 2016 turned around and supported Conor Lamb in 2018. Claiming credit for the creation of this plant, plans for which were announced in 2012 during the Obama administration (Colvin and Boak 2020), Trump took this opportunity to remind attendees, employees of Shell who were compensated to attend the event, of his devotion to their hometowns, their industries, and their struggles. This devotion, he claims, is unshared by Democrats up and down the ballot. "I don't think they give a damn about western Pennsylvania, do you?" he questioned (Law 2019).

Democratic nominee Joseph Biden was not as clear on his position on fracking, to the dismay and frustration of voters not only in the area but across the Rust Belt. In an exchange with CNN's Dana Bash during the July 2019 Democratic primary debate, Biden asserted, "We would make sure it's [fracking] eliminated and no more subsidies for either of those [coal or fracking], either—any fossil fuel" (Lybrand 2020). His campaign quickly put out a statement clarifying that he supported eliminating subsidies. Two months later, in another Democratic primary debate, he claimed opposition to "new fracking," a statement that again had to be spun by his campaign to reiterate their previous clarifications. An article by Savador Rizzo for the *Washington Post* in March 2020 highlights the problem with "Biden's fracking fracas": "Pushing for a total ban could hurt his general election chances in the swing states where fracking has propped up the economy, such as Ohio and Pennsylvania. Anything less than a total ban could detract from Biden's appeal among liberals and climate-change activists in the Democratic base" (Rizzo 2020).

The Lamb campaign recognized the problem presented not only by the fracking issue but also by Biden's inconsistencies. Beyond questions from local voters and news outlets, Lamb felt the need to clarify both his and Biden's positions, once they were challenged in the national setting, in order to unify the Democratic messaging. In February 2020, he penned an op-ed for the *Wall Street Journal*, pointedly titled "Joe Biden Does Not Support a Fracking Ban" (Lamb and Hamm 2020). He challenges the assertions of an earlier editorial by economist Stephen Moore, who claims that Biden's tightening of regulations is not only economically disastrous for the United States but also politically disastrous for Democrats who needed the votes of oil, gas, and shale workers in Ohio, Michigan, and Pennsylvania (S. Moore 2020). Lamb writes:

> The longtime antiunion advocate claims that former Vice President Joe Biden supports "ending the shale oil and gas revolution." That's simply not true.
>
> Certain Democratic presidential candidates have promised to "ban fracking," and I've publicly criticized them for doing so. Vice President Biden has criticized them, too. He has explicitly promised not to ban fracking, and when confronted by an activist who was upset with his position, Mr. Biden told him plainly: "You ought to vote for someone else."

I'm glad Mr. Moore acknowledges that "Pittsburgh has become a global energy hub." Those of us who live here are well aware of that fact, but he fails to mention that the vast majority of Democratic leaders in our region are vocal supporters of the industry. However, Western Pennsylvania Democrats look beyond corporate boardrooms. The pipe fitters, laborers, engineers and other tradesmen and women, and their families remain our highest priority. (Lamb and Hamm 2002)

In three short paragraphs, Lamb eloquently clarifies the position of the Democratic presidential nominee while simultaneously reaffirming that Democrats both up and down the ballot are supportive of the industries and the workers. Lamb was also a member of the Democratic Party's climate change platform panel, co-led by former secretary of state John Kerry and New York representative Alexandria Ocasio-Cortez (Cole 2020a). While campaign manager Abby Nassif-Murphy cites Lamb's involvement on the task force to protect jobs, the Parnell campaign sees his participation as proof of his liberalism. Parnell campaign manager Andrew Brey attacked Biden's "radical anti-energy agenda that will kill Western PA jobs," continuing that "Lamb's quest to end fracking may impress socialists like Bernie Sanders and AOC, but it won't impress the union members and workers who earn their living in the oil and gas industry, or the constituents of PA17 who benefit from it" (Cole 2020a).

Along with fracking, ensuring support from blue-collar workers across the region, especially union members, also served as a major campaign focus for both candidates. Although Democratic candidates have long enjoyed the support of various labor union leaders, rank-and-file members trended toward Trump in 2016 (Osborne 2020). While most major public-sector unions endorsed Biden, Trump received some endorsements from local unions and vocal support from some members.

Lamb enjoyed strong union support beginning in his special election, with leaders making a special push to assure their members that someone like Lamb, or the Democratic Party, could meet their needs better than Republicans or President Trump, who won in Lamb's original district by double digits. In 2018, Cecil Roberts, preacher and president of the United Mine Workers of America, presented Lamb as a "God-fearing, union-supporting, gun-owning, job-protecting, pension-defending, Social Security-believing, health care-greeting and sending-drug-dealers-to-jail Democrat," as quoted by Daniel Marans of the *Huffington Post* (2018). Marans goes on to say this:

Elements of the rally—the religiosity, the pro-gun rhetoric and the romantic attachment to coal country—would surely make more socially liberal Democrats squirm. But for better or worse, Roberts' speech was the rhetorical capstone of a campaign that has sought to bring rank-and-file union members who voted for Donald Trump or past Republican congressional candidates back into the Democratic fold.

This summary highlights one of the key issues that has plagued Democrats in western Pennsylvania (and across the United States) for years: how to assure more moderate or conservative-leaning voters that the Democrats are more interested in protecting their interests than impinging on their rights, especially when it comes to economic or social issues.

This sentiment carried through to 2020 as well. On a September 2020 train tour of the state, Biden was joined by Lamb and fellow Democratic representative Mike Doyle (PA-18), as well as Tom Conway, international president of the United Steelworkers, which endorsed Biden earlier in the campaign (United Steel Workers 2020). In a contest that featured extremely limited campaign events, Biden's choice of event not only reflected his affection for Amtrak but also demonstrated the campaign's realization that union labor and working families were politically in play in the region. Union leaders, such as Jim Kunz of Operating Engineers International Local 66, reminded their members that "the appointments Trump has made to the federal bench and the National Labor Relations Board have been devastating to working men and women," and that the unions "are asking members to put their employment ahead of other concerns they may have about the Biden-Harris ticket and fears they might support limits on gun rights" (Erdley and Lindstrom 2020). In fact, most of Biden's visits to the area featured some event with union members, including a visit to the Community College of Beaver County the night before Election Day.

Republican candidates had good reason, however, to believe that union members might show up in strong numbers in the 2020 election—they had turned out in large numbers for Trump in 2016. Many were concerned about Biden's agenda, fearing his plans for new climate change legislation could hurt or even eliminate jobs. As one union member put it, "If I don't have a job, it doesn't matter what I fight for on the union end with collective bargaining. If I don't have a job, I don't have a seat at the table" (Siegel 2020). The Republican Federal Committee of Pennsylvania embraced this notion, sponsoring advertisements and mailers warning against reelecting Lamb, who "embraces Joe Biden's socialist extremism and will turn back the clock on the Obama-Biden years when unemployment hammered our communities" (Republican Federal Committee of Pennsylvania 2020). Unions such as the United Steelworkers were excited by Trump's protective trade tariffs and promises to revitalize their industries, with former Steelworkers president

Leo Gerard praising Trump for being able to "see the steelworker agenda," which could have a major impact on swaying members from their traditional allegiance to Democrats (Schwartz 2018).

In addition to the strong ties that Democrats typically enjoy with unions, many members cite their disappointment with Trump's lack of delivery on campaign promises as a reason to support Biden. The "Energy Dominance" agenda touted by the Trump White House aimed to create a "golden era of American energy" by easing rules and regulations (White House 2020), but unions and workers did not see tangible, beneficial outcomes of this plan. Union leader Kunz faults the president for his inaction. "The president talked the great fight, but he has done absolutely nothing to create additional employment in western Pennsylvania" (Siegel 2020).

Parnell, looking to play up negative perceptions of the opposition instead of running retrospectively on his party's and president's agenda, also made a play for union members in his district. During his speech at the Republican National Convention, he tried to appeal to union members or more moderate Democrats, nicknamed "Casey Democrats," for their policy stances that mirror those of the late Democratic governor Bob Casey Sr.—that is, Democrats who might favor more conservative social policies on issues like abortion and guns (Bowman 2020b). When Parnell returned from Afghanistan, he "watched with alarm as the party of my grandfather—a lifelong union Democrat—turned against the very people it professed to represent," criticizing the "contempt" that the "New Democrat party" has for middle-class Americans (Cole 2020b). Interestingly, at a time when many Democrats in vulnerable districts stayed away from the convention to avoid tying themselves to the national party (Bowman 2020a), Lamb eagerly used his address to counter his opponent's claims and shore up support for both himself and Biden in his district.

Both candidates also received national attention when their first debate was broadcast on local station WPXI as well as C-SPAN. Aside from a discussion on fracking, the two spent much of the thirty-minute debate discussing health care, with Lamb warning voters of Parnell's opposition to the Affordable Care Act and Parnell accusing Lamb and other congressional Democrats of stalling on much-needed COVID-19 relief legislation (Routh 2020). As a member of Congress, Lamb cast a vote in May—before the primary—against the $3 trillion Health and Economic Recovery Omnibus Emergency Solutions (HEROES) Act; he was one of only fourteen Democrats to oppose the measure (Potter 2020). In Lamb's official statement, he calls the bill "not focused," but journalist Chris Potter contends that Lamb's nay vote was strategic, in order to prevent Republicans and Parnell from using a yay against him (Potter 2020). Parnell criticized Governor Tom Wolf's handling of the crisis, saying Wolf's plan to delay fully reopening the state until a "foolproof" vaccine is available is "absolutely absurd" and would significantly hurt businesses (Montanaro 2020). Parnell himself publicly flouted the statewide mask order, often posting images on his social media accounts of himself surrounded by supporters, maskless.

The frenetic and nationalized campaign continued into its final days. Lamb canvased for himself and Biden with the Allegheny-Fayette Central Labor Council (2020) on October 31st. Parnell spoke in advance of President Trump at a rally in Butler County on November 2nd, while Lamb joined Biden at the Community College of Beaver County the same day. Lamb praised Biden for returning to the area: "What it tells me is that he knows Beaver County is a place where people are pretty independent-minded and willing to listen . . . and above all they value jobs and the rights of working people and the middle class," a feeling reiterated by many of the members in attendance (Prose 2020).

The race lived up to expectations of a close contest, with each candidate raising nearly $4 million (Ballotpedia 2020a). ProPublica (2020a, 2020b) reports significant levels of outside spending on the race as well: Groups spent $164,850 in support of Parnell and $308,541 for Lamb; receipts for spending against Lamb totaled $151,494, while spending against Parnell topped $525,000.

The State Legislative Contests

We find mixed results in terms of the nationalization of the state legislative contests. While State House District 28 features some support from the state and national parties and discussion of nationalized issues, including the "Defund the Police" movement, the personal competitiveness of the race emphasizes the local focus of the politics. In State House District 30, strong focus on the candidates' personal qualifications and constituent service leads this to be a much more localized race.

PA District 28 candidate Rob Mercuri and campaign manager Corey Barsky, a 22-year-old Republican activist and veteran of the 2018 Rothfus campaign, both stated during interviews that local and state Republican Parties were supportive, but they cite significant and early support from the outgoing incumbent, Mike Turzai, as one of the most substantial influences on the campaign. The Mercuri family has had a connection to Turzai going back to the 2000 election, when Mercuri's father Vince ran an unsuccessful challenge against state representative Frank Dermody. Mercuri's involvement in Republican circles in the district kept the two in touch over the years. "He was aware of my interest in running for office someday, and so when he was thinking about how to . . . extricate himself from the position, he called me and said, uh, 'Would you be interested in running?'" Barsky credits Turzai's early endorsement of Mercuri as vital in helping to get the campaign up and running quickly in terms of establishing infrastructure and an early donor base.

Both Mercuri and Democratic challenger Emily Skopov recognize that the shifting demographics and high socioeconomic status levels in their district led voters to focus more on economic concerns, with Skopov realizing early on the benefit of framing issues from an economic or fiscal perspective. "Our narrative was very much constructed with the Republicans and the conservative Democrats in mind. . . . We had a cohesive narrative, it was just that Democrats want to keep hearing about other things," says Skopov.

One such issue that Skopov mentions as presenting a challenge was the call to "defund the police" in the wake of high-profile cases of police brutality. This is also the most nationalized aspect of this race, centering on an issue that was the focus of great national debate. While Mercuri's website includes a platform position of supporting police departments, firefighters, and first responders (Friends of Rob Mercuri 2020), Skopov did not include specific language regarding this issue. When speaking with constituents, the Democratic position and use of the "defund the police" language was frequently brought up, and Skopov feels that it was used "effectively against Democrats in districts" such as hers (Herring 2020). Campaign manager Nichole Remmert believes this was a strategic ploy by the opposition to drive the campaign off message. "Rob and his puppet-masters, they did that, even though they knew that was not a position Emily supported." Skopov notes, "We were on record, I mean, we have phone calls and emails and texts to people as early as June saying 'this "defund the police" is a big problem. . . . This Black Lives Matters stuff, the way it's being, like, messaged, is a big problem.'" The attention given to this issue by Democrats in her district forced her campaign to respond. "I literally had something posted on Facebook that said 'I support my police department.' I went and met with all my police departments," although Skopov's appeals to organizations such as the Fraternal Order of Police were unsuccessful, as they gave their endorsement to Mercuri. Mercuri's campaign manager Barsky believes these types of reactionary moves on the part of the Skopov campaign were beneficial for his candidate. The active Republican primary allowed Mercuri to begin to push his key issues—public safety, education, and fiscal responsibility—early, and the Skopov campaign admits that efforts by the Mercuri campaign and other outside groups, including the Pennsylvania Commonwealth Fund, hit early and hard to drive the conversations.

Coordination with the congressional candidates in PA-17 seemed to occur in limited ways for both Mercuri and Skopov. Mercuri attended multiple events with Parnell in the district, but keeping his own identity, separate from Parnell and even President Trump, was crucial. "I think our strengths played off each other. I think we had nuanced differences, though, that voters were able to discern over time," Mercuri notes. "[Parnell] was a little more tied to some of the national themes than I was. . . . He kind of ran a 'President Trump coattails' strategy where, you know, he was at every Trump rally." Mercuri believes this difference, especially his attention to local issues and his personal ties to the district, led him to outperform both Parnell and Trump in the district. "Trump's brand of politics, which, Parnell, even though he was hard-hitting and he was aligned with the president, he was still a nice guy, he was still a nice, projected image." Kozak agrees, noting that Mercuri "attempted to remain focused on local issues, continuing the path that Turzai set forth, and the shortfalls of the Wolf Administration's response to the virus."

When the same comparison was made between Mercuri and Trump, especially by the Skopov camp, Mercuri said that "burned him a little bit." Even though he is a Trump supporter, he noted his concerted effort in the campaign to focus locally and meet people, not get tied up in the personalities and issues on the top of the ballot. This included running a persistent and impressive ground strategy, with Barsky citing outreach to over 12,000 households through personal canvasing, 20,000-plus phone calls from campaign staff and volunteers, over thirty mailers, and the strategic placement of three billboards. Barsky notes that normally he would not have wasted valuable resources on billboards, but strategic placement on busy roads and near grocery stores was useful to catch the eye of those who ventured out for necessities during the pandemic.

As neither candidate was serving in the legislature, they had no direct impact or influence on state policies relating to the COVID-19 pandemic, but the issue loomed large over the campaigns. Thus, each candidate took a localized approach in this aspect of their campaign. Both included COVID information on their campaign webpages. Skopov listed a link to the Pandemic Unemployment Assistance application, as well as a series of direct links from Lamb's official congressional webpage (Emily Skopov for Pennsylvania 2020). Mercuri's site bemoans the "lack of transparency and leadership from our state government," and highlights three steps that Mercuri believes are necessary to support small-business owners: a payroll tax moratorium, a 50% occupancy capacity level, and providing incentives for workers to return to work (Friends of Rob Mercuri 2020).

While their official statements were geared toward supporting citizens throughout the pandemic, outside groups began to target each candidate for their positions. Conservative PAC Commonwealth Leaders Fund, which contributed over \$200,000 in total to the Mercuri campaign (Ballotpedia 2021), sponsored mailers that, according to Skopov, misrepresented her position on business closures during the pandemic (Deto 2020b). The mailer features an out-of-context reference to a headline chosen by an editor for an opinion piece Skopov penned for the *Pennsylvania Capital-Star* (Skopov 2020). The actual title, "This Turzai bill putting Pennsylvania back to work is bad for Pennsylvanians," is edited on the mailer, which ends up quoting Skopov as saying that "putting Pennsylvania back to work is bad for Pennsylvanians," omitting the reference to Turzai's proposal. House Bill 2400 would have eased restrictions on public and private construction activities, as long as Centers for Disease Control and Prevention (CDC) measures could be adhered to at worksites (Pennsylvania Legislature 2020). Skopov states her preference to get Pennsylvanians back to work safely, with legislation providing more guidance than a one-sentence "ill-informed policy" (Deto 2020b).

At times, attacks on both candidates went from policy-oriented to personal, localizing the focus of the race. Skopov accused Mercuri of an anti-Semitic attack against her after a mailer sent by the Commonwealth Leadership Fund criticized her "Beverly Hills politics," which she asserts is a dog whistle for her Jewish faith (Vellucci 2020). Skopov was angered that parts of her background, including her time as a screenwriter and producer for shows such as *Xena: Warrior Princess*, *Farscape*, and *Andromeda* (IMDB 2021), as well as her religion, were used as a negative condemnation of her. She said in our interview on December 8, 2020, "I think, my path to this was very different, I think I'm not your typical candidate in that sense, which, unfortunately turned out to be the way they weaponized that against me, I think ultimately, my opponents did and interest groups that supported them."

In an interview we conducted on December 15, 2020, Mercuri calls the independent nature of third parties a "double-edged sword":

> They have their interests in mind first, whether it's, you know, an issue they care about or an election priority they care about, or some messaging they want to get out. They don't care how that synchs up with your messaging as a candidate, or your particular campaign. And oftentimes they—you don't even know what's coming, and you'll just, you'll get a mailer with your picture on it, with messaging on it, and it probably comes from . . . their impression of you, or the way you fill out a survey as a candidate. And so usually their facts are right but the way that they position them and the messaging of it might be something that, um, as a candidate you don't want to talk about, or you're not focused on even after you win as a legislator. . . . So third parties, they do amplify, but they don't always amplify in a productive way.

Mercuri's survey comment is a reference to multiple mailers, sent to constituents by Pennsylvania Fund for Change, in which Mercuri is sharply criticized for his stance on same-sex marriage. According to a questionnaire the candidate submitted to iVoterGuide, Mercuri "strongly agrees" with the position that "Governments should not discriminate against individuals, organizations or small businesses because of their belief that marriage is only a union of one man and one woman," but is neutral on the statement that "Governments should define marriage as between one man and one woman; no other definition of marriage should be legalized or supported with taxpayer or public funds" (iVoterGuide 2020). Pennsylvania Fund for Change seized on these answers to create mailers with headlines such as "With Rob Mercuri, Bigotry Is Always on the Menu" (2020c), "Rob Mercuri Is Too Extreme" (2020a), and "Robert Mercuri: Extremely Wrong for Us" (2020b). Mercuri says his answers were taken out of context. "They say I want to turn back the clock on gay marriage—which I don't. But that didn't matter, that wasn't the survey question. So they took that and ran a whole ad campaign on 'he's not raising his kids to love others or treat them with dignity or respect.'" Although the issues in question are ones featured in national discussions, the targeted attacks on Mercuri's answers, in particular, localize and personalize the race.

Interestingly, a litany of other disparagements is included on the mailers, including Mercuri's desire to defund Planned Parenthood, his refusal to wear a mask at public events, and his desire to have businesses reopen before coronavirus testing was in place. In reference to the mask claim, the mailer cites Mercuri's Facebook page, which features multiple posts showing photographs of Mercuri standing in close proximity to other people without wearing a mask; multiple shots feature the Allegheny County Young Republicans, and one in particular shows Mercuri, Young Republican members, and Sean Parnell in a tight group, all unmasked (Rob Mercuri for State House 2020). When questioned about these specific mailers, Mercuri notes his frustration with the attacks. Despite photographic evidence to the contrary, Mercuri asserts that the accusations were not true and that "whoever sent them [the mailers] was not at all for us; in fact, they were dead set against us." He also believes photos were more helpful to him than harmful—and more harmful to his opponent. "I wasn't sure if my opponent even would have wanted something like that to be so widely broadcast, because it did, I think, turn a lot of people off."

Not all western Pennsylvania elections shared the somewhat nationalized, contentious nature of the elections discussed above. Sharing the eastern border of District 28 is District 30, a tall, narrow, L-shaped area (Ballotpedia 2020b). Over the past decade, the district has maintained Republican representation, with Lori Mizgorski carrying on the Republican streak after defeating the Democratic nominee, Betsy Monroe, by 4.6 points in the 2018 election cycle (Ballotpedia 2020b). Mizgorski is a native of Shaler Township with ample government experience. A former member of the Shaler Township Board of Commissioners, Mizgorski was appointed to the Conservation and Natural Resources Advisory Council during Republican governor Tom Corbett's administration, charged with providing recommendations regarding conservation and stewardship of the Commonwealth's natural resources. Upon taking office, Mizgorski prioritized legislation concerning redistricting, transportation, education, and renewable energy. Her 2020 reelection campaign highlighted her cosponsorships on House Bills 22 and 23, which focused on reforming the Pennsylvania redistricting process (Pennsylvania General Assembly 2020).

Near the end of her term, her legislative priorities shifted to COVID-19, creating a prominent, localized feature of her campaign platform, detailed under "Issues" on her websites (Lori4PA 2020; Lori Mizgorski PA State Senate 2020a). She voted to expand testing, supply additional personal protective equipment (PPE), and provide immediate assistance to hospitals. As unemployment numbers rapidly rose, she also voted to eliminate the weeklong waiting period to attain unemployment compensation. She did adhere to the Republican Party's desire to reopen industries by fighting to safely reopen the real estate industry to provide essential housing, and she voted to get construction workers and contractors back on the job. Also, according to her site, Mizgorski sought reelection to further her goals of investing in education and school safety; she had previously supported funding increases to public education and school safety grants without raising taxes.

Mizgorski did not receive influential endorsements from President Donald Trump or former Pennsylvania Speaker of the House Mike Turzai, and there was little evidence of coordination with state or national party groups. Instead, her most prominent endorsements came from the Shaler Township commissioners James Boyle, William Cross, Susan Fisher, and David Shutter as well as her predecessor, former state representative Hal English (Lori4PA 2020). As for organizational endorsements, Mizgorski was backed by the Laborers' District Council of Western Pennsylvania, Fraternal Order of Police Fort Pitt Lodge #1 and Lodge #91, and Humane PA (Lori Mizgorski PA State Senate 2020a). Although the organizational endorsements are fewer than received by the Democratic nominee, Lissa Geiger Shulman, as the incumbent Mizgorski did not need to attain as much organizational support as the upstart campaign of her opponent.

Democrat Geiger Shulman's grassroots challenge to Mizgorski centered on the environment, education, health care, and child care, and she garnered the support of local Democratic leaders, including state senator Lindsey Williams, state representative Sara Innamorato, and state representative Dan Miller (Lissa Geiger Shulman for State Representative 2020). Unlike her opponent, Geiger Shulman received top-down endorsements from Democratic nominee Joe Biden, former president Barack Obama, Pennsylvania governor Tom Wolf, and former Pennsylvania governor Ed Rendell. Her constituent-friendly campaign consistently shared messaging on social media channels, including involvement in community events, COVID-19 information, and voter registration. As it did for most candidates, the worldwide pandemic forced Geiger Shulman to adapt her campaign plans into virtual outreach. Her heightened visibility and her ability to conduct campaign events under CDC guidelines with Democratic peers such as Skopov and Senator Bob Casey allowed her to gain traction.

Geiger Shulman criticized her opponent's voting record, specifically on the issue of education. She condemned Mizgorski's vote on House Bill (HB) 800, a bill that would have expanded publicly funded vouchers for students who attend private and religious schools (Deto 2020a). The bill passed largely along party lines and was vetoed by Governor Tom Wolf. However, both candidates display similar and vague legislative goals for the education system. Geiger Shulman takes issue with the framework of Mizgorski's stance, claiming that if HB 800 had passed, it would have resulted in millions fewer dollars in resources for school districts and could have led to property tax increases for homeowners in various school districts.

In a further attempt to connect with District 30's constituency, Geiger Shulman desired to engage in a virtual debate with Mizgorski. However, Mizgorski—who was practically silent on the virtual campaign trail—failed to respond to the debate request. Shulman voiced her displeasure with Mizgorski's lack of engagement to local media:

> My opponent has already dodged other forums held by local organizations representing District 30 constituents. For more than a month now, the nonpartisan League of Women Voters has been trying to contact her. It seems clear that she does not want to be held accountable for her record over the last two years nor does she offer solutions for the urgent challenges facing our communities. (Deto 2020a)

Toward the end of the campaign, Mizgorski took to Facebook to make a rare statement regarding negative advertisements: "You may have seen my opponent's negative ads attacking me. They tried this same tactic in 2018, and they're doing it again. My opponent and her extreme outside-the-state donors . . . are bankrolling her campaign. . . . They are spending more than $300,000 in negative TV ads to try to deceive you" (Lori Mizgorski for State Representative 2020). Since Mizgorski's voting record was not addressed directly in debate, her lack of direct engagement may have worked to her benefit. Although the District 30 race remained mostly civil, both sides succumbed slightly to the typical party-affiliation blame game, although nowhere near the level of combative rhetoric displayed in District 28 or elsewhere.

Results

Once polls closed, four days passed before a winner was announced in the congressional contest, due to delays in counting mail-in ballots in Allegheny County. On Saturday, November 7th, the Associated Press called the race for Lamb (Associated Press 2020). Parnell, however, refused to concede or accept the results. During the counting process he repeatedly posted on social media that he would not declare victory or concede until "every legal vote has been counted," echoing similar sentiments declared by President Trump as the votes in the presidential contest were tabulated across the country, even after Lamb declared victory (Smith 2020). Following the lead of President Trump and Republicans across the country, Parnell and other state Republicans filed suit to challenge all mail-in ballots in the state, alleging that PA Act 77, the legislation that implements statewide mail-in voting, is unconstitutional (Ward 2020). On December 8, 2020, the U.S. Supreme Court rejected the Republicans' attempt to reverse the certification of the state's electoral votes for Joe Biden, opting not to intervene in the lawsuit (Sherman and Levy 2020).

Official vote counts in the district show Lamb won 51.1% to 48.9% over Parnell (222,242 to 212,279, a difference of 9,963 votes), as shown in Table 8.2, and Lamb was sworn in for a second full term of office on January 3, 2021.

In the highly contentious Mercuri-Skopov race (District 28), over 44,000 ballots were cast, including almost 23,000 mail-in ballots (Pennsylvania Department of State 2020). Election Day turnout heavily favored Mercuri, while mail-in votes were almost 2 to 1 for Skopov. In the end, Mercuri edged out Skopov by a margin of over 3,000 votes.

Mizgorski defeated Geiger Shulman in District 30 by a 9.6-point margin and quickly declared victory. On the same day, Geiger Shulman conceded on Facebook: "It is with a heavy heart that I must share that I have just conceded my race for state representative in Pennsylvania's 30th house district. . . . We proved that our county Democratic Party is out of touch with grassroots voters and energy" (Lissa for PA [@LissaforPA] 2020). Although Mizgorski accepted the election results in her own race, she supported an audit of the 2020 elections at the top of the ballot. Along with Speaker of the House Bryan Cutler (R-Lancaster), Mizgorski posted this statement on her website:

> This is not about who won or lost but about restoring faith in the foundation of our government. We all want to know our votes were fairly counted in this election and we want to ensure they will be fair-

TABLE 8.2 COMPARISON OF 2020 PRESIDENTIAL ELECTION RESULTS WITH SEVENTEENTH CONGRESSIONAL DISTRICT AND 28TH AND 30TH PENNSYLVANIA STATE HOUSE DISTRICT RESULTS

	Trump (R)	Parnell (R)	Difference		Biden (D)	Lamb (D)	Difference
Seventeenth Congressional District	48.1%	48.8%	Parnell +0.7		*50.6%*	*51.1%*	Lamb +0.5
	Trump (R)	Mercuri (R)	Difference		Biden (D)	Skopov (D)	Difference
PA 28th State House District	48.2%	*53.7%*	Mercuri +5.5		*50.7%*	46.2%	Skopov −3.1
	Trump (R)	Mizgorski (R)	Difference		Biden (D)	Shulman (D)	Difference
PA 30th State House District	*49.5%*	*54.8%*	Mizgorski +5.3		49.4%	45.1%	Shulman −4.3

Source: Compiled from precinct data from the OpenElections Project. Accessed March 2, 2021. Available at https://github.com/openelections/openelections-data-pa.git.
Note: Winning percentages are in bold italics.

ly counted in all future elections. . . . In order for the citizens of our Commonwealth and our country to move forward, we must ensure the validity of the results. (Lori Mizgorski for State Representative 2020)

Mercuri, her new Republican colleague, has not, as of this writing, called for the same type of investigation into the election.

Democratic Dissatisfaction

One of the most common themes from the Democratic candidates is dissatisfaction with the direction and messaging of the Democratic Party nationally, highlighting the frustration with the divisions both linear and hierarchical within the Democratic Party. Both Emily Skopov and her campaign manager Nichole Remmert have strong feelings about the perceived lack of support from local and state Democratic organizations. Like Mercuri, she appeared at events with other party members, including Lamb, and she was one of the few state legislative candidates to receive an endorsement from Biden, a distinction that was not extended to Lamb in this cycle. However, her inability to attend the Emerge candidate training program for female Democrats in both 2018 and 2020, coupled with disagreements with organizations such as the House Democratic Campaign Committee and prominent national groups such as EMILY's List, left Skopov feeling that "nobody was doing it for us." Both Skopov and Remmert have been publicly critical of the lack of a cohesive national Democratic strategy and messaging plan for candidates across the ballot, especially those in state and local races—from tweets critical of other more progressive minority legislators in the area, to interviews with the *New York Times* (Gabriel 2020). "We need to be better at a united front," Remmert implores. "We're not willing to have honest conversations even behind closed doors about the fault lines and blunders of the Democratic machine." This plea implies that the campaign did not feel that appropriate attention and support was given to down-ballot candidates, highlighting a more localized race, rather than one that was supported by the state or national party.

Skopov is not alone in her belief that more progressive individuals and policies are hurting the broader Democratic Party. In a postelection interview with the *New York Times*, Lamb gives what he calls an "honest account" of his perceptions of what cost Democrats in down-ballot races: "The rhetoric and the policies and all that stuff—it has gone way too far. It needs to be dialed back. It needs to be rooted in common sense, in reality, and yes, politics. Because we need districts like mine to stay in the majority and get something done for the people that we care about the most" (Herndon 2020). In an interview, Lamb is specifically critical of New York representative Alexandria Ocasio-Cortez, who is much further to the left of Lamb:

> She can put her name behind stuff and that's, I guess, courageous, but when it's a damaging idea or bad policy, like her tweeting out that fracking is bad in the middle of a presidential debate when we're trying to win western Pennsylvania—that's not being anything like a team player. And it's honestly giving a false and ineffective promise to people that makes it very difficult to win the areas where President Trump is most popular in campaigns. (Herndon 2020)

This criticism is a part of the rampant blame-attribution taking place in the aftermath of less-than-stellar Democratic performance in down-ballot races. It also serves to highlight the nationalization of prominent issues across the party, and how while there may be some coordination efforts with down-ballot candidates, these efforts might not always be effective or translate across to candidates in other states. Though Biden won the presidency, Democrats are facing a smaller majority in the House than they had during the 116th Congress, with Republicans gaining a net seven seats. More progressive members of the party, including Congressional Progressive Caucus cochair Pramila Jayapal (D-WA), believe that the left-shift of the party helped turn out younger, more diverse voters (Snell 2020). Interestingly, the same complaints were not made by the Republicans who were interviewed.

Conclusion

While we find evidence of a nationalized congressional race in PA-17, we see that the state legislative candidates participated in much more localized contests. The most apparent nationalization of the Parnell campaign is the frequent linkage between Parnell and Trump, both in terms of policies and in terms of personalities. Parnell used social media in much the same way Trump did, especially as both began to challenge the results of the election. Parnell and Trump took an energetic—sometimes combative—approach to their campaigns, especially criticisms of their opponents and the electoral process, and both lost. Constituents may have taken a retrospective voting approach in evaluating President Trump's performance during his time in office, especially in terms of major district issues (e.g., fracking, unions).

As for the Democratic ticket, Biden and Lamb may have defeated their opponents, but they did so by very slim margins. They spent most of their campaigns in a reactionary, defensive stance to appeal to moderate or swing voters, a group becoming increasingly important not only in western Pennsylvania but across the country. Biden was able to run on the perceived failings of four years of a Trump administration, selling voters a Democratic vision that promoted new solutions to their concerns. Lamb vocally supported Biden on these key issues, but he recognized the importance of maintaining the broadest base of support in a politically divided district. Lamb was also portrayed as Nancy Pelosi's puppet, although he ran and voted as a more moderate Democrat. There is some (off-the-record) speculation, however, that the Lamb campaign may not have wanted a Biden endorsement for fear that it would hurt him with swing voters in the district. Regardless, Lamb endorsed Biden and displayed public support for his campaign on social media and at rallies in western Pennsylvania to combat the nationalized Trumpian messaging.

Down the ballot, some candidates desired to distance themselves within their respective parties to avoid nationalized messaging concerning economic and social issues. Within the Republican ticket, Mizgorski and Mercuri did not engage in debate with their opponents, nor directly engage with them on social media. They were also more wary of a more nationalized approach to their contests, despite the perceived ties to other Republican candidates. Mercuri, although he noted in our interview that he agreed with many of Trump's positions on issues, was resistant to fully tying himself to the president and his politics. However, both Mercuri and Skopov also noted that it was difficult to avoid questions about the top-of-the-ticket race—and the positions of Trump and Biden—when meeting with constituents. Skopov also reiterated frustrations with differentiations between what powers and abilities lie with the state legislature and governor versus Congress or the president, especially in terms of pandemic relief.

Skopov found herself falling victim to what she felt was increasingly partisan messaging driven by factions in the national Democratic apparatus, to which she attributes her loss to Mercuri. These internal divisions—or a lack of nationalization—are, she believes, what hurt state-level candidates and what caused only minimal success for Democrats in Congress. Candidates Mercuri and Mizgorski accepted their district results, although Mizgorski questioned the validity of the election in general. Parnell and Trump contested their losses, declaring election fraud due to mass mail-in voting as a result of the COVID-19 pandemic. Parnell's continued support of Trump-aligned Republicanism is perhaps unsurprising, given his close performance as a first-time candidate, the strong support he received from not only President Trump but other prominent Republicans across the country, and the media attention that he received over his candidacy. However, his extremism brushed some in the Republican Party the wrong way even during the election. Two months before the election, Paul Kane noted that "Parnell has dabbled in bizarre conspiracy theories, including a recent suggestion that Lamb served as a source for leaks about Trump's refusal to attend a military service in France in 2018—leaks that clearly could only come from the president's inner circle" (Kane 2020). Despite these misgivings, with Pat Toomey's announcement that he will not run for reelection to the Senate, both Lamb and Parnell are being discussed as potential 2022 candidates.

Overall, the most nationalized race in our case studies was the congressional race that garnered national attention. While the Democratic incumbent, Lamb, mixed local issues and ties to the local community with nationalized themes, the Republican challenger, Parnell, tied his campaign closely to President Trump and national issues. In the state legislative races, on the other hand, candidates from both parties focused primarily on local issues and, with the exception of the COVID-19 pandemic, generally steered clear of national themes. In the end, party, incumbency, and local concerns seemed to outweigh national issues and themes in the Seventeenth Congressional District. The voters returned all legislative incumbents to office, choosing Democrats for federal office (Biden and Lamb) and Republicans for state legislative seats (Mercuri and Mizgorski).

REFERENCES

Allegheny-Fayette Central Labor Council (@AlleghenyLabor). 2020. "@ConorLambPA & @Senatorcosta getting us fired up this morning before we hit the streets & the phones for @JoeBiden & all of our Labor-endorsed candidates." Twitter, October 31, 2020. Available at https://twitter.com/AlleghenyLabor/status/1322571043823902722.

Associated Press. 2020. "Biden Takes Pennsylvania; Lamb Wins in 17th House District." November 7, 2020. Available at https://apnews.com/article/election-2020-virus-out break-senate-elections-harrisburg-pennsylvania-51190cdb0901096d8cebd4d4a52d 2ef0.

Ball, Molly. 2020. "'You've Got to Have Purpose.' Joe Biden's 2020 Campaign Is the Latest Test in a Lifetime of Loss." *Time*, January 30, 2020. Available at https://time.com /longform/joe-biden-2020/.

Ballotpedia. 2020a. "Pennsylvania's 17th Congressional District." Accessed December 12, 2020. Available at https://ballotpedia.org/Pennsylvania%27s_17th_Congressional_Dis trict.

———. 2020b. "Pennsylvania House of Representatives District 30." Accessed January 5, 2021. Available at https://ballotpedia.org/Pennsylvania_House_of_Representatives _District_30#cite_note-1.

———. 2021. "Rob Mercuri." Accessed January 20, 2021. Available at https://ballotpedia .org/Rob_Mercuri.

Blade, Rachel, and Jake Sherman. 2017. "Tim Murphy Resigns from Congress." *Politico*, October 5, 2017. Available at https://www.politico.com/story/2017/10/05/tim-murphy -resigns-from-congress-243510.

Bowman, Bridget. 2018. "Can Unions Push Conor Lamb to an Unlikely Victory in Western Pennsylvania?" *Roll Call*, March 8, 2018. Available at https://www.rollcall.com /2018/03/08/can-unions-push-conor-lamb-to-an-unlikely-victory-in-pennsylvania/.

———. 2020a. "Battle for Congress Seeks a Slice of the Spotlight as Democrats 'Convene' to Anoint Biden, Harris." *Roll Call*, August 17, 2020. Available at https://www.rollcall .com/2020/08/17/battle-for-congress-seeks-a-slice-of-the-spotlight-as-democrats -convene-to-anoint-biden-harris/.

———. 2020b. "Both Parties Featured This House Battleground at Their Conventions." *Roll Call*, August 24, 2020. Available at https://www.rollcall.com/2020/08/24/both -parties-featured-this-house-battleground-at-their-conventions/.

Boyle, Matthew. 2020. "Exclusive—Sean Parnell: Democrat Conor Lamb Does 'Nothing but Toe the Line' for Nancy Pelosi." *Breitbart*, June 22, 2020. Available at https://www .breitbart.com/politics/2020/06/22/exclusive-sean-parnell-democrat-conor-lamb -does-nothing-but-toe-the-line-for-nancy-pelosi/.

Cole, John. 2020a. "Lamb Serves on Biden-Sanders Climate Change Panel That Provides DNC Platform Recommendations." *PoliticsPA*, July 14, 2020. Available at https://www .politicspa.com/lamb-serves-on-biden-sanders-climate-change-panel-that-provides -dnc-platform-recommendations/95072/.

———. 2020b. "Parnell Touts Trump in RNC Speech." *PoliticsPA*, August 24, 2020. Available at https://www.politicspa.com/parnell-touts-trump-in-rnc-speech/95531/.

Colvin, Jill, and Josh Boak. 2020. "Trump Claims Credit for Shell Plant Announced Under Obama." *Associated Press*, August 13, 2020. Available at https://apnews.com/article /00061b19834849f8b6e1aa73ecdf54e4.

Cook Political Report. 2020. "2020 House Race Ratings." November 2, 2020. Available at https://www.cookpolitical.com/sites/default/files/2021-01/2020%20Final%20House %20Ratings%20January%202021.pdf.

C-SPAN.org. 2018. "President Trump in Moon Township, Pennsylvania." *C-SPAN.org*, March 10, 2018. Video. Available at https://www.c-span.org/video/?442305-1/president-trump -campaigns-rick-saccone-pennsylvania.

Czachor, Emily. 2020. "Pennsylvania House Speaker Resigns Amid Accusations GOP Reps Hid a Member's Virus Infection." *Newsweek*, June 10, 2020. Available at https:// www.newsweek.com/pennsylvania-house-speaker-resigns-amid-accusations-gop -reps-hid-members-virus-infection-1510003.

Davis, Susan, and Scott Detrow. 2017. "A Year Later, the Shock of Trump's Win Hasn't Totally Worn Off in Either Party." *NPR News*, November 9, 2017. Available at https:// www.npr.org/2017/11/09/562307566/a-year-later-the-shock-of-trumps-win-hasn-t -totally-worn-off-in-either-party.

Deto, Ryan. 2020a. "Geiger Shulman Calls for Debate in Pittsburgh's Most Competitive Race, Mizgorski Silent." *Pittsburgh City Paper*, October 5, 2020. Available at https:// www.pghcitypaper.com/pittsburgh/geiger-shulman-calls-for-debate-in-pittsburghs -most-competitive-race-mizgorski-silent/Content?oid=18121324.

———. 2020b. "Mailers in North Hills State House Race Share 'a Bald-Faced Lie,' Says Candidate Emily Skopov." *Pittsburgh City Paper*, July 15, 2020. Available at https:// www.pghcitypaper.com/pittsburgh/mailers-in-north-hills-state-house-race-share-a -bald-faced-lie-says-candidate-emily-skopov/Content?oid=17656125.

Emily Skopov for Pennsylvania. 2020. "COVID-19 Topics." Accessed January 5, 2021. Available at https://www.electemily4pa.com/covid-19-topics/.

Engelkemier, Paul. 2017. "Saccone Wins PA-18 Nomination." *PoliticsPA*, November 11, 2017. Available at https://www.politicspa.com/saccone-wins-pa-18-nomination/85345/.

Erdley, Deb, and Natasha Lindstrom. 2020. "Biden Scores Big Union Wins on Train Trek Through Western Pennsylvania." *TribLive*, September 30, 2020. Available at https://trib live.com/local/westmoreland/biden-scores-big-union-wins-on-train-trek-through-west ern-pennsylvania/.

Fischer-Baum, Reuben, and Kevin Uhrmacher. 2018. "PA-18 Will Be Split in Four Come November. Here's Why the Special Election There Still Matters." *Washington Post*, March 8, 2018. Available at https://www.washingtonpost.com/graphics/2018/politics/pennsylva nia-18-preview/.

Friends of Rob Mercuri. 2020. "Issues." Accessed January 5, 2021. Available at https://www .robmercuri.com/issues.

Gabriel, Trip. 2020. "How Democrats Suffered Crushing Down-Ballot Losses Across America." *New York Times*, November 28, 2020. Available at https://www.nytimes.com/2020 /11/28/us/politics/democrats-republicans-state-legislatures.html.

Gonzales, Nathan. 2018. "New Pennsylvania Map, New Pennsylvania House Ratings." *Roll Call*, February 21, 2018. Available at https://www.rollcall.com/2018/02/21/new-penn sylvania-map-new-pennsylvania-house-ratings/.

GovTrack. 2021. "Rep. Conor Lamb." Accessed January 3, 2021. Available at https://www .govtrack.us/congress/members/conor_lamb/412744.

Herndon, Astead. 2020. "Conor Lamb, House Moderate, on Biden's Win, 'the Squad' and the Future of the Democratic Party." *New York Times*, November 8, 2020. Available at https://www.nytimes.com/2020/11/08/us/politics/conor-lamb-democrats-biden.html.

Herring, An-Li. 2020. "Western Pa. Democrats Poised for Reckoning after Rash of Down -Ballot Losses." *WITF News*, November 11, 2020. Available at https://www.witf.org/2020 /11/11/western-pa-democrats-poised-for-reckoning-after-rash-of-down-ballot-losses/.

Herring, An-Li, and Luck Perkins. 2018. "Conor Lamb Beats Fellow Incumbent Keith Roth fus in Race for 17th Congressional District." *90.5 WESA*, November 6, 2018. Available at https://www.wesa.fm/post/conor-lamb-beats-fellow-incumbent-keith-rothfus-race -17th-congressional-district#stream/0.

IMDb. 2021. "Emily Skopov." Accessed November 10, 2020. Available at https://www.imdb
.com/name/nm0804662/.

Isenstadt, Alex. 2018. "Republicans Trash Their Candidate in Pa. Special Election." *Politico*,
March 7, 2018. Available at https://www.politico.com/story/2018/03/07/republicans
-pennsylvania-special-election-445221.

iVoterGuide. 2020. "Candidate Profile." *iVoterGuide.com*. Accessed December 5, 2020.
Available at https://ivoterguide.com/candidate?elecK=700&raceK=1792&primarypa
rtyk=R&canK=52703.

Kane, Paul. 2020. "Rep. Conor Lamb, Who Showed Democrats How to Win in Trump
Districts, Works to Deliver Pennsylvania for Biden." *Washington Post*, September 16,
2020. Available at https://www.washingtonpost.com/powerpost/biden-pennsylvania
-democrats-congress/2020/09/16/2fe2b97e-f83a-11ea-a275-1a2c2d36e1f1_story.html.

Kiely, Eugene. 2020. "Trump Wrong About Conor Lamb's Vote on Pelosi." *FactCheck
.org*, May 26, 2020. Available at https://www.factcheck.org/2020/05/trump-wrong-about
-conor-lambs-vote-on-pelosi/.

Lamb, Conor, and Harold Hamm. 2020. "Joe Biden Does Not Support a Fracking Ban."
Wall Street Journal, February 2, 2020. Available at https://www.wsj.com/articles/joe
-biden-does-not-support-a-fracking-ban-11580670403.

Law, Tara. 2019. "Shell Union Workers Had to Choose Between Attending President Trump's
Speech or Losing Pay: Reports." *Time*, August 18, 2019. Available at https://time.com
/5654772/shell-union-trump-speech-no-pay/.

Levy, Marc. 2020. "Biden Adds to Stable of Endorsements in Pennsylvania." *AP News*, January 6, 2020. Available at https://apnews.com/article/a508529f92e5d4e3932a95af74f40c21.

Lissa for PA (@LissaforPA). 2020. "It is with a heavy heart that I must share." Facebook,
November 6, 2020. Available at https://www.facebook.com/LissaforPA/posts/3309779
982477123.

Lissa Geiger Shulman for State Representative. 2020. "Lissa Geiger Shulman." Accessed
January 6, 021. Available at https://lissaforpa.com.

Lori4PA. 2020. "You may have seen my opponent's negative ads attacking me. They tried
this same tactic in 2018, and they're doing it again." Facebook, October 24, 2020.
Available at https://www.facebook.com/Lori4PA/posts/839018326841479.

Lori Mizgorski for State Representative. 2020. "Mizgorski: Pennsylvanians Must Be Able
to Trust Election Results | PA State Rep. Lori Mizgorski." Press release, November 10,
2020. Available at http://www.repmizgorski.com/News/18544/Latest-News/Mizgorski
-Pennsylvanians-Must-Be-Able-to-Trust-Election-Results.

Lori Mizgorski PA State Senate. 2020a. "Endorsements." Accessed January 6, 2021. Available at https://lorimizgorski.com/endorsements.

———. 2020b. "Issues." Accessed January 6, 2021. Available at https://lorimizgorski.com
/issues.

Lybrand, Holmes. 2020. "Fact Check: Biden Falsely Claims He Never Opposed Fracking."
CNN News, October 23, 2020. Available at https://www.cnn.com/2020/10/23/politics
/biden-fracking-fact-check/index.html.

Marans, Daniel. 2018. "Unions Show Their Force in Pennsylvania District Won by Trump."
Huffington Post, March 13, 2018. Available at https://www.huffpost.com/entry/conor
-lamb-organized-labor-shows-force-pennsylvania-special-election_n_5aa7e620e4b
04042d27e853e.

Montanaro, David. 2020. "GOP Candidate Parnell Blasts Pa. Governor's 'Absolutely Ab-
surd' Benchmark for Full Reopening." *Fox News*, May 25, 2020. Available at https://www

.foxnews.com/media/gop-candidate-sean-parnell-pennsylvania-gov-wolf-vaccine
-reopening.

Moore, Daniel. 2020a. "Conor Lamb Wins Another Two Years in Congress, as AP Calls
17th District." *Pittsburgh Post-Gazette*, November 7, 2020. Available at https://www
.post-gazette.com/news/politics-state/2020/11/07/Conor-Lamb-defeats-Sean-Parnell
-House-District-17-Mt-Lebanon-Associated-Press/stories/202011070068.

———. 2020b. "In Race Between Conor Lamb and Sean Parnell, a Referendum on a Moderate Democrat in Trump's Washington. *Pittsburgh Post-Gazette*, October 25, 2020.
Available at https://www.post-gazette.com/news/politics-nation/2020/10/25/Conor
-Lamb-Sean-Parnell-17th-Congressional-District-Trump-Pelosi/stories/2020102500
03?cid=search.

Moore, Stephen. 2020. "Democrats' War on Fracking Will Cost Them in Battleground
States." *Wall Street Journal*, January 22, 2020. Available at https://www.wsj.com/articles
/democrats-war-on-fracking-will-cost-them-in-battleground-states-11579734852
?mod=article_inline.

Osborne, David. 2020. "Unions Were Democratic Shock Troops—until 2020." *Philadelphia
Inquirer*, October 14, 2020. Available at https://www.inquirer.com/opinion/commen
tary/unions-trump-support-biden-pennsylvania-election-2020-20201014.html.

Pennsylvania Department of State. 2020. "Election—County Breakdown Results." Accessed January 5, 2021. Available at https://www.electionreturns.pa.gov/General/Co
untyBreakDownResults?officeId=13&districtId=100&ElectionID=83&ElectionType
=G&IsActive=1.

Pennsylvania Fund for Change. 2020a. "Rob Mercuri Is Too Extreme." Mail piece in the
author's possession.

———. 2020b. "Rob Mercuri: Extremely Wrong for Us." Mail piece in the author's possession.

———. 2020c. "With Rob Mercuri, Bigotry Is Always on the Menu." Mail piece in the
author's possession.

Pennsylvania Legislature. Assembly. H.B. 2400. Amendment to the Administrative Code
of 1929, providing emergency COVID-19 provisions. Available at https://www.legis
.state.pa.us/CFDOCS/Legis/PN/Public/btCheck.cfm?txtType=PDF&sessYr=2019&s
essInd=0&billBody=H&billTyp=B&billNbr=2400&pn=3520.

———. Redistricting Reform Constitutional Amendment. H.B. 22. 2019–2020 sess. Available at https://www.legis.state.pa.us/CFDOCS/billInfo/billInfo.cfm?syear=2019&sI
nd=0&body=H&type=B&bn=22.

———. Redistricting Reform: Independent Redistricting Commission for Congressional
Districts. H.B. 23. 2019–2020 sess. Available at https://www.legis.state.pa.us/cfdocs
/billinfo/billinfo.cfm?syear=2019&sind=0&body=H&type=B&bn=0023.

Potter, Chris. 2019. "President Trump Rips Paris Agreement, Democrats While in Pittsburgh." *90.5 WESA*, October 23, 2019. Available at https://www.wesa.fm/post/pres
ident-trump-rips-paris-agreement-democrats-while-pittsburgh#stream/0.

———. 2020. "Lamb Breaks with Democrats on Coronavirus Relief Bill He Calls 'Not
Focused.'" *90.5 WESA*, May 16, 2020. Available at https://www.wesa.fm/post/lamb
-breaks-democrats-coronavirus-relief-bill-he-calls-not-focused#stream/0.

ProPublica. 2020a. "Conor Lamb." Accessed December 8, 2020. Available at https://pro
jects.propublica.org/electionbot/candidate/H8PA18181/.

———. 2020b. "Sean Parnell." Accessed December 8, 2020. Available at https://projects
.propublica.org/electionbot/candidate/H0PA17115/.

Prose, J. D. 2020. "'There's So Damn Much at Stake,' Biden Tells Labor Crowd in Beaver County." *Beaver Times*, November 2, 2020. Available at https://www.timesonline.com /story/news/2020/11/02/biden-touts-labor-ties-election-eve-swing-western-pennsyl vania/6131529002/.

Republican Federal Committee of Pennsylvania. 2020. "Don't let them lock it back down." Mail piece in the author's possession.

Rizzo, Salvador. 2020. "Fact-Checking the Biden Fracking Fracas." *Washington Post*, March 19, 2020. Available at https://www.washingtonpost.com/politics/2020/03/19/fact-check ing-biden-fracking-fracas/.

Rob Mercuri for State House. 2020. "Great turnout for our Day of Action for these two Young Republicans, Sean Parnell and Rob Mercuri! Thanks to all who came out and knocked with masks in this heat." Facebook, August 1, 2020. Available at https:// www.facebook.com/Mercuri4PA/posts/200231638188204.

Routh, Julian. 2020. "Healthcare, Economic Relief at Center of Lamb-Parnell Debate." *Pittsburgh Post-Gazette*, September 26, 2020. Available at https://www.post-gazette .com/news/vote2020/2020/09/26/Conor-Lamb-Sean-Parnell-Pennsylvania-s-17th -Congressional-District-debate/stories/202009260057.

Said, Samira, and Vanessa Yurkevich. 2020. "This Single Issue Could Decide How Western Pennsylvania Votes." *CNN News*, October 28, 2020. Available at https://www.cnn .com/2020/10/28/us/fracking-western-pennsylvania-election-voters/index.html.

Schwartz, Ian. 2018. "United Steelworkers' Leo Gerard: Members Won't Forget What Trump Did, He Stopped Wealth Transfer." *RealClearPolitics.com*, March 8, 2018. Available at https://www.realclearpolitics.com/video/2018/03/08/united_steelworkers_leo _gerard_members_wont_forget_what_trump_did_he_stopped_wealth_transfer.html.

Scolforo, Mark. 2020. "Pennsylvania House Speaker Says He'll Leave Office Next Week." *AP News*, June 10, 2020. Available at https://apnews.com/article/e8300cc19de0055485 01a2290a539f78.

Sherman, Mark, and Marc Levy. 2020. "High Court Rejects GOP Bid to Halt Biden's Pennsylvania Win." *AP News*, December 8, 2020. Available at https://apnews.com/article /high-court-reject-gop-bid-halt-biden-win-0b7005328243eeca23f8bc3368549879.

Siegel, Josh. 2020. "Biden's Liberal Climate Policies Feared by Unions in Pennsylvania." *Washington Examiner*, July 16, 2020. Available at https://www.washingtonexaminer .com/policy/energy/biden-liberal-climate-policies-feared-by-unions-in-pennsylvania.

Singer, Jeff. 2018. "Under Swingy Pennsylvania's New Map, Trump Won 10 Districts and Clinton 8. The Old Split: 12–6 Trump." *Daily Kos*, February 19, 2018. Available at https:// www.dailykos.com/stories/2018/2/19/1742923/-Under-Pennsylvania-s-new-map -Trump-won-10-districts-and-Clinton-8-The-old-split-12-6-Trump.

Skopov, Emily. 2020. "This Turzai Bill Putting Pennsylvania Back to Work Is Bad for Pennsylvanians." *Pennsylvania Capital-Star*, April 12, 2020. Available at https://www .penncapital-star.com/working-the-economy/this-turzai-bill-putting-pennsylvania -back-to-work-is-bad-for-pennsylvanians-opinion/.

Smith, Lydia. 2020. "Pennsylvania GOP Candidate Refuses to Concede Until 'Every Legal Vote' Counted." *Newsweek*, November 6, 2020. Available at https://www.newsweek.com /pennsylvania-gop-candidate-refuses-concede-until-every-legal-vote-counted-1545496.

Snell, Kelsey. 2020. "House Democrats Dissect What Went Wrong and How to Rebound from Losses." *NPR News*, November 15, 2020. Available at https://www.npr.org/2020 /11/15/934586955/house-democrats-dissect-what-went-wrong-and-how-to-rebound -from-losses.

United Steel Workers. 2020. "USW Endorses Joe Biden for President." Accessed May 20, 2020. Available at https://www.usw.org/news/media-center/releases/2020/usw-endorses -joe-biden-for-president.

U.S. Census Bureau. 2017. "My Congressional District." Accessed January 5, 2021. Available at https://www.census.gov/mycd/?st=42&cd=17.

Vellucci, Justin. 2020. "Jewish Candidate for PA Statehouse Attacked for Her 'Beverly Hills Politics.'" *Pittsburgh Jewish Chronicle*, August 23, 2020. Available at https://jewishchron icle.timesofisrael.com/jewish-candidate-for-pa-statehouse-attacked-for-her-beverly -hills-politics/.

Wallace, Danielle. 2020. "RNC Speakers: What to Know about Sean Parnell." *Fox News*, August 24, 2020. Available at https://www.foxnews.com/politics/rnc-speaker-sean-par nell-republican-convention.

Ward, Paula Reed. 2017a. "Democrats Choose Conor Lamb, a Former Federal Prosecutor, to Replace Tim Murphy." *Pittsburgh Post-Gazette*, November 19, 2017. Available at https://www.post-gazette.com/news/politics-local/2017/11/19/Conor-Lamb-Dem ocrats-pick-replace-Tim-Murphy-18th-Congressional-district/stories/201711190199.

———. 2017b. "Rep. Tim Murphy, Popular with Pro-Life Movement, Urged Abortion in Affair, Texts Suggest." *Pittsburgh Post-Gazette*, October 3, 2017. Available at https:// www.post-gazette.com/news/politics-nation/2017/10/03/rep-tim-Murphy-pro-life -sought-abortion-affair-shannon-edwards-susan-mosychuk-pennsylvania-chief-of -staff-congress-emails-texts/stories/201710030018?utm_term=Autofeed&utm_cam paign=Echobox.

———. 2020. "Rep. Mike Kelly, Sean Parnell Continue to Pursue Legal Challenge to Pa. Election Results. *TribLive*, December 2, 2020. Available at https://triblive.com/local /regional/rep-mike-kelly-parnell-continue-to-pursue-legal-challenge-to-pa-election -results/.

Weigel, David, and Josh Dawsey. 2020. "Biden Campaigns in Close Pennsylvania Congressional Race." *Washington Post*, March 6, 2020. Available at https://www.wash ingtonpost.com/powerpost/biden-campaigns-in-close-pennsylvania-congressional -race/2018/03/06/cd280e34-2153-11e8-badd-7c9f29a55815_story.html.

White House. 2020. "American Energy Dominance: Bad for Bureaucrats, Great for Our Country," July 29, 2020. Accessed December 20, 2021. Available at https://trumpwhite house.archives.gov/articles/president-trump-is-restoring-american-energy-domi nance/

INTERVIEWS

Barsky, Corey. Campaign Manager for Rob Mercuri. December 8, 2020.

Kozak, Alexandra. Government Relations Specialist. December 10, 2020. Email message to author.

Mercuri, Rob. Candidate for the 30th Pennsylvania House District. December 15, 2020.

Remmert, Nichole. Campaign Manager for Emily Skopov. December 15, 2020.

Skopov, Emily. Candidate for the 30th Pennsylvania House District. December 8, 2020.

9

Conclusion

What Have We Learned about Nationalization?

STEPHEN K. MEDVIC, MATTHEW M. SCHOUSEN,
AND BERWOOD A. YOST

The belief that American politics has become nationalized is widely held among both pundits and scholars. Systematic evidence of the phenomenon is typically found in patterns of voting behavior. Indeed, the correlation between vote shares in state legislative races, for example, and vote shares for president is extraordinarily strong. And popular commentators are quick to share anecdotes when state or local candidates weigh in on national legislation or link themselves (or, more likely, their opponents) to national partisan figures.

This book takes the nationalization thesis seriously. It does so by examining the thesis from a perspective that has yet to garner much attention in the literature on nationalization, namely, from the perspective of candidates and their campaigns. We have analyzed the 2020 presidential, congressional, and state legislative races in Pennsylvania in the aggregate (i.e., statewide), and our case study authors have done so "vertically," that is, up and down the ballot within selected congressional districts. By doing so, we provide the first systematic study of nationalization within campaigns.

What follows in this chapter is, first, a detailed summary of our findings, where we see that the evidence for nationalization in congressional and state legislative campaigns is mixed at best. We then consider theoretical aspects of the nationalization thesis: Why should we expect nonnational campaigns to be nationalized in the first place; why is voting behavior as nationalized as it appears to be when campaigns, generally, are not; and what explains variation in levels of nationalization between campaigns? Finally, we identify limitations to our current study and suggest areas for future exploration.

Summary of Findings

Throughout this book, we have examined three sets of actors who are involved in campaigns and elections: voters and their behavior, parties and their surrogates, and candidates and their campaigns. The evidence for nationalization is strongest among voters, as we might expect based on previous research, although even here the evidence is somewhat mixed. In the activity of parties and outside groups, and in the behavior of candidates and their campaigns, we see considerable evidence of localized messaging.

Voters

Voters' expressed preferences and behaviors support the idea that voters are nationalized at some levels of aggregation, but nationalized behavior is less persistent at lower levels of aggregation. The success of incumbents in these case studies offers some evidence of more localized politics. The following conclusions about voting behaviors, based on our aggregate analysis and the vertical analysis in the case studies, begin with the strongest evidence for nationalization and end with two counterfactuals that weaken those claims.

- There is a strong correlation in county-level voting patterns for different offices. In the 2020 election in Pennsylvania, the correlations between presidential vote share and congressional vote ($r = 0.987$), state senate vote ($r = 0.950$), and state house vote ($r = 0.881$) were high.
- Postelection survey interviews showed that nearly nine in ten supporters of both Trump (87%) and Biden (87%) supported candidates from the same party in other state and local elections. These postelection interviews found that 41% of voters voted straight Republican, 42% of voters voted straight Democrat, and the balance, about one in six voters, split their tickets.
- Polls conducted during the fall showed that well over four in five voters agreed that the candidates they prefer in congressional, state house, and state senate elections align their views with the views of the candidate they support for president.
- District-level returns show split results between presidential preference and district-level preference in eight of eighteen races in our case studies. Two congressional races, in the First District and

the Eighth, resulted in different partisan selections for president and Congress. Six (of twelve) state house races had different results (see Table 9.1).

- Nationalization is thought to make appeals to incumbency and candidate traits and experience much less important, but our case studies show that most incumbents won (fifteen out of sixteen in these races), in some cases overcoming significant partisan disadvantages (see, for example, Chapters 5 and 7).

Parties and Party Surrogates

There is some evidence, particularly among Democratic campaigns in southeastern Pennsylvania, that the parties coordinated their activities with local campaigns, but party coordination for federal and state-level candidates was minimal in other places. In addition, party spending that joined federal campaigns with state campaigns and incentivized coordinated messaging was almost nonexistent. Among our key findings are the following:

- Beyond the respective party campaign committees (and party-aligned super PACs), advertising data suggest that very few organizations make message appeals in more than one campaign. That is, there is very little spending by outside groups that might link various races to a singular message.
- The above point is particularly true with respect to spending by outside groups in races at different levels of government. Only four groups spent money in more than one type of race, and three of those were active only in federal races for president and Congress.
- Party committees stay entirely in their own lanes. That is, national committees spend in the presidential race, Hill committees spend in congressional races, and state party committees spend in state legislative races.
- Advertising by parties and outside groups tends to follow the lead of the candidate that the parties or outside groups support. If a candidate makes nationalized appeals, so too will the parties and outside groups; if messages are more local in nature, the parties and outside groups will typically reinforce those messages.

Candidates and Campaigns

Campaign messaging is wildly divergent. Some campaigns see a strategic advantage in nationalizing at least part of their messages, or the campaigns

TABLE 9.1 DISTRICT CHARACTERISTICS AND ELECTION OUTCOMES FOR CASE STUDY DISTRICTS

District	PA-143	PA-144	CD-1	PA-150	PA-154	CD-4	PA-119	PA-120	CD-8
Population density: people/square mile	380.5	1,057.3	1,117.4	1634.7	3752.1	1532.1	331.1	1,025.3	262.1
Population white	92%	87%	82%	75%	61%	80%	83%	89%	78%
Population black	1%	2%	4%	9%	25%	10%	2%	4%	6%
Population Hispanic	3%	4%	6%	5%	5%	6%	11%	5%	13%
Foreign-born	6%	8%	11%	11%	10%	10%	6%	3%	7%
Median household income	$103,081	$98,634	$93,474	$107,381	$92,490	$91,030	$50,676	$55,888	$56,149
Bachelor's degree or higher	52%	46%	43%	48%	57%	49%	19%	28%	24%
Registered Democrat	38%	38%	43%	43%	69%	49%	48%	49%	49%
Registered Democrat—Registered Republican	-5.5	-7.7	3.2	2.6	49.6	13.3	9.8	9.6	11.6
Ad nationalization score	—	—	4.3	—	—	3.2	—	—	4.3
District winner party	R	R	R	D	D	D	D	R	D
Presidential winner party	D	D	D	D	D	D	R	R	R
President and district winner same party	No	No	No	Yes	Yes	Yes	No	Yes	No
Incumbent win	No	Yes	Yes	Yes	OPEN	Yes	Yes	Yes	Yes

Source: Data compiled from preceding chapters.

District	PA-105	PA-199	CD-10	PA-6	PA-9	CD-16	PA-28	PA-30	CD-17
Population density: people/square mile	1,058.5	278.8	689.3	113.1	331.1	204.8	1,409.3	1,205.6	882.9
Population white	74%	87%	73%	93%	90%	89%	86%	94%	87%
Population black	12%	4%	11%	2%	5%	4%	2%	1%	6%
Population Hispanic	5%	4%	9%	2%	2%	3%	2%	1%	2%
Foreign-born	9%	5%	8%	2%	2%	2%	9%	4%	5%
Median household income	$74,626	$64,204	$67,155	$56,527	$47,324	$54,627	$110,430	$91,459	$70,857
Bachelor's degree or higher	38%	31%	32%	28%	23%	28%	66%	51%	43%
Registered Democrat	40%	35%	40%	35%	45%	40%	38%	44%	49%
Registered Democrat—Registered Republican	-4.4	-13.9	-4.1	-16.9	1.4	-6.1	-6.9	2.1	11.5
Ad nationalization score	4.1	—	3.0	—	—	2.3	1.5	2.7	3.3
District winner party	R	R	R	R	D	R	R	R	D
Presidential winner party	D	R	R	R	R	R	D	R	D
President and district winner same party	No	Yes	Yes	Yes	No	Yes	No	Yes	Yes
Incumbent win	Yes	Yes	Yes	Yes	Yes	Yes	OPEN	Yes	Yes

Note: Data compiled from preceding chapters.

have candidates with a personal affinity for such messaging, while others are much more focused on local messages. Although most campaigns referenced national issues or personalities at some point during the campaign, these references were very often presented with local context.

- Advertising for the state's congressional races had an almost equal balance of national and local messages, shading just a bit toward the nationalization end of the scale. On the one hand, the contests in both the First and Eighth Districts had an average score of 4.3 (with 5 as the highest level of nationalization), indicating a fairly high level of nationalization. Ads in the Fourth, Tenth, Sixteenth, and Seventeenth Districts were either balanced between national and local messages or were decidedly local in their emphasis (with average scores of 3.2, 3.0, 2.3, and 3.3, respectively). The average nationalization score for all congressional ads aired in Pennsylvania in 2020 (including those not covered in the case studies) was 3.5.
- Advertising for state house races had relatively little nationalization of messages, although it should be noted that the ads are not entirely localized. As in the congressional races, some races were more nationalized than others. With a score of 4.1, the most nationalized of all state house races was the contest in the 105th District, which was discussed in Chapter 6. Several districts, such as the Thirtieth, had messaging that balanced national appeals and more localized ones, but most races had scores on the localized end of the scale. The average nationalization score in all state house races was 2.5.
- Looking in the aggregate at the case studies does not show the level of campaign nationalization one might expect based on existing scholarship. The presidential race, while obviously national in scope, did contain localized messages. Congressional contests straddled the divide between national and local. Because members of Congress deal with national issues, those issues were the focus of many of the appeals made by, and on behalf of, congressional candidates. But U.S. House members also represent local districts, and thus campaign ads often attempt to tie these candidates to the district or to present the candidates as "one of us." Finally, state legislative campaigns are heavily localized. National issues undoubtedly find their way into candidates' messages, but the bulk of the messaging consists of local appeals based on parochial issues or candidate traits.
- The evidence from the Bucks County races (Chapter 3) illustrated how competitive districts often constrain nationalized campaign-

ing. Every district studied in Bucks County was won by Biden, but these districts also all elected Republicans down-ballot, including the sole defeat of an incumbent state house Democrat. In these districts, Republicans focused on atypical issues (for example, environmental protection) that were more in tune with the district and local concerns than with national Republican priorities. Bipartisanship was a common theme among these Republican candidates. In fact, Republicans in these races "consistently avoided identifying as Republican."

- The unusual case among those studied was in southeastern Pennsylvania. Democrats running in the Fourth Congressional District worked to express a consistent message that every vote mattered and that change would occur only if Democrats were elected across the board. Even here, though, Republicans were not nearly as unified, because the candidates were running individualized campaigns with varying degrees of allegiance to the national GOP and President Trump.

- In the Eighth Congressional District, the challenger tried to nationalize the election, while the Democratic incumbent Matt Cartwright focused more on local issues and constituency service.

- In central Pennsylvania (the Tenth Congressional District), Republican incumbents largely talked about local issues when promoting their own campaigns and accomplishments, but they were much more nationalized when discussing their opponents, attempting to connect their Democratic challengers to unpopular national Democratic figures.

- As the 9th State House District illustrates, candidates who consistently message about the specifics of local issues can win, even when the candidate differs from the partisan leanings of their district, and even when their opponent runs a primarily nationalized campaign.

- In the Seventeenth Congressional District, the Democratic incumbent, Lamb, mixed local issues and ties to the local community with nationalized themes, while the Republican challenger, Parnell, tied his campaign closely to President Trump and national issues. In the state legislative races, on the other hand, candidates from both parties focused primarily on local issues and, with the exception of the COVID-19 pandemic, generally steered clear of national themes.

- A nationalized strategy is never used by both candidates in a single race. In all the races in our study, not one race featured a predominantly nationalized Democrat squaring off against a predominately nationalized Republican.

Theoretical Considerations

Having concluded that there is mixed evidence to support the nationalization thesis, we now take a step back and consider the question of nationalization from a theoretical perspective. In the discussion that follows, we take up three questions about nationalization. First, why would candidates below the presidential level nationalize their messages in the first place? Second, if campaigns are not heavily nationalized, why is voting behavior nationalized? And, third, what might explain the variation in levels of nationalization we found among campaigns? Of course, our answers to these questions contain a considerable amount of speculation. Nevertheless, we offer those answers in the spirit of building theoretical explanations of a phenomenon—nationalization—that is more nuanced than many have previously thought.[1]

Why Would Any Local Campaign Be Nationalized?

Countless observers have declared American politics to be nationalized. As noted at several points throughout this book, virtually all of the evidence for nationalization is taken from voting behavior and election results. Still, the assumption among observers seems to be that, at all levels, elite political actors—candidates and elected officials, party operatives and activists, and members of advocacy groups—are also behaving in nationalized ways. With respect to legislators specifically, Hopkins (2018) maintains, "Nationalized political behavior is likely to make legislators more unequivocally focused on national partisan and ideological questions. . . . Legislators are no longer as willing to buck their party in favor of a local interest. Every vote becomes a partisan test of strength rather than an opportunity to fashion a bill-specific coalition" (238).

It is not immediately clear why politicians, and the party and interest group activists who work to elect them, would emphasize national issues over local issues. After all, every elected official but the president represents a state or a (more or less) local district. Thus, we might expect candidates for nonfederal offices to focus on the concerns of their districts, which almost by definition will be state and local concerns. Even congressional candidates, running in what are essentially local areas, would be rational to address the specific needs of their districts, which will vary tremendously across the country, and to highlight their own ability to serve their would-be constituents.

So why might local campaigns be nationalized? One explanation, which Hopkins (2018) emphasizes, is the disproportionate attention voters have begun paying to national politics. The corresponding lack of attention to local politics is likely rooted in the well-documented decline in sources of local news, particularly with respect to newspapers (Sullivan 2020; Abernathy 2020). Of course, national news sources, and especially cable news stations, focus almost exclusively on national politics. As a result, state and local candidates may feel that they have to enter the national debate in order to gain attention.

Hopkins also notes that campaign contributions, at least to U.S. House and Senate candidates, have increasingly come from outside candidates' districts or states. In 1990, 31.4% of itemized contributions (i.e., those over $200) came from outside the state; by 2012, that number had risen to 67.8% (Hopkins 2018, 76–77). Similarly, Gimpel, Lee, and Pearson-Merkowitz (2008) found that by 2004, 45% of all itemized contributions to House candidates came from donors who live outside both the recipient's district and any adjacent district (378–79). Presumably, these figures have increased over time as the internet has become more integral to fundraising efforts. Thus, the potential to raise money from a national donor pool creates an incentive to nationalize one's appeal.

Finally, partisan polarization, or at least ideological sorting between the parties, and negative partisanship may force candidates to signal their connections to the team. Blurring partisan distinctions, which are established nationally, will fail to generate the kind of support candidates need to be successful. This is particularly true in primaries, although nationalized partisan signals sent in order to win a nomination will likely carry over to the general election.

The evidence we have provided in this book suggests that down-ballot candidates do make nationalized appeals but are just as likely, if not more likely, to make localized appeals. Our strong hunch is that nonnational campaigns, were they to take place in a vacuum, would be entirely localized. But national politics creates pressures and incentives that encourage candidates for state and local offices to at least nod to national concerns.

Nevertheless, local appeals are essential to candidates' bids for office, including those seeking a seat in Congress. Indeed, even presidential candidates feel the need to make some localized appeals in swing states, as when President Trump ran ads about fracking in Pennsylvania during the 2020 campaign. Candidates can signal to voters that they understand their needs by addressing local concerns. In addition, establishing a connection with voters in a particular location is a way of building trust with those voters.

If Campaigns Are Not Highly Nationalized, Why Is Voting Behavior?

To the extent that voters behave in nationalized ways, it is largely for the reasons that candidates feel the need to nationalize their campaigns. A decline in local sources of news, for example, means the information that voters get on a daily basis is increasingly national in scope. Between elections—that is, for a majority of the time in any given two-year election cycle—the focus of news about politics is on national political figures who are engaged in battles over how to govern the nation. Those battles, in turn, are treated as zero-sum games, where any victory for one side is treated as a loss for the other. Furthermore, these battles are highly polarized, contributing to an "us versus them" mindset and, ultimately, to negative partisanship. Even in those rare moments when voters are exposed to coverage of state or local policy debates and governmental decisions, the framing is likely to emphasize partisan disagreement. Thus, while the issues being highlighted in media coverage of state and local government may not be national, the familiar partisan heuristic—Democrats-versus-Republicans—is.

Contributing to this way of understanding the political world is the fact that, over time, party elites have sorted themselves along ideological lines. That is, virtually all liberals are now Democrats and nearly all conservatives are Republicans. Because the parties have become more ideological cohesive at the elite level, voters have also become sorted by ideology (Levendusky 2009). Importantly, as Levendusky notes, "When a voter moves from unsorted to sorted, he becomes much more firmly anchored to his party and much more supportive of it both in the voting booth and beyond" (2009, 3).

Voting behavior is also a function of the alternatives that voters are given (Fiorina 2017). When those alternatives, up and down the ballot, are between a liberal Democrat and a conservative Republican, voters have only one choice to make—namely, which party to support. The result is less split-ticket voting and patterns of voting that look nationalized.

This binary choice means that candidates' messaging and campaigns should have little impact on voters' decisions. Taken to an extreme, voters need to know nothing other than their own, and the candidates', party affiliations in order to know which way to vote in every contest. However, this level of apparent nationalization did not appear in the 2020 elections in Pennsylvania. Our case studies identified eight legislative races (including those for Congress) out of eighteen in which the winning presidential candidate and the winning legislative candidate were of different parties. This suggests there is local information (most often incumbency status) that will override sheer partisanship in the voters' calculations.

While an increase in partisan voting behavior is consistent with the expectations of nationalization, it does not necessarily mean that campaigns and elections have become more nationalized. Could ideological sorting, partisan gerrymandering, and other social and political factors explain the changes in voting behavior without producing an increase in nationalization? Our work, as well as the work of the only two other studies that examine nationalization in congressional and state-level campaigns, suggests that the answer is yes. Holliday (2020) finds little evidence of nationalization in gubernatorial campaigns. Liu and Jacobson (2018), in studying 2016 congressional campaigns, found that nationalization was less likely to occur in competitive races and when the Republican candidates were incumbents or women. Our findings are consistent with these other two studies, suggesting that nationalization in down-ballot campaigns is less common than previously believed and is likely to occur only when candidates find it in their electoral interests to tie themselves to national themes or figures. And if campaigns are less nationalized than we previously thought, perhaps voting behavior, while more polarized and partisan, is less nationalized than we previously believed. Perhaps future work would benefit from maintaining a cleaner distinction between polarization as a feature of voters and nationalization as a feature of political discourse. While these concepts may be reinforcing, they are not exactly the same.

Why Are Some Campaigns More Nationalized Than Others?

Because every campaign in our study contained both local and nationalized components, our research suggests that campaigns for congressional and state legislative office exist along a continuum from localized to nationalized. While some campaigns were predominantly local, others were more balanced between local and national issues, and still others tended more toward national themes. Although this study does not lead to definitive conclusions, it does suggest there are three types of factors that help explain the level of nationalization in a campaign:

- Structural factors, including the size of the district and whether the candidate is running for federal- or state-level office
- District-level factors, including competitiveness and partisan distribution
- Candidate-level factors, including incumbency and background

Structural Explanations

In our study, candidates running for the U.S. House of Representatives were more likely to use nationalized themes than candidates running for state legislative office. We suggest that the reason is twofold: federalism and constituent representation. In the United States, candidates running for a federal legislative office are more likely than candidates running for state legislative office to address national issues and interact with national political figures. Put another way, congressional candidates are almost always addressing national issues because their policy domain strongly overlaps the president's policy domain. State legislative candidates, on the other hand, typically do not address the same issues, or they address the issues from a different perspective. For example, state legislative candidates rarely concern themselves with whether the president of the United States should be investigated or impeached. Even when there is issue overlap, such as the economy, taxes, or the pandemic, state house candidates typically focus on the governor's or the state's response to the issues rather than the federal government's actions, thus running less nationalized campaigns.

A second structural explanation relates to the size and scope of the contested district. As the size of a district expands and the number of constituents increases, candidates are more likely to employ a more nationalized strategy. The average member of the U.S. House of Representatives has about 750,000 constituents, while the average member of the Pennsylvania State House has fewer than 63,000. Given that U.S. House districts are ten times larger than Pennsylvania house districts, candidates running for federal office are less likely to know their constituents personally and also less likely to use local appeals. In other words, the smaller the size of the district and the smaller the number of constituents, the more likely the candidate is to use more personal and localized appeals. While most candidates running for office claim that they have local ties and understand local concerns, our study finds that state legislative candidates stress these connections more than U.S. House candidates do.

If these structural explanations are correct, the level of nationalization in a campaign should decrease as we move from federal office to state office to local office. The level of nationalization should also decrease as the number of constituents decreases. In other words, nationalization should decrease as we move from the U.S. Senate to the U.S. House to the state senate to the state house to, finally, local legislative offices. Clearly, more empirical research is required to test this explanation, as the data in this study are limited to U.S. congressional and state house races.

District-Level Explanations

At the district level, the district's partisan makeup and level of electoral competitiveness directly affect the level of nationalization. In a district with a strong partisan advantage that is less electorally competitive, the candidate representing the dominant party is more likely to mount a nationalized appeal, because the candidate's reelection coalition is likely to be made up of fellow partisans who support the party's national figures and themes. Conversely, a candidate with a strong partisan disadvantage is less likely to stress national themes in an effort to craft a campaign message that will appeal to voters in both parties.

Recall from Chapter 7 that Mike Kelly ran for reelection in the safe Republican Sixteenth Congressional District and employed a more nationalized campaign, while his Democratic challenger, Kristy Gnibus, focused on a more personal narrative (mom and schoolteacher) and tried to distance herself from national Democratic figures and themes. Similar examples exist at the state legislative level. In an open-seat race for Pennsylvania State House District 154 (Chapter 4), a district that strongly favors the Democratic party, Napoleon Nelson ran on nationalized Democratic themes such as ending racism and creating a fairer tax system, while the Republican, Kathy Bowers, who did not mention on her official campaign website that she was a Republican, focused more on local issues.

As legislative elections become more competitive, however, candidates are more likely to favor a mixed or more localized campaign strategy because they need to expand their electoral coalitions beyond their party identification. In the highly competitive Eighth Congressional District race (highlighted in Chapter 5), the Democrat, Matt Cartwright, fought to save his seat by focusing on his local roots, his constituent service, and his understanding of issues that matter to voters in northeastern Pennsylvania. Likewise, Chapter 3 highlights two candidates who were able to win close elections using local appeals. Brian Fitzpatrick kept his seat in the First Congressional District by focusing on local issues. At the state level, Todd Polinchock (PA-144) completely avoided mentioning President Trump or any national issues and used a bipartisan approach to defeat his Democratic challenger. In both of these races, Republicans were able to win in districts that favored Biden over Trump.

These district-level observations suggest that partisanship and competitiveness can influence the level of nationalization in a campaign. If these observations are correct, we should see highly nationalized campaigns employed only by candidates running in safe districts—districts in which the partisan advantage strongly favors their party. As elections become more competitive, however, the level of nationalization in campaigns should decrease. Given that only one candidate can have a strong partisan advantage in any race, the district-level explanation suggests that we should never see both major-party candidates employing nationalized campaign strategies in the same race.

Candidate-Level Explanations

In addition to the type of office a candidate is seeking and the makeup of that candidate's district, several candidate-specific characteristics also seem to influence the level of nationalization in a candidate's campaign. These characteristics include incumbency and background.

The incumbent advantage—including greater name recognition, fundraising prowess, and connection with constituents—gives incumbents more flexibility in deciding how they want to structure their reelection campaigns, including defining the balance between nationalized and localized messaging. At the congressional level, our findings suggest that incumbents in safe districts were more likely to nationalize their campaigns (Dean and Kelly) than candidates in more competitive races (Fitzpatrick, Perry, Lamb, and Cartwright). In state legislative races, most incumbents favored a mixed or more localized campaign strategy. Even in districts that were not competitive, incumbents were unlikely to employ a nationalized strategy. They either campaigned very little in general or focused on their service and their connection to the local community.

U.S. congressional challengers, on the other hand, employed different strategies than incumbents. Challengers running against safe incumbents in districts with a partisan advantage strongly favoring the incumbent were more likely to take a localized or mixed approach in an effort to appeal to voters of both parties (Republican Barnette in the Fourth and Democrat Gnibus in the Sixteenth). Challengers in more competitive U.S. House races, however, seemed equally likely to run nationalized, mixed, or primarily localized campaigns. In the First Congressional District, Democratic challenger Finello ran a mixed campaign, striking a balance between local and national themes. In the Tenth, Democratic challenger DePasquale ran a more localized campaign. On the Republican side, both challengers (Bognet in the Eighth and Parnell in the Seventeenth) ran more nationalized campaigns. While these findings might suggest that Republican challengers in more competitive elections are more likely to employ a nationalized strategy, the limited number of cases makes it difficult to draw specific conclusions.

It is hard to determine the reasons for this variation in the challengers' campaign strategies. Their personal traits, their backgrounds, and the competitive nature of the primaries in which they ran may have influenced the level of nationalization they introduced in their general election campaigns. For example, in the competitive Seventeenth Congressional District race, the Republican challenger, Sean Parnell, ran a nationalized campaign against a highly vulnerable incumbent. Given the competitiveness of the district and a partisan balance that slightly favored the Democrats, one might have expected the challenger to run a mixed or more localized campaign, but Parnell was a *Fox News* contributor who strongly supported President Trump, so in this case the candidate's background and personality did not lend themselves to a bipartisan or localized campaign. In fact, Parnell announced his candidacy on *Fox and Friends* in front of a photo of himself with President Trump. Likewise, in the competitive Eighth Congressional District, the Republican challenger Bognet also chose to run a more nationalized campaign. His decision might have been influenced by the fact that he was a longtime

Republican operative who worked for strong Trump loyalist Lou Barletta, or it may have been the result of his running in a highly competitive Republican primary as the "Trumpiest" of all the candidates. Or perhaps his strategy was the product of some combination of background, primary, and personal preference.

At the state legislative level, challengers tended to run either mixed or localized campaigns. Although some used nationalized messaging and even welcomed endorsements from their presidential candidates, most challengers did not tie themselves to national issues or political figures.

Another individual-level factor that might influence the level of nationalization in a candidate's campaign is the reputation that candidates—particularly incumbents—build over time. Incumbents may seek to forge a relationship between their behavior in office and their message on the campaign trail. For candidates who have made their mark as bipartisan or independent-minded lawmakers, running highly nationalized campaigns might not make sense. Likewise, candidates whose time in office has been characterized by polarizing, partisan behavior might have more success running nationalized campaigns. For example, two congressional incumbents, one Democratic and one Republican, built reputations as being bipartisan and independent, stressing their commitment to constituent service. Fitzpatrick (in the First) and Cartwright (in the Eighth) both ran more localized campaigns and won in competitive districts. The Democratic incumbent in the Fourth (Dean), on the other hand, has been a polarizing figure on Capitol Hill (e.g., as an impeachment manager), and she ran a more nationalized campaign in her safe congressional district. But not all incumbents stress or emphasize the reputations they have developed in Washington. Perry, the Republican incumbent in the Tenth Congressional District, is a highly nationalized and polarizing figure in D.C., but during his campaign he downplayed his strong support for President Trump and national Republican issues, instead running a mixed campaign featuring both local and national themes. Perry's case suggests that a candidate's past behavior and reputation are not always strong predictors of a particular campaign strategy.

Our study suggests that multiple factors influence the varying levels of nationalization we see in political campaigns. Structural factors, such as federalism and district size, can influence a campaign strategy, as can a district's competitiveness and partisan makeup. In addition, individual-level factors, such as incumbency, past political activity, and personality, can influence the degree to which candidates choose to nationalize their campaigns. Undoubtedly, more research is needed to clarify the relative importance of these factors and the specific ways in which they influence campaigns.

Limitations of the Present Study and
Avenues for Future Research

We believe we have provided ample evidence to conclude that, whatever else may be happening in American politics at the moment, campaigns below the presidential level are not, generally speaking, thoroughly nationalized. In fact, taken as a whole, campaigns are at least as likely to emphasize local concerns as they are to focus on national issues and personalities, and in many cases, particularly below the congressional level, they are more likely to be localized.

Having drawn this conclusion with some confidence, we also acknowledge certain limitations to the present study. For example, the study was conducted in one (presidential) election cycle in a single state that happens to be one of the most important battlegrounds in the nation. In addition, the campaign took place amidst a highly unusual circumstance (i.e., the pandemic) in which in-person campaigning was limited, at least for one party. How generalizable, then, are our findings? We would argue that, if anything, most of these factors should have produced a heightened level of nationalization, particularly given the intensity of the presidential campaign in Pennsylvania and, in particular, President Trump's presence in the race. Still, we realize that without additional evidence, from another cycle (or several) and other states, our conclusions must be tentative.

We also recognize the difficulty in defining and measuring nationalization, and we know that some will disagree with our conceptualization. Nevertheless, nationalization is too often treated as synonymous with polarization or partisan sorting, particularly with respect to voting behavior. We have tried to move beyond this conceptual blurring, but further refinement of the definition of *nationalization* is certainly warranted.

Having said this, we once again believe that, if anything, we are likely to have overrepresented the level of nationalization in campaigns. Whether in campaign advertising or in other appeals to voters, as well as in coordination between campaigns, we have treated any reference to a national issue or personality, or any link to a presidential campaign (including appearances at rallies), as a piece of evidence for nationalization within a given campaign. However, there may be a difference between identifying oneself or one's campaign with national concerns and attempting to nationalize one's opponent. Take, for instance, a candidate who claims her opponent supports President Trump 100% of the time or is in favor of defunding the police. On the one hand, this candidate is invoking a national figure or a nationally debated issue. On the other hand, the underlying message of these negative attacks is to create a contrast between an opponent who does not represent local values or local issues and thus is not one of us, and a candidate who understands local concerns and issues and thus is one of us. The point is simply that we have erred on the side of nationalization in categorizing candidates' appeals.

In addition to replicating this study in future election cycles and in additional states (not to mention for other offices, like governor or municipal offices), as well as clarifying nationalization conceptually, further research could address a number of questions. For instance, how is nationalized thinking primed among voters? Is a certain threshold of nationalization required to trigger nationalized behavior? Furthermore, what role do environmental or structural factors play in making nationalized behavior, among elites or voters, prominent? Federalism, the two-party system, primaries, gerrymandered districts, and the media landscape, to name only a few, are likely to influence the level of nationalization we observe—but how, exactly, do they do so?

There is still much to learn about the nationalization of American politics. By moving beyond voting behavior, we have provided evidence that we believe complicates the story of nationalization. But that evidence is, in many respects, preliminary, and we encourage others to examine this phenomenon with the aim of better understanding American democracy in the twenty-first century.

NOTE

1. Hopkins (2018) offers a comprehensive treatment of alternative explanations for nationalization in Chapter 6 of his book *The Increasingly United States*.

REFERENCES

Abernathy, Penelope Muse. 2020. *New Deserts and Ghost Newspapers: Will Local News Survive?* Chapel Hill: Center for Innovation and Sustainability in Local Media, University of North Carolina.

Fiorina, Morris P. 2017. *Unstable Majorities: Polarization, Party Sorting and Political Stalemate.* Stanford, CA: Hoover Institution Press.

Gimpel, James G., Frances E. Lee, and Shanna Pearson-Merkowitz. 2008. "The Check Is in the Mail: Interdistrict Funding Flows in Congressional Elections." *American Journal of Political Science* 52:373–94.

Holliday, Derek. 2020. *Nationalized Elections, Localized Campaigns: Evidence from Televised U.S. Debates.* Los Angeles: UCLA Department of Political Science.

Hopkins, Daniel J. 2018. *The Increasingly United States: How and Why American Political Behavior Nationalized.* Chicago: University of Chicago Press.

Levendusky, Matthew. 2009. *The Partisan Sort: How Liberals Became Democrats and Conservatives Became Republicans.* Chicago: University of Chicago Press.

Liu, Huchen, and Gary C. Jacobson. 2018. "Republican Candidates' Positions on Donald Trump in the 2016 Congressional Elections: Strategies and Consequences." *Presidential Studies Quarterly* 48, no. 1: 49–71.

Sullivan, Margaret. 2020. *Ghosting the News: Local Journalism and the Crisis of American Democracy.* New York: Columbia Global Reports.

Contributors

Sophie Ackert is a 2021 graduate of Dickinson College.

Andrew Bloeser is Associate Professor of Political Science at Allegheny College.

Christopher Borick is Professor of Political Science and Director of the Institute of Public Opinion at Muhlenberg College.

Kristen Coopie is Director of Pre-Law at Duquesne University.

Angela M. Corbo is Associate Professor and Chair of Communication Studies at Widener University.

J. Wesley Leckrone is Professor of Political Science at Widener University.

Stephen K. Medvic is the Honorable and Mrs. John C. Kunkel Professor of Government, Director of the Center for Politics and Public Affairs, and Codirector of the Floyd Institute for Public Policy at Franklin & Marshall College.

Sarah Niebler is Associate Professor of Political Science at Dickinson College.

Olivia O'Donnell is a 2021 graduate of, and current law student (JD '24) at, Duquesne University.

Matthew M. Schousen is Professor of Government at Franklin & Marshall College.

Benjamin T. Toll is Assistant Professor of Political Science at Wilkes University.

Tarah Williams is Assistant Professor of Political Science at Allegheny College.

Berwood A. Yost is Codirector of the Floyd Institute for Public Policy and Director of the Center for Opinion Research at Franklin & Marshall College. He is also Director of the Franklin & Marshall College Poll.

Index

Congressional districts are spelled out, for example First Congressional District (PA). State legislative districts are listed as PA, followed by their number, for example, PA-143.